Having Coffee with the Special One

Patty Scott

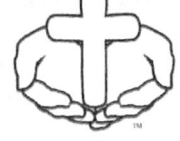

Give "God" His Glory, LLC

Copyright © 2020 by Patty Scott

All rights reserved. No part of this book may be used or reproduced or used by any means, graphic, electronic, or mechanical, including photocopying, recording, taping or by any information storage retrieval system without permission of the author except in the case of brief quotations embodied in critical articles and reviews.

Give God His Glory, LLC publishing firm's books can be ordered through booksellers or by contacting:

Give God His Glory, LLC
3602 S. Cooper Street
Arlington, Texas 76015
(817) 266-3297
info@GiveGodHisGloryPublishing.com

The author of this book does not dispense medical advice or prescribe the use of any technique as a form of treatment for physical, emotional, or medical problems without the advice of a physician, either directly or indirectly. The intent of the author is only to offer information of a general nature to help you in your question for emotional and spiritual well-being. In the event you use any of the information in this book for yourself, which is your constitutional right, the author and the publisher assume no responsibility for your actions. This is a work of fiction. Names, characters, places, and incidents either are the product of the author's imagination or are used fictitiously. Any resemblance to actual persons, living or dead, events, or locales is entirely coincidental.

First edition August 2020

Book design by Aleisha Wikked

ISBN 978-1-7344405-0-8 (hardback)
ISBN 978-1-7344405-1-5 (paperback)
ISBN 978-1-7344405-2-2 (e-book)

Library of Congress Control Number: 2020910730

Acknowledgments

I would like to thank God for his input and spending so much time with me. Thank you for your guidance and help in making this daily journal of our time spent together and sharing these moments with you. And thank you to all readers that encourage me to write and to finish the stories.

I am so thankful that God has shown me that he will get me through the rough times, and that he does answer prayers, not only mine but others too. Just know that God is with you always and he does care about you. It's easier to use Kira's character to get through the heart felt moments. I hope you enjoy the journey and there is something in here that will help you too.

God bless you all always.

Kira thanks him for his mercy and forgiveness; and for showing her the way to trust in him again and that there are others that can be trusted. Trust was something she lacked within her. She is sharing her journey where she took the time and grew in her faith and opened her heart and mind unto Jesus Christ.

Having Coffee with the Special One

Kira hopes that you'll feel the love and take the walk with her, find the peace that surpasses all understanding and keeps your hearts and minds open unto Christ. Love and faith have taken over her as she goes through this process. Healing and guidance in his word. If God had stopped the accident that day, it's hard to say if I (Kira) would have gotten this close to him. You know he could have stopped it if he had the desire, but he had a greater purpose for what had happened.

A special thanks to Anna and Mary Kay for your time and help with typing, editing and feedback on this manuscript. It's very time-consuming: and I know the work that goes into a successful story. There were many days when I am sure you just wanted to play rather than sit and type. I thank you very much for all that you helped me with, especially Anna too, because she also spent two days with me helping me complete and submit **The Porcelain Rose and The Hidden Truths**, my first book.

A special thanks to my daughter Aleisha for doing the great job she has done on the books covers. They match so well to what the story is all about and illustrate the daily walk that Kira did with the Lord for six months. She does a great job at graphic illustration; and she knows how to put life into the cover.

Also thank you to my friends and family for their tolerance and input to help make this story come to pass. Without our friendships and times together some of this wouldn't have been completed. Some of the characters can relate to some of the stories with my friends and families, so hopefully it will give the full effect of how God is in your life and once you're truly his you always will be no matter what.

A special thank you to all the readers, I hope something will touch your heart and lives and know that God will stay by your side no matter what.

In this daily journey of the walk with Jesus Christ and writing about it, I have learned a lot about myself and about why things happen as they do. Each time I read this myself, I can see where God even changed me and gave me his peace. It showed me that no matter if Jesus Christ loved me, he was there to help me clean out the gunk within me that I had been holding in and on to for years.

This was written after the forgiveness process was introduced in **The Porcelain Rose and The Hidden Truths.** In addition, I have gone through some traumatic events, so this was completed right after my 60th birthday.

A friend that I sit with at church gave me a very beautiful devotional written by the very gifted author Sarah Young; and I am ever so grateful that she gave that to me, for it really started the cleaning of my heart and soul and helped the Holy Spirit come alive in me again. If you haven't read any of her devotionals, I ask you to do so, I promise

Having Coffee with the Special One

you'll love them, and you'll feel the peace and the presence of Jesus Christ in them. This has hit home, and I hope it can help others too and touch your heart.

This is basically a daily journal so remember, it's what was going through Kira's thoughts as the walls were being torn down brick by brick; and healing after a long process of forgiving others and learning to trust the Lord and again to trust others. It's interesting how things that bothered you come out and sometimes you didn't even realize that it was even bothering you.

Enjoy, God Bless you and may you have his peace.

I love to tell the Story of Jesus Christ and his Glory...to tell the old, old story of Jesus and his love. You remember that song? It sticks with me at different moments........

Day One, as Kira gets ready to sit down and spend time with the Special one:

Good Morning Jesus, how are you doing today?

As she does every day, Kira prepares for her daily time to soak in the warmth and love of the Lord. Kira had forgotten and didn't appreciate just how nice it was to lollygag in your jammies in the morning until she wanted to get dressed. It was so nice not to have to jump up and get dressed every morning just to rush somewhere—mainly to work.

It was wonderful just to sit and relax, to be with the Lord, have a cup of coffee and talk. Not that Kira didn't appreciate having work in the first place, but it was so nice to just sit and be with the Lord without interruptions or the telephone ringing.

The wonders of you Lord!

Kira wanted her career (ha!) and she knew she wasn't completely ready to relax everyday of her life Lord. But she was telling you that it was so awesome to get to sit and spend time with you with a cup of coffee. She did not appreciate the simple things in life much after her teens, did she?

With friendships, Lord, Kira tended to ruin them, or she didn't know how to nurture them, maintain them, and keep them alive. She asked: help me to maintain the good ones.

Something that just hit her is that things are working Lord, you know what we talked about in the past, you know the issues between Kira and her staff and her family, is it because she has stayed away and didn't expect anything from you or get into your way? Lord you're answering my prayers that I prayed for, thank you. Kira was having a

Having Coffee with the Special One

hard time with some of her family members, she was sad because she had to stand by and watch them struggle, it's good for them, but that doesn't make it any easier to stand back and watch them go through the struggles.

Kira does want friends but she just doesn't want a lot of demands on her or her time. She doesn't ask for much does she? Kira knows you listen to her when she asks you to, God, by the way you take care of the world and because when she gets so overwhelmed you give her a sense of peace and calm. Kira knows she isn't calm or peaceful, God, but she is still learning. She doesn't want to be responsible for other people anymore. God you take care of all of us. You watch over all of us now....oh never mind you already gave her the answer. It's because you're the Almighty and can deal and tolerate more than we can. We don't have any of the power in comparison as you. How can Kira even try to put you in the category as she and others as we are mere humans. We don't have the strength for any of this, and God, you show us that we can't do this on our own. We need you and we need you now.

Patty Scott

Kira had gone to Bible classes, and she belonged to a woman's group in her church in Colorado, and in Texas. Lord, she has done a lot. She went through "The Purpose Driven Life" but she doesn't think all that had soaked in nor meant so much to her at that time. And she felt it had not done so much for her as what she was experiencing now at this time. Now it was meaning so much more to her. Maybe that was the beginning of what all started years ago when she finally gave in, let go and let you take it away from her. Kira opened her heart and mind unto you Jesus Christ. Kira asked you; you listened to her.

A thought just came to her mind *"Trust in the Lord with all your heart"*. Sort of like love, honor and cherish. These words mean a lot and they have powerful meaning behind them. They aren't to be minimized, and Kira's thoughts were heading to this:

If you know one thing about the Lord our Savior, know this. He had to struggle and deal with bad things in life too. Why should our lives be any better than his was? Would any of us have wanted to suffer on the cross as he did for us? Lord why don't we look at things like that, why didn't I look at things like that in the past? Why did I think that my life should have been easy, why do I think I shouldn't have suffered any negativity in my life?

Having Coffee with the Special One

Kira has realized that she sure took you and your love for granted, didn't she? Kira asked what one of us would suffer like that or even endure the suffering as you did for us. She knows she needed to remember her life is good compared to that. She is sure she wouldn't have wanted to be nailed to a cross. It's the hard truth Lord: to endure all the whips, the cuts and vinegar in the wounds, we wouldn't have even been able to put up with a small amount of that pain that you endured for us.

Thank you, Jesus, for thinking we are worth it. Your love is just so deep for us and so strong. Kira has had to remember that you suffered and died for her. Yes, God's angels do take care of us and they see much more than we think about. "I see you watching over my shoulders writing about you. I love you Jesus; Kira says that she is so glad that God has a sense of humor. Kira loves these mornings with the Lord and the time she gets to spend with him, and she trusts you Jesus. **She has learned to trust you.**

Thank you for allowing her to share and discuss you with her staff Lord. It's difficult to work with others that aren't on the same path and faith path. Kira doesn't know if she would be able to encourage them and/or inspire them the way you would want her to, to give them hope and peace, as she has learned to enjoy herself. Kira messes up too, and people depend on her, hmmm. No, they should depend on God not Kira.

Kira is only a means for people to get what they need while God is working through her. He is the help and the way. You just lifted a heavy burden from me. I just realized another one of my errors: I am just a steward for you Lord. I am to bring them to you and to know you, while you do the rest. So, I shouldn't have to worry where their faith is, it's up to you not me. Why do I always put responsibilities on my shoulders that don't belong there? How did or when did I ever think I had that kind of power?

Lord it's hard at times, but Kira is starting to really understand where she went wrong. Where her thinking was wrong and the way she looked at things. Kira knows that she still needs improvement, she knows that life is a journey not a destination. How many times in the past years had she heard or read that in her studies? Lord you're showing her the way she hopes that she can learn to understand Tim better too. She really is at a loss there. Just when she thinks she knows someone, she finds out that she didn't, or maybe she just thought she did, and instead of really trying to know him, she just assumed. Of which that can cause a lot of the problems just assuming.

There are some that just want to blame others for everything that goes wrong in their life, and until they own it, it won't be resolved. Kira knows that she has to try not to come on so strong, give anyone the impression that she is in the attack mode, she

Having Coffee with the Special One

has to learn the difference between being aggressive and being assertive, as it was pointed out to her so kindly. She needs to learn to teach them how to think not what to think; it's not her place to try to control others' thoughts. She needs to learn how to be a little softer and kinder, speak with a different tone in her voice. Change her stance when she talks to someone. Body language tells a lot too and sometimes she puts them on the defense right away, and that just sets the mode, for disaster.

Kira learned that God is a gentle man, but don't take her wrong. If someone didn't listen to him or got out of line with him, he can and does get angry. We are like his children, no matter how old we get, and we still need to listen to the Lord. As it says in the Bible: "Vengeance is mine sayeth the Lord" so that shows he can get angry at times. Kira remembered reading that back in San Diego, and that was something she took seriously when she backed off from trying to resolve an issue that she couldn't get resolved.

Kira had a disagreement with one of her associates and then apologized to her. It was about the same time that Linda had invited Kira to go over to her office and meet with a couple of Linda's clients who were having some issues with their hard-to-handle tax situations. At the time, Kira was glad to go over to meet and help them out. Kira didn't have ill intentions it was a really busy time for her.

Linda and her clients were waiting for Kira when she arrived, and they they went into the conference room. They all sat down and Kira took over the conversation (no harm intended!.) Linda's clients asked their questions and Kira answered them to the best of her ability, then they all talked a little longer before finishing up the meeting. Kira had to get back to her office because she had a deadline to meet and she was behind.

Kira ran into Linda a couple weeks later at a meeting they have with other industry associates once or twice a year....and Linda hardly talked to her at the event. In fact, she [can't read the words] avoided Kira. Kira thought that was weird. She was hoping to get to talk to Linda when the meeting was over, but Linda just shot of the room and left.

Again, Kira thought that was weird. She thought "oh well, I'll just call her when I get a chance". Kira just couldn't figure out what she had done wrong and was sort of anxious to have a conversation with Linda. Kira isn't one to leave things like that and walk away.

A couple of days later, she called Linda and wow— did she get a shock of her life when Linda just went off on her and hung up on her. Kira was in shock that Linda acted that way and thought "this is nuts". But there wasn't much that Kira could do about it. Kira thought she would wait a few days and see what was going on but had a hard time reconnecting with Linda.

Having Coffee with the Special One

Finally, a few months later she called and was able to talk to Linda. Linda told Kira that the clients (they both had met with) were mad at Linda and told her she didn't know what she was doing so they weren't going to bring their business to her anymore. Linda had been so upset over that, instead of talking to Kira, she took it out on Kira.

Later Kira found out that the clients themselves were not getting along and had been fighting with each other after one of the persons had lost his wife of several years. As a result, they took it out on Linda. In turn, Linda wanted to blame Kira and it just spiraled out of control after that.

As Kira is learning now, when she would take the time to sit and listen to the Lord, he would show her the way and let her see the light. He showed her many things and she felt it too. She knew it was him that was guiding her and leading her. She could just tell how it would happen, and when she would acknowledge it as being the Lord, it would really change the way she looked at things and let them affect her.

As enlightening as it is to see where she had been going wrong and how she was hanging on to feelings and thoughts, it's also sad to see or find out how she wasn't trusting in the Lord with all her heart. A person can't change if they don't open themselves up to it or recognize that they need to change.

Kira was putting more importance on the negative activity in her life which gave her anxiety, rather than on God who gives her peace. It also was kind of hard to understand how she could put God on the same level as a human being. How could she lower the importance of him and him being in her life? She just didn't understand how she could have done that, even though she knows what she thought at times which wasn't always the purest or the best way to think.

In some ways it was very embarrassing for Kira to find and see what was happening to and in her. In a way she was shutting down. But the best part was God will forgive her. And he did forgive her and showed her the way back to him and his peace. She really hadn't realized how far she had gotten from the Lord even though she was going back to church and talking with him. She realized.... she wasn't listening.

She had known all her life that God is there, and God is real, but she didn't realize how she had gone astray from his love and his presence. How she had just sort of left him out of her decisions, her prayers, and her life, it just happened slowly and unnoticed. How did that sneak up on her like that?

Having Coffee with the Special One

"Kira is feeling you Jesus". She learned you really can feel his love and peace and you can see him everywhere in your life when you take the time to look and listen. In songs on the radio, billboards, out of the mouths of babes, he is everywhere you just must seek him, seek the kingdom of God and he will let you know he is there.

One day at church Kira had asked Rile, a short, petite woman she sits with on Sundays, why she hadn't heard what God was saying to her? Rile leaned over and whispered in Kira's ear, "it was because you hadn't been listening."

The pastor had said something in the sermon that triggered Kira's attention about talking to God and she told Rile: I talk to God all the time. Rile said, "But you're not listening to him."

Kira just didn't realize how one sided she had become. She was shutting everyone out in her path and in her life. "Because she knew better". Well, guess she didn't. Kira was wondering why everything in her life had to be so hard. It seemed everything she tried to accomplish was just so hard! Her loan officer at the bank even asked her why do you have to do things the hard way. Of which you do know, that when it's God's way it's the hard way, because it's the right way, it's a road less traveled, and it's rough along the way.

Patty Scott

To Kira at the time, she just thought it was supposed to be that way, to her it just seemed normal. You know the adage: if it's "easy it's wrong". Something I remember hearing a long time ago. God's way is not always the easy way, but it sure is a lot easier when you bring him along with you than when you don't bring him. You need to trust in him and let him be the boss. Kira must chuckle now because she was such a strong-willed child and had the attitude that she could take care of herself and would get through what was happening. Well it was true she would get through it, but she wouldn't do it as well alone if she doesn't let God guide and direct her.

The hurt and the pain in her mind is what she allowed to give her the drive and the reason to succeed. Geez!! she didn't stop and think of the blessings she had and how it was God. It's God that gives her a much better life than she has ever planned for herself or she ever could even have imagined that she could have.

All Kira knew when she was growing up, was she knew it didn't have to be that way and she didn't have to live that way for ever. But she just didn't know how her life was going to change, and who was going to change it. Even then she doesn't remember, thinking that God would change it, she just knew it didn't have to be that way. She didn't have to live like that.

Even when Kira fell in love with the man who she married just a year out of high school before she

Having Coffee with the Special One

turned 18, she found out later that it was wrong, wrong, wrong from the very beginning, to marry him. (She chuckles.) Her mom tried to tell her that she didn't have to marry him.

It was through that piece in her life that Kira learned how to really love, and it really did help her in succeeding in life. She knows now it was all God giving her direction and guiding her; it wasn't the pain and the anger that pushed her. He was molding her into the person that she is today and will be tomorrow. He had a plan and a better one than what she had planned with her ex-husband Nevan.

Kira was so thankful she finally went through the forgiveness process with Nevan. They forgave each other. Nevan forgave her and stopped being mad at her for letting him down and not being able to change who he was. She forgave him for hiding from her, lying to her and for not telling her the truth about it all.

Nevan blamed Kira for things she had no control over. She was so hurt he wouldn't let her in. Kira didn't understand any of it. It's so nice to know the truth because the truth helped set her free.

Not only was she free, but Nevan was free too and could be himself; no longer did he have to hide.

Years later, Kira got a phone call at work from Nevan's sister Chari, letting Kira know that Nevan was in the hospital and they did not expect him to make it. Kira's emotions were like a roller coaster. Does she go or does she stay and say good-bye to him here at home, with her current husband Tim? Kira decided and told Chari she would be there as soon as she could get there.

Chari said Nevan was malnourished and had double pneumonia with fluid in both lungs. He was running a high fever and wasn't responding. She made the decision that she would go see him and say goodbye, and that was going to be the last time to see him. She did go and say goodbye to him, but he did live a little longer than was expected. Kira didn't have contact with him after the visit though. No real reason, she just didn't.

While driving to a client's office Kira thought that she had been so stupid in not allowing God in to help her and guide her. She thought I can do this on my own; I don't need anyone. Kira remembered even saying that; and saying it out loud and not only once but several times. On top of that, she really believed it too!

At the time she didn't really think about it as keeping God out. Kira kept thinking he made her this way. Yes, she had the thoughts that she was self-sufficient. (Chuckle.)

On the way to her client's house she passed a church, and on their billboard was in big bold print:

Having Coffee with the Special One

*"**God loves you even when you do stupid things**".* She had asked him to forgive her for doing stupid things just prior to seeing the sign. He does answer you and listen to you as he proved by quickly answering her and confirming that he was listening.

For the past, oh I don't know, ten years or more, Kira felt so frustrated she didn't think she could explain herself or get her point across to people. She felt like no one was listening, when in fact it was her that wasn't listening. Her mind would swirl and turn like a rolodex thought would just fly through her, she was so lost in her head and you're right God, nothing got resolved at all!!

She wore herself out and she felt like a lost soul. Kira was so burnt out and so exhausted. She said she was sorry for that, Jesus. She wouldn't or couldn't listen to you or anyone else for that matter. You know her: she's like the horse with blinders on (or should she say stubborn mule?.) She wasn't sure at times if she was coming or going, and sometimes, forgot on the way there were others around her.

Dear God: Kira would pray; I am so sorry for getting wrapped up in "my way". Wow!! She didn't realize how much of a control freak she was.

Patty Scott

To keep her weight down, Kira controlled what she ate, to the point of where she could have fallen into the anorexia category. In some ways, Kira thinks she probably did, but you helped with that...yet she wasn't even aware totally how you did help in that area. Kira did fall into the trap of "thinking" she was eating to live not living to eat; oh, geez, living and breathing to stay away from so many foods continually consumed her mind and thoughts. She was so afraid of being fat or getting fat! She meant she thought about it 24/7. Kira said: God I'm so sorry and yes, I became a prisoner to that. This is an area where we cannot serve two Gods. Kira didn't even think how this could have been serving a God, and it sure wasn't the one true God.

Most of her life people she cared about and loved said something about her weight and used to tease her and called her "liberty bell". Kira is petite and thin, but she has bulging hips/thighs. It doesn't matter if she weighs ninety-nine pounds or one hundred and fifty pounds, they are there and noticeable. When she was younger and people said something about them and she would laugh and joke and say come on baby, hang on, hold on baby we are going for a ride! Kira used to laugh and say it's funny but "maybe it wasn't after all". Kira always joked about it, but it really did affect her to the point she was or is so obsessed with being skinny. "God please take this problem and thought

Having Coffee with the Special One

process away". Yes, the fear of being fat too!! Let me know that it will be okay, even if I put on weight, it's ok, if I don't go the other way, of which gluttony is also wrong, one of the sins.

Kira said: God is with me on this and is with me always. "Trust in the Lord with all your heart, lean not on your own understanding, acknowledge him in all your ways and he will lead you straight". Until now you haven't asked in my name, ask in my name and your joy will be complete. I didn't realize that I didn't ask in his name, Kira still needs help and work on how to pray, and realize that it doesn't take an hour long prayer to reach God, just say his name and he will be there, he is that close to you and to her. For some reason, we think it's hard to reach God when it really is simple, he keeps things simple for us.

Kira knew she is so blessed how much her adult children love her and care about her. She sat down to do her daily devotions and she caught site of the photo album, that her oldest son and his wife had made for her for her sixtieth birthday. On the cover was a photo of Kira when she was in sixth grade up through current years. No, it didn't have photos of all sixty years. There are five different photos from various years. It just gave her a warm feeling because she could feel the love and care that went into that album. You know pictures say a thousand words, and there were so many words and so much love in that album that included photos of her family, friends, and fun events.

Kira could picture Marie, her daughter-in-law, sitting there at her computer going through the photos and thinking about what was happening at those times, pondering over which ones to put into the album. Two of them are very bright and cheery showing the times Kira was full of life and love. Some of the fun times. Kira's oldest son wrote something in it and one of her grandsons Kristopher, and Marie also. It was and is a genuinely nice gift and something she can enjoy in years to come. Marie put a lot of time and thought into the completion of the album. Notice she didn't say treasure. Kira is so thankful to God that she has her children and that they all have the same dad. They bring so much joy in her life. The family is growing and Raelee keeps adding to the family.
There were times when Kira didn't think that way. There were times when they wore her down. Kira was so tired she didn't feel as though she really enjoyed them, not the way that God intended for a mother to enjoy her child. The sad thing is that we don't get this time back either. She remembers one time they were living in San Jose, and she was tromping up the stairs to go to the master bedroom. Her husband Tim was coming down the stairs as she was walking up them. Sub-consciously she looked at Tim and said to herself; now it's your time and your turn to take over the responsibility of these kids. This can't be changed either.

Having Coffee with the Special One

All three of the kids were remarkably close in age and she was dealing with three teenagers and they were messing with things they shouldn't have been, all three of them. That was a time when her husband no longer was on a ship in the Military and he was stationed at the reserve center. Kira was so worn out and worn down it was like she sort of washed her hands of her kids that day. (Sort of just went on strike.) Maybe that's a better way to word it.

The problem was she didn't bother to verbalize that with her husband, or her kids and she isn't sure, but she can pretty much say she probably didn't even sit down and discuss it with God either. You do know we are supposed to bring him in on everything in our lives, we are supposed to share and talk to him. But that was a day to where Kira pretty much let go of her kids in her mind. Oh no! she didn't stop loving them or raising them; it was just a moment where Kira quit fighting.

It was a wall she was putting up even within her own family, so it didn't hurt so much to watch them do what they were doing to themselves. Kira had no idea what all exactly they were doing but she knew she wanted them to stop! This was going to lead to nowhere good. It scared her for her kids. Kira was so naïve enough to think because she told them to stop, that they would, and they did. "Ha" It just made them hide it better while she got so busy with going to school and working, Kira just kind of didn't take on the roll or responsibility of being a mom or even a good wife. Even having to say this makes her feel as though it was wrong of her. Kira went into a mode of burying her feelings and thinking she was working toward something good in her life. How selfish was that? Here she got mad at her husband, why did she blame him for something she was doing on her own and not allowing God the space or room in her heart and mind? They lived in a really nice home; it was a Tri-level, one of Kira's favorite floor plans. Tim had a great job and was fulfilling a dream of his. The kids were great kids.

So, what was it that she was missing, what more could she need? It was the closeness she needed and the realization, that she needed to share with God and pray more and put him back in her life where he belonged.

Kira's mind was always churning, and she tried to decide to see how the outcome would be. It's not something that can be predicted. It was just another area her thinking she was or is in total control. Her mind was always locked in on thoughts that she was going to resolve the issue. Thinking she has control of how things could or would end up. Kira felt so done and that no one understood her. How could they when she was such a lost soul? She thought she could handle it all, you know. "I can take care of it myself!" "I don't need anyone."

Having Coffee with the Special One

She remembers thinking these thoughts as if it would make a difference. She didn't need anyone. But she does want them. Nevan wasn't her first love! God's her first love. How could she forget that? She had put too much importance on Nevan and she said that she is sorry for that Lord, She is sorry for not opening up to you and letting you really be in her life and the leader of her life, where you're supposed to be. The first and the head of the family.

When there was something bothering Kira, she would always get lost in thought and shut out everything including her husband, her family, and God. She would forget who was there to help her. The problem would become more important to her than it needed to be. An example would be that she would look at a tax case as if it was the most important thing in the world and if she didn't know the answer to the problem, it would roll around in her mind and consume her. During the process she would lose out on the present moment that she was in and she would miss precious time with her husband or family member. Kira wouldn't let go and turn it over to God and walk away from it. Now Kira can see where she gave herself more stress and anxiety than she needed in her life.

Kira was thinking: Lord there has been many times in my life where I pulled away from you and tried to do things my own way and I stumbled and fell. After the divorce of the first marriage where she was drinking and partying and got into doing things she shouldn't have been doing. Kira didn't take care of herself, as she should have, she was a real mess. You stayed with her and watched her self-destruct and ruin several relationships with friends, probably more than she wants to remember. You picked her up and loved her anyway. She made you watch her go through that and your spirit had to deal with what she was putting in her body, and how she treated herself. Our bodies are the temple where the Spirit resides in us, so how could I have treated is so poorly?

Yet, you forgave her before she could even forgive herself. Kira didn't even really forgive herself until now. This was one of the times in her life she was lost and was a mess. You saved her from that world. Even though she had gotten so bad because she wouldn't eat properly and passed out in the shower. You kept watching over her. You protected her and you kept her alive when you didn't have to.

You didn't have to do any of it, Lord, you could have just let her die. Of which she is incredibly grateful and thankful that you did Jesus, that you saved her. That was one of the times in Kira's life where you turned her around and helped her become a better person and get her away from that life. That was before she ran into Tim and they got together. Kira never turned back, and she thinks she even started putting weight back on after that. You could have let her go and let her die, but you didn't.

Even then Jesus, she didn't fully comprehend the magnitude of your love, help or protection as she does now. Now she knows just how much love and

Having Coffee with the Special One

care you put into her life and how you protected her. How could she do that to herself, and not care? And you cared for her and about her even when she didn't care about herself.

Lord, thank you for allowing her to live on. She is grateful for it because you gave her a good life, a wonderful life. She doesn't think she really appreciated it fully either from where she is now to what she was back then. She can look back and see where you pruned her and healed her and helped her grow in faith.

Still Kira sees though where she was strong-willed and didn't totally turn her life over to you. Kira can see now that she was on a growth journey and she still is learning and growing deeper in her faith and trusting, not only friends and family but God too. Trust never was easy for Kira, it didn't matter who she was with, she didn't know if someone was trying to help her or trying to hurt her, it was so hard for her to determine that.

Kira said: "Lord" I don't think I ever even really thought about it, trusting you or not trusting you, even though you're God Almighty. I just didn't trust you or anyone else in my life. I took things to heart too much and allowed the hurt and pain to control me.

In the past Kira really thought she was dealing with it and handling it. Now she knows that she wasn't. She remembers when she was living in California and there was a high-profile case in the news, and she was watching some of the news clips about how his wife was murdered. Lord, it brought out so much of the past of what she had to live through. Even when she was married the first time, things could have gone south there too, but luckily, they didn't. As a child having to live with the way her dad was and the meanness, Kira wouldn't have wanted to be on TV or even in a courtroom to tell the world what all her dad did.

Kira remembers all the pain being lifted from her and the walls crumbling—and the freedom. She remembered being so scared she didn't know what was going on within her or what was happening. You were cleansing her and cleaning out her heart. It just clicked: God was tearing down the walls and giving her a new spirit within her. It came out when Kira was ready to handle it. You picked her up and you carried her.

Kira had thought that she was going crazy. She didn't really understand at all what was happening or going on at that time. The thoughts of her dad and wondering and being scared and wondering what the heck was going on. Was she having a nervous breakdown, or what? You knew didn't you Lord? You knew it was time to clean out all the junk and the muck in her life. It was time to stop what was hurting her and keeping her frozen in fear that someone would find out how her dad was and use it against her. Kira learned that she wasn't at fault and she couldn't help what her dad or others did.... she wasn't responsible for other peoples' actions. How did she ever get to thinking

Having Coffee with the Special One

that she had that kind of power or control? When did she start thinking that way?

When Kira was younger, she took to heart what people said, and unfortunately, she let what one woman said when she was around her influence her in the wrong way. Kira overheard someone say that if a family member committed suicide or had mental problems then others would follow. Kira was really scared and hoped she was not one of them, and she hoped she didn't follow in the footsteps of her dad. Kira had recently turned forty when that case was on TV, and her dad was close to forty when he committed suicide. She was hoping that wasn't what was happening to her. You know at that time all the muck that was in her head she had tied it all together and it scared the heck out of her! Where you showed her that it was time to let it go and let you come into her heart and mind.

As Kira sat and thought: God you pulled her out of more than one dark moment in her life. With the beginning of her childhood life…her current life with her husband and family….and then the life she had with her ex-husband Nevan.

All the healing you did in Kira. You started tearing down the walls and lifting her from the pain she held inside of her. You pulled her through it all you taught her to forgive and to let go, let go so that she could remember the good times, the love and the joy you put into her life, her siblings her mom, you showed her just how much she was really loved even when she didn't feel like it at the time. You took away the anger and placed it with love and peace. It was amazing how you replaced the negative thoughts and replaced them with loving and caring thoughts.

How after all those years, Jesus, you have made her whole. Kira doesn't even know if she can explain the magnitude of the power of the Lord, of how he can change the way you look at life and the way that you think.

Kira hates to admit it, but she truly hated what her dad did and what he put her family through. Yes, she knows hate is a strong word, but she did hate what he did. Kira said: "Jesus I release them completely into your hands and I put my trust in you". Kira hopes that Nevan did truly turn his life over to you Lord before he died for his sake. Jesus, you helped her move on and she gets to see the beauty in her life, and she has the life you planned for her. You gave Kira the family that she wanted, and you gave her the beautiful grandchildren that she absolutely loves.

Kira is so thankful and grateful for the life you have given her. She didn't appreciate what you did for her; really until now and she is sorry for that, Lord. Lord, you have given so much even when she didn't deserve to have what you have given her! Kira didn't always acknowledge that it was a gift

Having Coffee with the Special One

that you had given her, at times she did God: but not at all times and not to your glory as she should have, Kira is aware of that now; now she tries to make a special effort to make sure she thanks God for all he is doing in her life, believe me; she still messes up at times, but at least she is aware of trying to always be grateful. That just makes her life so much more pleasant, even in the times of trials and tribulations, of which if you're alive you'll go through them. So just hang on and let God lead the way.

Jesus, I have wallowed in a lost state and let my life go amuck, Kira said. She hopes that she can do, as you want her to do and stay on your path. She knows still that she has a lot to see and to learn. Kira hopes that she remembers this lesson well and she doesn't fall back into the black hole where she fell before. God has worked too hard to get her to where she is today.

Kira realized that she does monitor what the Lord does…. what is his job?! She keeps pulling things back into her grip when all she needs do is let go. Let go and Let God. How many times does she have to be reminded of this? How many times will he tell her to let go? All she must remember is that he will complete it: but it will be in his time not hers.

Kira tries too many times to rush things and get quick results. Especially where her family is concerned. Kira wants so bad for them to have a good life and to succeed but that isn't what they want, or she wanted for that matter.

Kira asks: Who am I to say what is right for them? Who am I to tell them what they should be doing? You're their guide, I'm not.

You know Kira has been carrying the weight of her family on her shoulders and she worries about them. So much that it really affects her work and her whole being. It was wearing her out and it wears her down.

When did Kira start thinking that she had so much power and control? When did she put you on her level? How could she have done that? How could she have put you anywhere close to a human being? Jesus, you are Kira's love even when she was so wrong to do that to you and really her family too. All of this goes through Kira's head, and she would discuss all of this with the Lord.

As Kira prays: Lord, please remove the yolk and the walls that I have built that holds me back. Let the spirit in me move and put me in the right direction you want me to follow. You have given me all that I have and use me as the tool to get me where you want me to be. You're guiding me even

Having Coffee with the Special One

though I stumble along the way. Hopefully, I will always remember that now.

Kira says: I know you're with me and guiding me. We aren't powerful enough to ruin the plan you have set for us, as I got reminded again from Gay, one of my siblings.

Kira started shutting down and pulling away from people: she didn't want to sit around and eat foods that would make her gain weight, so she wouldn't go to lunch with friends or co-workers. She cared about how she looked more than enjoying the friends that she had and the moments they had together.

She quit doing things that were good for her. Kira shut out the people who cared about her the most. She didn't realize it until currently just how much she had closed herself off to the people around her. Kira realized it when she attended her friend's office's annual open house. Kira didn't get to talk to Glenda that much, but she did greet Kira with a hug. During the open house, Glenda didn't talk to Kira, and Kira didn't go over to talk or hug her. Glenda had to say hello to a lot of other guests. Kira is seeing just how much she had pushed relationships to the side, the back burner and did not take the proper time for them to flourish or to build on them. Sometimes Kira guesses that it just must hit you in the face before you realize that what is important in life. You must try to keep it alive.

Patty Scott

When Kira moved out of an old house into a new one, she got a glimpse at how cluttered and messed up she had let her life get. All the dust that gathered behind furniture and her closet was a cluttered mess. Kira was so embarrassed that she had let it get so bad. It's so nice to be able to see the beauty now, to be almost free from clutter. (Like that will ever really happen, Kira is such a slob.)

It lifts her spirits to be free from the burdens she carried until she learned to turn them over to you and to listen to you, Lord. Even when it's very hard, at times, to swallow how she has been acting and allowing work to take over her life. Kira knows that she didn't want to be in that position, when she was younger, she was responsible, but she didn't eat sleep and breath work. Looks like she forgot what really was and is important in life.

It's funny she has been striving to be good and one of the best in the field of the tax business and all that has done is cause her pain and grief at times. Because of the way she handled it, not because she went into that business. Thankfully, you have maintained what she has left, and you're helping her and guiding her to do what is right. Kira forgot the most important factor in the equation, of which is you. Kira put the wrong things first. She

Having Coffee with the Special One

can't blame anyone but herself for that. No one else had control over how she acted or how she placed the importance of things in her life, it was only her to blame.

As Kira sits down with her cup of coffee, first thing she does is to say: Good morning God. I slept well last night. Thank you for that. I did dream, but I can't remember what they were about now.

Kira keeps thinking about the other day, when she realized that she had been stupid and saw the sign at the church that said: "You love us even when we are stupid". Ha ha. She still gets a chuckle out of that.

Well you hit the nail on the head again this morning. As Kira woke up and went to the bathroom you were on her mind: she needs to hurry and get up so she can have her time with you. The kids are showing up for dinner tonight, so she won't have the time to spend with you in devotion. Isn't that one of the items you keep telling her, is to take it slow and not be in a rush?

It's not entirely true, that she won't get to spend time with you. She will be seeing her grand kids and spend time with them and enjoy them, so in a way she is with you surrounded by love. Lord, I am starting to see just how time is just flying by. Kira thinks: It seems like I don't take the time to slow down...so my life is just slipping away. She isn't sure how to say it to you, but you know what she is feeling. She thinks about the lady at church who told Kira she better not let life slip away from her and work until she dies, or something to that affect.

We are talking about retirement, right? Kira asks. She hopes one day she can and will, but she doesn't know if that's what your plan is for her or not. Kira is just off key this morning isn't she, just out of sorts a bit?

You do know that the steroids and the medication that they have her on is making her ADD worse. You know sort of scattered brained and can't stay focused. Please forgive Kira if she gets off track at times and loses her thoughts.

As usual there is so much stuff running through her mind, she doesn't really know where to start. Yet you know before her what she is thinking or what you want to cover and talk about, you're the one that says, "Wait patiently". Before she even understood it, yet now she knows. Another aha moment, from you. The light just went off.

Can we go back to what you were saying about Kira with her time schedule and what you were saying also where you told her to hang on to your yokes

for now? Here Kira was praying for them to be removed, she didn't know that it was you holding her back. She is sorry as she wasn't sure if she should write it that way, but she knew she could

Having Coffee with the Special One

feel that there were "blockers". Kira felt that there were blockers holding her back instead of looking at it the way she should have been looking at it.

Kira was seeing the negative side not the positive side that was coming from you. She thought it was the evil one getting in her way. She kept wanting to push forward rather than just sit back and enjoy the slow down and the moment you had her in. It's so good to feel the love and joy in her life again, Lord; you know the mess she was in and she kept trying to make people leave her alone. She was trying to find fault in everything they did just so she had a reason to stay away from them and keep them away from her.

What the heck! Why did she do that? Love and joy are much more fulfilling and so much more enjoyable, and it makes your life more pleasing to live in. Why does she have to do things the hard way Jesus, why did she fight things so much? She wasn't being fair to Tim her husband who is a very big part in her life and deserves to be treated better. She hadn't been very nice to him either. It was almost like she blamed him for every single bad thing that happened in her life, and it was his fault. How fair was that to him? Yet he stayed with her through it all and he loved her anyway. An example of unconditional love.

You know when she waits on you and you do things in your time; they go so much smoother and she gets so much more joy out of doing it. Yet there is the big difference of when she isn't letting you control the outcome and the steps she takes or uses there is a battle to get the job done.

What makes Kira even think that she can take control back from you anyway? How did she think she was more powerful and mighty than you? How could she do that to you? This happens more often than she even cares to admit.

When she realizes that it's what you want her to do and when you want her to do it, it's much more peaceful and flows so much smoother. As you say there is a time and a season for all things, yet she tries to push them along, and it just doesn't work. Why is that so hard to remember at times?

That's what you're talking about. You're putting the joy back into Kira; it's all your workings in her. Now she can understand that part "She thinks she took credit instead of giving it to you. She is sorry". Mental note, for Kira, stop taking credit for what you do in her life!! She is glad that you're helping her understand where she has been going wrong and why her life turns into the mess and the clutter that's everywhere. Her job, her marriage, her relationship with her children, friends, all the people who mean something to her. Kira guesses that in a way sort of this is kind of like taking others for granted, thinking they should always, bend to what her way is, she has got to remember that her way is not the only way and may not always be the best way to get something done. Bring God into all your decisions, you might even find, that you change your mind on some of them.

Having Coffee with the Special One

Something of an enlightenment: Loving one another Lord, is the focus in life isn't it ... relationships and friendships? Kira didn't know how many times she had ruined the ones or just picked some of the wrong people for friends that she had in the past. She knows it wasn't all her, but she also knows, that maybe she could have salvaged some of them. Yes, she knows that it takes two Lord. She knows she can't take credit for everything that has gone bad in her life, and she also knows there was a purpose and a reason for it. Some she would rather not go through but did, and sometimes there is no reason at all... it just happens. That's the way it is!

Even in the movies and books they show that it all boils down to loving one another and being kind to each other ... and you're the lead of us all. Yet Kira chose to push those she loved away and try to just stay a loner. Kira remembers what it felt like when she was so in love with Tim before she let fear and mistrust take hold. Lord she knows what the feeling of love is when you put it in me again it's so much nicer, there is so much more joy.

She is glad that you want to and desire for all to build an intimate relationship with you one with deep meaning and she understands more what it really means to have this kind of a relationship with you. Kira guesses she never looked at things this way, and she didn't realize that's what you really wanted. A deeper meaningful relationship with you.

Kira says: Thank you for thinking that she is worth it and for taking the time to show her this and Jesus, how to. Kira thinks just knowing how to, makes it easier to do so. Not everyone has learned on how to Lord. It doesn't really require an arm or a leg or any money, it's something that's free, and so freely given to us.

Then why is it so hard for us to do? Why is this so important item; one that's so hard to make important? It's also the knowing how to do it, through scriptures and worshiping, this is how we learn what kind of relationship that Jesus wants with us. Kira was striving for perfection and in the wrong way. She fell into the trap of expecting people to be perfect. She pushed for the perfect office, the perfect staff, the perfect tax person, the perfect, the perfect, and the perfect. Kira thinks it was her misunderstanding what she thought had to be done and how it had to be done, instead of really studying your word she would miss interpret what you were saying or the minister was saying and she would handle things in the wrong way at times. Often, sometimes, because she wouldn't listen.

Kira asks: Lord, help me to do this the right way, help me to accept people's limitations. Help me to realize I have them too and help me to remember

Having Coffee with the Special One

you're our guide, our Alpha and Omega, you're the one.

Yes, Kira realized that she messed up her life by seeking perfection!

There are so many trials and tribulations going on in her life in these times, and there always has been. She remembers when she lived in Colorado and her friend Kendra said to her one day, Kira, you have such an exciting life, there never is a dull boring moment. Kira thought she was crazy because she thought her life was a mess, but Kendra was right Kira's life wasn't ever boring and she never had a dull moment. The kids themselves helped with that too.

There were so many blessings and teachings in the experiences that Kira was going through. She guessed that she looked at them differently now because she was just more aware of them. Now she looks at them as teachings and can maintain an attitude of gratitude. Believe her, she will still get frustrated and must stand back, take a deep breath, and remember God is in control.

But when he is in control and on your side, then who can be against her? Why does she still allow the crap to get under her skin at times? Is it because she wasn't putting her trust in you and you had to pull her back into your light? Jesus, for the most part, Kira thinks that she does better then wham! something comes along and knocks her for a loop, taking her back to square one.

Then at other times, even though this is not a fun time to be going through, the thoughts about what she is going through is not at the forefront of her mind even though they are still there. Like when the computers are acting up at the office, we all get locked out or information gets dropped even when we know we did the work, Kira just wants to scream. But when she gets up, walks away and doesn't let the negative situation control how she feels, she realizes that's thanks to you, it's your peace that surpasses all understanding and keeps her heart and mind open unto you. Even though the problem is still there, it just isn't grabbing her uncontrollably. Kira isn't going to lie, she really wishes that her life and her surroundings, would get somewhat back to calmness, and give her a break for a while.

So many things at one time!

Kira knows God that you say you'll not give us any burden that we cannot bear, but Kira thinks that you think there is more in her than she thinks there is. She just wants to sit down and cry at times, she is so tired of fighting the battles.

(Jesus: She wants you to fight them for her.)

She wants you to resolve them and make them leave her alone. Kira wants to be that little child

Having Coffee with the Special One

that she sees you holding on to as you're walking along the beach. In her mind, she is always giggling, and your eyes sparkle as you look down and smile upon her. But she's an adult and she need to get through these trials, if for nothing else, to show others that you're there and you're helping her. It's just at your pace not hers. She hates to say it, but one of the hardest things for her to accept is she can't tell you what to do and she can't tell you when to do it.

So, what does it mean when you tell her to be bold then?

She needs to understand that she needs to learn what you mean when you tell her to be bold. In Kira's way of looking at things and friendships, she kind of looks at you just as she would a friend, except she thinks that she has more respect for you. Respect is also an important factor in relationships. However, Kira had lost respect for others. She just didn't see if they could go on hurting her, then how could she respect them and if they wouldn't even recognize that they did something wrong then how could she respect them? One example was her dad, she had lost all respect for him. He never did as far as she could remember say he was sorry or admit that he ever did anything wrong.

Also how does she be bold yet learn to let go and let you deal with it? Release the hold that she has so tightly? Then there is the next thing of doing all that she can and letting you do the rest.

God she sure hopes that she will learn all of this and remember it so she can go on to the next thing that you want her to learn. She knows there will be something else if she is on earth and following you there will be something else.

As you know Kira sure was having an exceedingly difficult time of understanding what that truly meant, "To let go and let God". That was extremely hard for her. Everyone was telling her she was such a control freak. She didn't understand that either until now! She even said it, she always said she didn't want to control your life, but she does want to control hers. Boy was that the wrong attitude to have! It's amazing what all you taught her in such a short period of time—only 6-months—and this all was brought to light.

God, Kira is also learning that you're in control of her life. She makes too much of a mess of things. Kira got them into debt with the business purchases, living on the edge, and pushing her loved ones away, what else? She knows there is more. Let's get it all out! She buries everything so deep inside of her.

Kira built the walls, and you just keep showing her where she needs a cleaning and sometimes a deep cleaning. Not really what she signed up for or even thought would be happening. Kira wanted you to change everybody else, and she realized it was her that needed to change.

Having Coffee with the Special One

Lord you know that trust was an issue Kira had. It's not so much that she didn't trust you (yes it was) she didn't want to admit it, but she didn't trust you either. She never looked at her mistrust in people as mistrusting you. Kira knows she has been wrong. Going through this time with you Lord has opened her eyes and let her see just what she was and wasn't doing. She had been so afraid of getting hurt and wanting and expecting everything to be perfect, she never looked at the flaw in herself, to where she was so mistrusting. It ended up her not putting her trust and faith in you. Kira allowed fear to lead her, not trust and faith in you. Fear is such a liar.

Kira sees changes in society as a whole and in individuals. There are so many countries at war! In her opinion, it's because they're pushing you out of their lives and countries, not putting you first.

Kira knows that there for a while she wasn't even keeping you first in her life. How does it get this way?

God we all need to put you back where you belong in our lives. We all get so busy and we are forgetting that you're the one and only. You're the only one that takes the time and care to show us that we are worthy of your grace and mercy. Who else is going to take the time to show us that? Who else even cares enough about us to do something like that for us? There is so much proof that you're there, yet we at times forget that it's you.

We get this false pretense that we can do it without you, yet look at the mess we are in. We need to get our trust in you back to where it belongs and let you have our little children, in schools and in our homes, put you back to the top in their lives. These thoughts just continue to go through Kira's head, and she wonders just where she went wrong, and forgets to notice the changes.

Kira always needs to reaffirm her trust in you. For example, when she crosses a flyover, she is so afraid, and she still needs to reaffirm her trust in you, so she isn't afraid. And God you know the panic she has in receiving gifts. Kira knows it may sound dumb to others but Lord it's very hard for her to receive gifts from others.

She knows that this is sort of off track, but it's a perfect example not fully trusting and looking at things the wrong way. At times she felt guilty in her life for the gifts you gave her, like the nice homes or the nice car, and she

tried to act like she didn't have anything so it wouldn't bother others. She also didn't want the things to control her. She didn't look at them as gifts from you and it probably seemed as though she didn't appreciate what you gave her and still give her. She just didn't really know how to handle all that she was given. She had so much and not everyone in her family had what she had.

Having Coffee with the Special One

Then one day Kira learned that it's up to God what he blesses others with during their life. She learned that maybe she didn't need what her neighbor had, so maybe that's why some don't get much because they don't need what others need. You know that makes sense, and she has learned to appreciate and not be scared to have what God decides to give her. Don't compare and don't wish you had what others did, because really there is a lot of responsibilities that comes with these gifts too. So maybe think twice for what we pray for, because we might just get what we ask for and more. (Chuckle)

Kira had noticed a change in herself. Actually, she noticed more and more changes in herself, and realized that once you start looking for God in all of your life and seek to have a relationship with him, then you start to recognize that all things come from the Lord. He wants others to have the blessings so why not enjoy what he gives us? He had afforded Kira to have many gifts and blessings, all that came from you.

Kira read in one of her studies, a guy had a sign on his Mercedes Benz which read "Don't let this car fool you...my treasure is in Heaven". That simple message stuck with her. It showed her that the Lord keeps things in the proper order and puts you first in his life, but he also appreciates and enjoys the gifts that you afford him to have. Kira hopes she can think of that and make sure she keeps you in the proper place you belong in her life. She does enjoy what you give her and afford her to have. It's you who decides what gifts others will have and it's not our place to say whether they deserve it or not.

The time off with our family and friends, the ability to travel is what Kira enjoys so much. The ability to do the work that she does and the great sales you find for her when she goes shopping is great, and she enjoys it. Jesus thank you for blessing me in all the ways that you chose to do so. You kept me alive, you helped my kids take care of me and you're holding me. This runs through Kira's mind a lot. There is so much to be thankful for, and grateful for as life is the main one. You don't know how close we are that it could change in a split second. It could be a car wreck. You could fall off a building. Or you could be close to drowning. Remember, it could be that fast.

God if it wasn't your will Kira wouldn't be here today. All the times in life where she messed up or wasn't paying attention you were there watching over her and blessing her. You showed her the ways that she didn't want to go, and you showed her why she didn't want to go there. Kira needs to learn that you're giving all that she has to her, it all comes from you.

No one can be cursing you and loving you at the same time, you have told Kira that more than once. Lord, she loves you and she thanks you for not giving up on her.

Having Coffee with the Special One

Kira really is enjoying this walk, this journey with you Lord, even though she is getting to see where she's been most of the problem in the situations. This doesn't flow well when it's her trying to think of what to say does it? It all comes from you. You'll lead her and guide her. It's hard to swallow, when you find out you're part of the problem.

We don't deserve the kindness from you. Kira remembers the pastor saying a few weeks ago in a sermon that we don't deserve what you give us. If we got what we deserved, it wouldn't be a pretty picture. It made her think of how when she was messing around with things she shouldn't have been, after her divorce and not eating like she should (her and her worry of getting fat) and not thinking of what it was doing to her or what she was doing to herself. Kira is sorry if she repeats herself at times, it's because something else comes to light and makes her think of things again in a different way.

God you saved Kira rather than her going down the death road or some other path. You saved her from herself, she was her own worst enemy. "You could have let her go but you didn't." That was a turning point in her life. She was on a four- or five-year road of destruction.

Patty Scott

Kira fell for the wrong people. Except Heff, he was a decent guy from what she could remember of him. Kira lost him because she was such a mess, but who knows, maybe he was in her life just to meet Dot. She wouldn't lie— it hurt to lose him to her, but it was her own fault. What ever happened to him or them, Kira wondered? At times old moments will pop into her head, and she will think of them.

Kira was also thinking about the day she and Sheila were talking about the day that the Lord had knocked her in the head. Not that she liked it, but that was probably one of the best things for you to do, was to knock her in the head and make her realize what she was doing. (guess knocking her in the head is the only way, you can get her attention.)

It was at that time also when Becky—an old high school friend—called Kira out of the blue and told her if she didn't stop doing the bad things she was doing, she wouldn't be Kira's friend anymore. She still remembers that day and that phone call. Becky was one of Kira's closest friends even though they weren't hanging out together at that time. Yet she cared enough to call Kira. It also made an impact on Kira and her life.

You used Kira's friends, and the people she cared about to get through to Kira. Kira still missed and thinks of Becky often. Kira is so sorry that she died so young. Becky had long black hair, black rimmed glasses and was skinny as a bean pole even though

Having Coffee with the Special One

she ate like you wouldn't believe. She just burned it all off.

Y et another day...

There are times when Kira just sits and thinks about guilt feelings that are instilled in us from other people. Kira always thinks people have an agenda when they give gifts, or they are kind. That isn't fair to them or her for that fact. You can't assume the worst in people because there are some that want to be around you because of who you are or who you know. All in all, really there are more good people in this world, and shouldn't assume the worst of others. It's not only from you God, it's from friends and family too, that Kira struggles with these feelings!

It's dumb of her too because she does love receiving gifts and cards from people and especially small little notes from her grandkids that they leave on her desk at the office. The little "I love you" notes, it really is the little things in life that mean so much and you miss when they don't happen anymore.

Kira has some of them on her wall as well so she can keep them close to heart, look at them once and a while, and really think and see what is important in life. They make Kira stop to take time to think about them, their little smiles, and their hugs. She doesn't know if they know how much they mean to her, but they do mean a lot to her and she tries to let them know too.

When people want to give gifts, she has got to stop second guessing and assuming there is a hidden agenda, because just maybe there isn't one. There are also other reasons why Kira is leery of accepting gifts especially if it's someone that's related to the work life. You know Lord, that's one of the areas that really bothers her when receiving gifts. But you have taught me to understand that even in the work world, some people just want to be nice. There may be some that don't but in general people have good hearts and they want to say thank you. you can kind of tell by the way they act or their body language when they give it to you.

In life there are a lot of quirks aren't there? When someone acts like they want to help you, what do they want from that? Kira remembers years ago when they were going through the financial disaster. Now she realizes that she didn't put her trust in you and what happened is they ended up giving up too easily with the result having their credibility and integrity questioned.

Kira felt like she was lower than dirt. She went against her word. She had vowed not to be that way again, she will put her trust in you to the end Lord, she won't give in to fear. Just please let her know that there is an end and it will be over. Rather it's losing a material item, or whatever it may be, don't let her give up and them get the best

Having Coffee with the Special One

of her. Let truth and justice prevail and stand out. They gave up, she knows the difference now between letting go versus giving up and having no hope. (Faith)

Now Kira can see, it was because she didn't turn to you and she didn't trust you. Because of the way she acted, and she felt, she didn't have the peace that you give her. She didn't rise above the circumstances, and she let them swallow her up. She knows that she didn't put her faith in you like she should have.

Each time in her life Kira sees where she messed up royally. Lord if she would have just had faith! But you know what, if she didn't have these trials and tribulations then she probably wouldn't be who she is today and maybe she wouldn't have learned just how important you're in her life, and how much you actually are in her life.

How did she ever think she was powerful enough to change your plans for her life? To change what you desire for her and where you wanted her to be. It's you who is helping her be the person that she is today. But she also thinks she wouldn't know the difference and wouldn't be able to tell what you have brought her to. She sees if she hadn't done it the way she did but had handled it the way she handles it now, there really is a big difference in the ways God, with you and without you.

Each time she goes through something devastating it shows her and reminds her that you're always

Patty Scott

with her. Each item has been a lesson, either to teach her or to enable her to help someone else. It's like footprints in the sand, you carry her some days, kick her in the butt some days and drag her some days. Sometimes you skip along the path holding on to her and she sings and giggles. Lord she does hope that she can make you laugh and chuckle at some of the stupid stuff she does.

Kira can picture it at times, don't you think at times it's fun? Sometimes Kira pictures you and her just sitting there talking and having a conversation and you smile your big bright smile, there is laughter in your eyes and that sparkle is there, it's so heartwarming. Kira thinks: Lord I know I could have them more often if I would just slow down and take the time. It really does lighten my load and my day. You make it all worth being here and knowing you. You really do love me and care about me, don't you? I am realizing that it's true love, not my imagination either. My first love...

Thoughts for today:

Man, Kira's attitude really was bad! Lord, look at how she treated church. Kira is so thankful that you forgive when people ask, she is so sorry. If it wasn't for church Kira wouldn't be where she is in her faith. She allowed one person to change how she viewed religion, and the funny thing is; that

Having Coffee with the Special One

isn't about religion, it's all about you and getting closer to you and building a relationship with you, Kira just never looked at it in that way before. She forgot or didn't think why she went to church in the first place and who it was for.

You do realize it was the minister at the church in California that she was thinking of. That was really kind of dumb of Kira to allow something like that to come between how she felt about God. Just because someone may word something wrong, or they personally may be in a better place than you, you shouldn't have let them push you away. That wasn't fair to them or to God or to you.

Kira is incredibly grateful you led her to the church she is attending now as she feels so much at home. She is remembering why she is there. It's for no other reason than to keep you close and to hear your word. She is glad she was led to her church. She knows it's not the religion it's the belief and faith in you and to be with other believers. Gather to worship and glorify you, it all comes from the Bible and your word is in the Bible, what you promise us. This is where we get to praise you and sing praises for your glory. Kira is like others as she struggled with her faith, and sort of broke away. Its' amazing how unconditional love works. God accepts us back as if we never left him once we ask for forgiveness and open our hearts to him.

Patty Scott

Today is the first day of the rest of your life. Think about this for a while. What does this really mean to you?

To Kira it means, she gets a fresh start, a new lease on life.

Good morning Jesus, how are you today?

Kira wants to tell you that she really is enjoying the time off, the time to relax, the time that you're giving her right now. She needed to slow down. She forgot just how good it felt to not be rushed and pulled in every direction (you know as she said earlier, about in her jammies.) God, she loves the peaceful feeling and your presence in her life. Last night at church she was thinking of the dancing spirits (she could picture in her mind) and relishing in the peace.

Thank you for having Tim go to church with her. It was so good to have him next to her, even though it was probably for the pie. All that matters is how you see her, not everyone else. Why or when did she start caring about that so much? It's your thoughts of her that matter and only that. Kira needs to keep remembering that it's none of her business what others think of her, those are their private thoughts not any of her business. Not sure if others really realize this either.

Having Coffee with the Special One

Kira has always loved the spirit you put in her Lord, but she guesses that she just forgot to thank you, to take care of it, feed it and let you know all the time. You have given her such a high spirit and an active one. She loves how it shows in her face and smile. You gave it to her kids too, which she is thankful for. God, she hopes that they will go back to you. She hopes that they will come back to what she has too. She wants to pray that you'll open their hearts and minds unto you Jesus Christ too.

Lord you do know that part of the fear is about completely letting go and turning my life over to you was because Kira wasn't ready to leave this world. She knows she wants to be in Heaven with you and when it's her time there is nothing, she can do to stop it or change it.

She just isn't ready to leave it, now. For some reason, she thought that letting go was sort of like giving up, and she didn't completely understand that. But it was quite the opposite. Kira thought when she truly had faith in you and gave up all control, that she would die. What she didn't realize as what it was so she could really live. Live the life of peace and happiness that you intended for her to have. She didn't realize well, in a way you do die, you're a born-again Christian. Everyone must be born again. That was interesting for her to learn.

Jesus, she still loves the kisses, the hugs and all that mushy stuff. She doesn't feel or think her job is over here. Does she have the right to even think or feel that way? It's not that she doesn't want to be in Heaven with you. She knows she is on a natural time clock, and there is nothing she can do to extend her life or shorten it because it's your plan, not hers.

Kira just doesn't want to be there yet (as if she could control that either.) Is that fair or right of her? There you go, getting her to digging out one of her deepest fears. She also feels that you're going to allow her to live to a ripe old age. Maybe banged up a little (from the car wreck), but a ripe old age. Kira can't help what she thought, and how her mind was working. Well yes, she can now that she knows. She knows that now but anyway there you have it. You said we would even touch on her deepest darkest fears, well that was one of them.

Lord, you did exactly what she said would have to be done. Knock her in the head to wake her up.

Kira will choose her words more carefully next time. Lord she is thoroughly enjoying the time you're giving her. Kira is enjoying feeling again, feeling your presence and your closeness to her. Please help her to keep this peace in her and your Spirit. Lord she loves it. She really loves the cleansing in her heart and mind. As you're fully aware, she was a mess inside and out. She is doing as you ask her to do, she is basking in your

Having Coffee with the Special One

presence. As she used to do in the sun, she just didn't connect the dots, she didn't realize that that was you wanting to get close and be close to her also.

As Kira is listening, you're telling her she needs to stop thinking. You're going to fix all her problems, and Lord she does understand what you're saying that you're not going to take her problems away but you're going to make a change in the way to approach the problems.

You're right, she shouldn't ask you to remove them, she should ask how would you handle this one and listen to what you say you're the Almighty, you wouldn't give her the wrong answer. Yes, she does have a lot of problems, It seems as though each day, more just keep adding up, Kira is trying so hard to rise above them all, and just forget about some of them, maybe they will end up taking care of themselves. Maybe if she would let go and just give her mind a rest that would be something nice, just give her peace. Just because we believe and have faith doesn't change the fact that we are still going to have struggles, in fact there are times when Kira thinks that because her faith is growing stronger, that the evil is just attacking her life and everything in it trying to pull her away from God, and this time she isn't going to let it happen, God has worked too hard in her and in her life to just let it all get taken away. There's nothing in this world that can take God's love away from us. Please if nothing else remember that because he really does love and care about us.

That was Kira's thoughts for today, and here are some others for us to discuss:

Jesus, on another subject, **YES**: Kira does want to win, that's correct. YES, she feels defeated at times and she doesn't want others to be let down. A perfect example was a confrontation she had. By the way Lord thank you for going with me yesterday. I felt your whole presence and I was so happy about the way it went. As you could tell, it was totally unexpected the way it went and that's what you're talking about isn't it, how to look at it in your light.

This is a perfect example where Kira went wrong in the past. She would get an attitude that they were wrong, and she was out to prove that they were wrong. She knows what you're talking about here. Kira could see that in her the difference from how she felt before, the nervousness inside and shaking feeling, where yesterday she was so calm and at peace. It just went so smooth. That's where in the past she had thought if it was easy it was wrong. God's way is the hard way, so she guesses that's not in stone and a given. Your way isn't always the hard way because yesterday was a very good example.

Kira is talking to God under her breath: Lord once I got here it was so smooth.

Having Coffee with the Special One

I need to quit acting like I'm going to take on "the world". This is where my associates are trying to tell me I do wrong isn't it? It was the difference of being aggressive or being assertive. I never looked at it like this in the past, I never really cared either.

I didn't have the compassion in the past as I do have now. I never really thought about how others felt, or how it would affect others. I hate to say it, but I guess I didn't even care much about others to even stop and think about them or how they would feel. I just saw that something needed to be done and I did it, without even thinking at times really. This is one area where Kira did need to change, she needed to stop and think about how she was affecting others.

Kira was wondering why she acted as she did and why her brain wasn't properly working. Now she knows you have showed her joy to bring her back into the now and to pay attention.

As you know Lord, she was really struggling but when she finally stood back and quit thinking about it, it finally clicked in her head: you're giving her a bit more clarity. God, all these years of her doing things the way she was, it just wasn't working for her and it made the way so hard.

Kira guesses when you don't put your trust in God or even others you kind of miss the boat and miss what they might be trying to tell you. Sometimes in life things are just unfair, and there isn't anything you can do about it. But knowing that and accepting it, might make it a little better or easier for you to get over it. Not everybody is honest and has good intentions. But she must also remember, there is one that you can trust always, and it's Jesus; he can't lie, he just can't.

Kira wonders just how many times she will also see areas where she didn't really trust God either. Why did it take her so long Lord to get it, for it to make sense to her? Last night she realized how overwhelming it had been to her to have to go through the forgiveness process and that there was no way she could have handled all the situations at once!

The forgiveness of her dad's actions, by writing him a letter and telling him even after he was dead. She finally forgave him and told him how he made her mad for the way he was and what he did. For her forgiving Nevan and him forgiving her, Lord: those were some powerful emotions that really knocked her for a loop!

Kira just can't seem to find the right words for how you moved her and healed her!! She felt awkward in the past when she prayed, and she felt like maybe she wasn't doing it properly or that she wasn't doing it in the proper place (grant it maybe in the bathroom, isn't the best place.) She wondered how she knew if she was doing what God wanted her to do or not, or if it was his will or hers.

Having Coffee with the Special One

Now she knows that when it comes from the heart and you feel such a peaceful feeling come over you, you know it's from God. He will also tap on your heart when he wants you to do something. Maybe it's that gut feeling you have or get at times, that's from God. Kira still has a hard time at times distinguishing if it's God's will or she is reading into it what she wants to hear or know, but overall, the outcome is up to him no matter what. If he wants it done, he will make sure you do it, like finishing The Porcelain Rose and like finally forgiving, it'll get done.

Now Kira just wonders why in the world did it take her so long to do that, other than it was for God's purpose, not hers. She even thought it was what she needed, but still it was for God's purpose because it happened the way it did.

Jesus, I can't tell you enough that there is such a difference in "my way" or your way.

It brings to Kira's mind another conversation that she had with her loan officer; God bless him. They were discussing terms for her loan on the building and the interest rate, and she had to keep the insurance she hated so much paying. When he asked her: "Kira what do you say?" she sort of chuckled and then he said, "it's what it is and my way or the highway." Something like that. (Geez isn't fun when people throw back in your face what you say to them.)

God how did he continually put up with me, and why? She really felt that way at the time. Kira thought it was a negotiation tool. She was so stubborn and headstrong. Grabbing the bull by the horns. But she does see there is difference in the way to accomplish what she wanted and bringing you into it. Kira has got to remember to sit and discuss these items with you first!! And yes, Lord you're right. She does think that she gets a defeated attitude. She needs to look at it differently. Just because she may have lost the battle it doesn't mean that she lost the war!!

As someone said a long time ago, it isn't always fun to find out where you were the main problem in the equation and the way you looked at things. Sometimes you bite off more than you can chew, and it's more than you bargain for. But if you're going to really get right with God then you really must face all things, where you were wrong and where the situation was just wrong. There always is a better way to handle things.

Maybe this is not what you may expect when you're to sit and pray with God, but it isn't all one sided. It's your asking for something, it's us listening, waiting for him to answer and telling him, sharing with him. Treat him as you would your spouse or someone you want to build a relationship with, then stop and listen to him. He won't always tell you what you want to hear, but he wants you to

Having Coffee with the Special One

get it all out even the stuff you bury deep inside and can be embarrassing to bring it up.

Does Kira ever know that, you'll see there are topics that are very hard to talk about and bring up, but you must if you want to be right with God? That's what Kira is finding out.

Kira thanks the Lord for what he is teaching her and showing her—even when some of this is hard to face and swallow— how she has been so one sided and so stubborn. Lord she can see where she really got lost in thought. It was like she was locked in her own head, kind of a prisoner to her own thoughts which had a hold on her. You know how you feel like you're in the fog, and not really paying attention to what you're doing? Well she sort of felt like she was walking around in a daze, always lost in thought.

She wanted to get out of it. She also knew that she tries to fix everything and believes there is an answer and a reason for everything. Nothing happens just to happen. There is a reason for it.

Kira does believe Lord, that if she remembers that when there is knocking on her heart, then it's from you. As you're aware, she was really struggling with that Lord, if it was your will or hers?

Kira had asked how a person like her would know if she was doing your will or her will. One day in church, the answer came to her when the minister said again that if it's God's will it comes from the heart and that God has been knocking on your heart. There were times when she felt like she wasn't doing things properly, as you're aware of that. She was having a big problem with slowing down and relaxing, and just taking it easy. She felt as though she might have missed out on life if she would have slowed down. Kira didn't realize that she would enjoy life a little better and live a better life. You have added to her life not taken away from it.

It's funny now, guess what she missed out on? It was what she wanted all along, but she didn't realize that this is what was missing: all she wanted was to be with her kids, and her family.

Kira thought she was letting them go to let them grow, that she had to stay out of their life because she didn't want to interfere with their family life or their growing up. But the fact was they all needed each other and could learn from each other. Kira was also so focused on making a successful business that she really forgot what was important in life and to her.

She hopes at least she was doing some little part correctly, Lord.

Kira knows she should have trusted you; it comes back to that a lot doesn't it? It almost always comes back to the trust issue.

Having Coffee with the Special One

She wishes that she had done a better job of letting you be her guide. You do know that it was all, about don't you? You knew that it was because you were a man too, she didn't figure that out until she began the journey with you. Kira didn't realize it all had to do with that. How in the world could she have again put God on the same level as a human man? How could she lower God to the level of a human being, yet you love her still...you forgive her....and you never left her side in all that was going on.

Kira put her adult kids to work for her company to try to give them a better life but that wasn't necessarily one of the best choices, for them or for her. Kira needed someone with knowledge, and Raelee had experience in her industry so it seemed to be a good fit. Kira had it in her head that if she learned it so could they, and because she loved her field in the accounting and tax world so much, that surely automatically they would love it too. Luckily, you made her aware of her errors, and slowly they left and went on to do what really made them happy, what they each really wanted to do in their lives.

Kira thanks you for the gift you gave to her. The gift of the mind that you gave her and that's why she was able to learn and understand the laws. Not everyone has that same gift, as you have pointed out to her many times. It was because it was your will for her to go that route, you put the want and the desire in her. Not everyone has that burning desire. She remembers the day like it was yesterday; the day that she fell in love with the tax world.

Kira also didn't look at others, "what's the word for it" limitations, or desires within if they had any that they would like to pursue?

In some ways Kira never really thought there were limitations, and she got upset with people who didn't seem to have the drive or the nerve to take it as far as they could in learning. She always thought that if she could do it, then so could Suzie or Pam or anyone. But thanks to constant reminders from others, it finally hit her that maybe—just maybe—not everyone loves it like she did, nor did they have the desire to flourish in the field as she chose to. There wasn't anything wrong with that either, but this was the flaw in her thinking wasn't it?

She just thought that there were no limits on a person's abilities. You know you can do anything you want once you put your mind to it. Well that does have some truth in it, but also only God can give you the level of knowledge that he wants you to have. Maybe he doesn't want everybody to be in that field because it takes all kinds of people to make this world. Kira wouldn't ever or couldn't ever be a nurse, or a doctor or a lawyer. No way. She has no desire whatsoever, so why couldn't she see that?

Having Coffee with the Special One

Kira messed up and sometimes still does, because she still pushes people and puts high expectations on them. She is the one that puts pressure on them. Help her to see when she should stop and get someone else Lord. Don't let her push too hard. Help teach her to know when it's time to let it go. Look for it in the first place....do they really want it, or do they just want something to do?

Kira keeps thinking we can do all things through Christ, who strengthens us.

Yet she hadn't ever thought that there might be a time when that's all they can do and that's all that he wants them to do.

Remember she isn't the one that's in control, and that just maybe God didn't want us to be able to do all things. Just maybe there are some areas where God doesn't want us to be, and Kira will need to learn the boundaries in that area.

She means if you could do miracles or other superior things, then what would you have God do for you if we could do it all on our own...now she can see that. How would we get the attitude that we didn't need God if we could do it all on our own? Kira gets that now. She gets that she needs God and she can't do it on her own.

Patty Scott

There is nothing in Kira's life that has been done on her own, even though at times, she always said she had to do it on her own, because no one else would be there for her , to do it for her or to help her. That sure was a closed-minded thought process wasn't it, or even a little selfish? She is fully aware, there is no way she nor other people have the energy or strength to do all of what you do Lord. To her it's too overwhelming to worry or care for so many people. You just amaze her each day, when she thinks about what all you do for her and for others....and wow, you can handle it! She sure can't.

One of the areas is where she may have lost loved ones or people who were close to her, through death.

There are times when she gets so overwhelmed with how many people she knows that have died, and especially just in the last six months, and how many are sick with cancer or some other life threatening disease she just can't handle it. What she can do is pray for them, because she sure can't cure them and she can't take away the pain or illness, but you can and you'll with the ones you chose to do so. It's not something that Kira has control over or that she can control, and it still puts a prickle in her heart because it hurts to see someone you care about suffer and be in pain. On the other hand, she sees how you're watching over them and taking care of them, healing some and well some not so much. Kira hopes that they don't

Having Coffee with the Special One

lose hope or that they don't lose the will to push on. Some of them are really in pain.

Here is another fault in Kira's makeup; she had to realize that when it's their natural time to go, that maybe Lord you don't want them to be on earth any longer. Who is Kira to say or think she can prolong their life any longer? It says in the Bible there is not one of us that can extend our life or shorten it, even one day longer than you have already set for us. so how could she think that just because she loves someone and spends time with them that she can prolong their days. Maybe she can just make it worthwhile to them. Maybe another laughter or a smile. Kira thinks that probably is another area in her life that she needs to back off and realize it's your will and not her will?

You know, Kira didn't realize that she was really such a control freak, she sure took on more than she needed to. This is an example of letting go and letting you, not giving up, just not trying to control it, or thinking she can change it. This control thing, it sure does get out of hand at times. Do we ever really learn the magnitude, and really get to where we are truly submissive?

Man Lord! Kira asks, "Please help me to stop wasting valuable time by trying to figure these things out in my head."

Kira gets such a choke hold on her thoughts and gets lost in them so much! Kira says she is sorry and doesn't want them to grab her like this. Please work on her mind and give her freedom from that. Lord, help her to be more aware so she can look up to you as it's happening.

Also as you're aware, there is another place that she feels so lost and confused which is in the relationship with her husband, She feels at times that there are so many demands put on her at work and in life in general, and the expectations that take so much out of her Lord, that she just doesn't think at times she can do it all. She gets worn down and it just wears her out. Really, she can't blame Tim because it really isn't him, it's just the way that she feels at times. You know something has to give and for some reason, she defaults to a relationship first, when in reality she probably just needs to learn how to say no and not take on so much, or volunteer to do so many outside projects.

Kira already is an over achiever and she pushes herself too much and too hard and yet at times she gets the feeling that it just isn't good enough. How can he or anyone else stop this in her, when she doesn't even know how to. All he is probably saying is hey I would like some time with you too. Relationships do struggle when you don't take the time to nurture them and feed them. Even our relationships with you, Kira didn't really know what it meant to have a true relationship with you until now, now that she is taking the time that's needed to develop it and nurture it. They said in church you want an intimate relationship with us, so it's up to us to build on that and develop it. You know full well how she feels, and you're always

Having Coffee with the Special One

aware of it because you're the one that knows her inside and out. You know; don't you the thing is, that you know both sides of the relationship you can see all, and you don't look at things the way we do, we need to remember to look at things through your eyes, we need to ask ourselves, is this worth the struggle, or the argument that it may cause, because maybe it just really isn't that important.

Why is it though that sometimes we just sit and complain instead of getting up and doing something about it? Kira knows that she is at fault in this area, and why can't she explain and get her point across? You know the battle they go through at times, yet she doesn't want to change what she is doing, and maybe that's what's causing some of the friction. How do you figure out the difference between, being strong and being stubborn? That's something Kira needs to work on, which would she rather be? (Chuckle) You know; do you want to be right or do you want to be happy?

Lord, Kira wants to be all you want her to be and she doesn't want to disappoint you and yet at times she thinks that she does disappoint you.

Yet you tell her at times through her devotions, that you're happy with the progress, and with what she is doing. Kira just needs to hang on to faith that you'll give her what she needs, and what you want her to have is up to you, not her. Even here, she must learn it isn't enough to just have faith, she also must believe. Kira needs to believe that you'll help her and show her the way. She can't always think you're going to fix everything, but she can bring it to you, and you'll help her to get through it. Maybe it was how she was perceiving it; was that the way it was supposed to be? Maybe it was because Kira owed so many demands to even take her away from you. How could she blame someone else for that, when she didn't even see it herself at first?

Exhaustion sets in when you work too much or put too many things to do on your plate. You get flat worn out. That's why, Lord, you allowed Kira to be taken out of the picture isn't it. That was the only way you were going to get her attention! You had to knock her in the head so she would listen to you and trust you completely. She had to completely let go and trust you.

At first, she was fighting it tooth and nail. Kira was afraid if she fell, she wouldn't get back up. Yet you carried her all the way and still are to this day. Kira didn't fall far, not like she thought she would, but she sure stumbled a lot! Lord thank you. You showed Kira that you were there, and you weren't going to let her fall, not too far anyway. That sure was hard for her to relinquish control over to you and submit to you. Being out of work and you being in control (as you were always anyway.) Kira realizing that it was you all along anyway, that was so different.

Having Coffee with the Special One

Lord, Kira whispers she hopes that she won't fail. This is an area where she can say, "bite me". At the time Kira felt like she didn't have much left to offer but look at what you're doing for her now, and in her life. She is rising above it. Kira didn't have or should she say, she didn't take the time to give them what they needed, and now she can be at peace and she can see if she just looks how you're making these things all work out for your good. Kira felt like she was an assembly line going through the motions. Now she can truly see where she forgets the initial intent and the whole meaning in the first place.

Kira really feels like she is on a roller coaster ride in life right now, with all that needs to be done. Lord, remember when Kira used to say come on baby we're going for a ride and she knows last year she could feel and see you were making some major changes in her life and she commented that people could either hang on or let go but she was taking the ride with you no matter what. If Kira remembers correctly you told her you wanted her to live on the edge with you, and she thinks she has been doing exactly that, living on the edge with you. You give Kira just enough to where she isn't drowning.

She really knows now that's what was going on!! Don't let her fall or break away from you as she did in the past when she hit rough patches and roads in life. Help her to remember in all that she does it's your work, and you have a plan—something better—for her and in her life than she could have ever planned for herself. You know blind faith, and trust. You know what is best for her. She really had to take the hard way of getting back to you didn't she Lord.

Kira couldn't just let go and let you; no ... she had to fight you all the way. Lord she does have and is facing many challenges ahead of her. Please back her and guide her as you're telling her your will. She really is looking forward to the results that you'll choose, and the end results are up to you, it's your choice not hers. Whether it's what Kira thinks she wants or not, it's up to you how this is going to end. Whatever the end results are, help Kira be joyful and thankful with gladness in her heart and mind for all the challenges you lay before her. It's not only the struggles in her business that she is having to face; it's several issues some of which she can't even talk about yet. It isn't that Kira wouldn't like to share it's that she can't at this time about these challenges she faces ahead.

Lord, will you teach Kira how to be strong and not just bulldoze people over. Help her learn the proper way to carry herself so people don't feel like a freight train coming when she is around. Help her know her confidence and know when she needs to "back off". She doesn't want to harm people as that's not her intent. This is an area that she has seen that you're working in her, and it's by faith alone, now she has a better understanding, and

Having Coffee with the Special One

knows when she is acting that way, and knows when to push and when to slow down, you showed her the way.

Can we ever say it too much? Lord, again, Kira wants to say thank you for the hope and the joy you give her. She loves that bubbly feeling that you put inside of her. She likes being filled with joy and hope, let the light shine in her and through her. She wants people to know that she is a child of God's and there is hope for them too. We can't have people lose faith or to lose hope. Sometimes that's all that they have. Kira has come to realize, Lord, sometimes that's all she has, too. It helps her to hang on to you. There are so many words in songs that run through her head, at times like this. Hang on there is more to come and know that you're not alone.

"Peace be with you" and "I will be with you always". Those words take on a whole new meaning and when Kira truly lets you in Lord, she can feel your presence, there is a soft warm feeling and a sort of like safety feeling. Kira can feel it move from her head to her toes like a river flowing through her. You know the warm fuzzy feeling, like a bubbling river. Or when someone you love shows up and gives you a kiss, you know that feeling. Kira guesses she never thought or realized that was from you. Kira thinks that she really took you for granted, she just never really thought about it like she does now.

Patty Scott

Kira still remembers the day that she was in church and the minister said something that grabbed her attention about us talking to you and taking all our worries and cares to you. At the time it didn't mean what it does to her today. She turned and said to Rile, I always talk to "God" (to you Lord) and she turned to me and said, "you're not listening to God". Lord, she would ask you questions out of frustrations and exhaustion and she wouldn't take the time to listen to what you were saying to her. She would basically blow you off or she just didn't let it soak in that you were talking back to her. Kira asks herself: Why did she allow the space between you two? Kira knows that she had excuses why she acted the way she did, but none of them are good ones as she sees it now. Every day you show her something different and you show her how you helped her and how you have healed her, and it's funny; now that she takes the time for you, she can really see you, Jesus she really sees you for the Lord that you are or as much as she can comprehend and you may let her see.

Kira prays: Dear God, I thank you for opening my heart and mind unto you, Jesus Christ. She is so thankful for the peace and the new spirit you have put in her, she doesn't think she can thank you enough, for all the time and trouble you have gone to for her. It makes her hunger for more. Kira really enjoys the quiet time with you and you answering her. Or should she say she's listening to

Having Coffee with the Special One

you. It's interesting what you tell her too, maybe it's not always what she wants to hear. Kira knows that she sure didn't give you much of a chance in the past, did she? How could she have even put you on the same level as her dad or any other man? How could she do that to you? Kira always thought that it was the way she was supposed to be, like, well, she was fighting to survive, using a survival mechanism. Why didn't she just let go and let you? "It would have been too easy".

Lord she thanks you for not giving up on her, you could have let her drown, or let her die, either case you could have let her go. Kira thanks you again for loving her even when she is stupid, or she does stupid things. That will probably come up several times because she did so many stupid things before. Lord thank you for giving her the gift of life again, thank you for saving her and showing her that she is worthy of your love, and worth it to you, thank you for your forgiveness and another chance in life. You know it's funny Kira used to say a cat only has nine lives yet her mom and her have used up as many or close to it, and God still takes care of them.

Yes: Kira knows that Heaven is her eternal home but on earth we are to share you and the peace and joy you give us. She remembers too; you saved her several times. It was before each time that her faith in you had grown stronger, it's a process, isn't it Lord. Each time you're going to do something great in our life, then the evil tries to destroy what you're trying to do, and we just have to hang on to what you want for us. You're aware of it too, and there is a reason you do it this way too, isn't there. Your will. That's where the free will comes in isn't it. You want us to ask you to come into our lives. You won't force us to do anything you won't force yourself onto us. We must open and welcome you in. "Ask in my name and it will be given to you. Until now you haven't asked in my name, ask and ye shall receive and your joy will be complete." All we must do is ask in your name. Why is that so hard for us?

Kira didn't have a "true" thankful attitude. She was allowing everything to get between her and you. She had forgotten all that she had, truly came from you. "Everything she has Lord, comes from you."

Thank you, Lord, for our business. Thank you for the opportunities that are brought forward. Thank you for putting the people in her life that you want in her life. Thank you for carrying her after she stumbled. You picked her up again every time that she fell. Even when she thought no one was there for her.

How selfish and how wrong of her. God why didn't she remember you were there for her if she just asked and if she would have bothered to listen?

She remembered the horrible attitude she had. Kira was just so tired of things not going her way and she felt so worthless!! Things just weren't

Having Coffee with the Special One

working out!! Yet! Look at all that you gave her. She really did need to realize it was thankfulness and gratefulness that was lacking in her. It wasn't hers in the first place. She was just a steward for the Lord....and it was his, she was just taking care of it for him.

And Lord, you freely gave it to her ... and everyone else! It's there for the taking and asking. All anyone had to do was ask, "In your name".

Kira got to see the flutters of fairy (angel wings.) The bright lights and the breeze of the wind with little glimpses of Heaven. Little tiny lights that move ever so quickly and flutter here and there. The little twinkling sparkle of light. Really bright, though small. The angels in Heaven. When Kira would investigate the sky, she realized that was what she was looking at when she would look to Heaven.

So even though Kira opened to you and "listened" and welcomed you in, the problems weren't going away. She just had to learn how to handle them and deal with them in another manner, and you were going to teach her. You're the strong one in her. Kira must make a mental note of that and remember God: you're her strength; not that she is tough and can handle it.

Wow! Putting things in proper perspective. Not that you made her strong. and she can handle it. You're her strength; you'll get her through it! This is the better way to look at things and get her mind straight. She could turn it all over to the Lord, and he will help her handle it, and teach her that some of it will just take care of itself. The Lord will guide her and instruct her when or what she needs to act on. Not until then.

How could she not want this or take the time to receive you in her daily life, Lord!

It's such a powerful feeling. How come she wouldn't want this daily, or open to you in the past? Why couldn't she or wouldn't she trust you completely? Yes, she knows she was really, mad at you for a while there. She guesses in a way she blamed you, for everything. Kira knows that she has had to realize where she was part to blame in every circumstance in her life that went wrong! Where she meant she was part to blame was because in her mind it takes two, it takes two to break it and it takes two to fix it. Is she wrong on that aspect too?

She had to learn that she doesn't depend on others for her happiness, and she doesn't have expectations, so she wouldn't get disappointed as often. Kira still needs work on this and needs to remember you can expect God to help you, but you can't expect others to read your mind or to entertain you. Don't depend on others for your happiness. If they want to be a part then let them, but don't try to force it.

Having Coffee with the Special One

You know Kira has been becoming more aware of the songs they sing in church—the words not just the music—and now they have a whole different meaning to her. No longer does Kira just sing the words...now they mean something to her.

When she says the Lord's prayer it really means something to her, and she can say it! Kira had sort of given up on saying it or with true meaning for a while. She guesses when you have pent up anger and ill feelings inside, then you can't say it. Now she knows when she says it, she truly is asking for your forgiveness of her sins that she commits—the known and the unknown ones—and she truly is forgiving those that have hurt her in the past. She isn't hanging on to ill feelings, there are some she still doesn't understand, but she knows in time if necessary, the truth will come to light and God will handle it. He has your back.

Is there ever a time when harm is there and that it doesn't affect two or more people at the time? Kira means look at how many people are affected when a family member gets a divorce.

Not everyone knows or realizes just how many people it affects in the family and who all are bothered by it at the time. So, know that it affects the whole group, friends included not just the people that are getting divorced. Kira only thought at first it was the couple that got hurt but it's not. And then in all the years it takes them to heal and forgive don't let that damage other relationships in the meantime. Kira knows after her divorce she did not give her current husband a chance and her not letting go of the hurt and anger, kept people at bay and far away from her. Well that was not doing anyone any favors. It sure wasn't glorifying you either.

Kira thought she was protecting herself when all she was doing was hurting everyone around her and herself during the process. When she had a choke hold on it, she was sort of not trusting you or worshiping you completely. The divorce was getting in the way of her relationship with you Lord. How could she have had faith in you Lord when she really didn't Trust? She is sorry for this.

Kira looked at it as giving her the drive to succeed. What a fool she had been, and you let her carry on that way, you gave her free will! She knows now that she had to do it when she was able to deal with the process. Man, it was such a powerful process! The forgiveness process…. will she ever be able to

tell others the magnitude how important it is to forgive? It's such a freedom, such a relief. Now that she has done it, she wonders how she lived without it, and more importantly, why? It really is an important factor in living a peaceful life.

Another day with you Lord: "Peace be with you and I am with you always".

Having Coffee with the Special One

Kira is taking the time now to really understand what that means.

To her Lord, can she really have peace without you being there too? No: if you're not present there isn't any peace.

Kira never really realized or thought about what it meant when she was in church and would say to the person next to her "peace be with you". Now it holds a totally different and true meaning. Kira guesses in a way it's like saying "God be with you". We are asking for you to enter them and be with them throughout their day. As you know Kira never really thought that much about it.

It's kind of embarrassing to confess this, but it's necessary. She was missing out on the blessings that God had for her...she sort of was missing the boat. Kira is sorry she missed the blessings you were trying to give her, and the importance of what it truly meant. She needed to really pay attention. You're all around us if we just let you in. You give us all the time in the world, you don't rush us, or yell at us. Then why do we expect you to answer us right away?

When Kira thinks about the anxiety, she had without acknowledging your presence, she hopes now she doesn't forget you're the one that gives her the peace and joy. You have said several times that Kira is the one that needs to relax, slow down and take time out for you and with you no matter where or when; you're always with her. "All she has to do is ask". Ask in your name and her joy will be complete. And yet you give us so much more, so much more than we can ever imagine or even ask for.

Here are some other thoughts and comments:

Kira guesses she is still a work in progress because she doesn't think she has yet to understand the true meaning of: "work like you don't need the money". She still falls short in this area, but she is trying (by the way, she thinks she is catching on to this.)

As now she genuinely enjoys the days off and the time you have given her, sometimes she thinks maybe too much. She is still working on the area of getting lost in thought trying to work things out in her head and you're right! she doesn't know the outcome or how it will turn out. She doesn't have the crystal ball "but you do" so she needs to have faith and trust you completely. Then she wouldn't have the anxiety and stress.

All she must do is trust you and now she knows to believe also. What you ask of us really is not that difficult and it should be natural, but isn't and why do we fight it?

You do know that Kira's church has lost a lot of the members but a friend of mine put things in perspective: Even churches need money to keep their doors open. What business can operate or function if they do not receive revenues to keep it in

Having Coffee with the Special One

service? It's up to us as members to give to the church. How can they minister and teach us if we can't keep the electric or gas on to have service?

Lord, Kira was struggling with this as you're aware. She also realized again that everything she has comes from you and because of you, it wasn't hers. She is just the steward of what you give to her to manage. You have always made sure that she had what she needed and more, and it's up to her and others to use their gifts in a manner that would please you.

God you always provide a way for us 'don't you' so who is Kira to question or hold back. "For I am with you says the Lord." He also won't ever ask you to do something that you can't afford.... you can't out give God.

Even though we are Christians, Lord, it doesn't mean we don't face trials and tragedies. When we give you thanks during a tragedy, we still go through the tragedy, but it's with a joyful heart. Kira gets that now. She knew you were with her last year during her car wreck, but you're with her every day of her life because she let you into her heart and mind. You got her through it, you saved her and even though it was a personal disaster (it could have been much, much worse too), Kira got through it without hurt, anger and hatred.

Lord, it's important that she learned this. Kira was able to get through the disaster without being ugly and you healed her. Kira wasn't that way in the past, there were times, when she was very hateful and not such a friendly person. There is so much of a difference in her now, Thank You Jesus.

Lord, Kira learned to let go and let you work in her and in her life and everyone around her. Oh, believe Kira, she fought at first and then she just realized she wasn't in control and she let it go. In her eyes there were many doors that needed to be opened. Lord, we will get back to this because you have opened her world here and in the forgiveness process. You have opened her eyes a lot here and yes! It was hard for her to see and admit to the error of her ways. Kira put so many walls up and you're tearing them down brick by brick. This is where Kira truly opened and let you in through her eyes, her heart, and her soul. You're her salvation. Kira just didn't want to put too much emphasis on the wreck because that's a whole different story, but it helped get her here to where she is today. It's part of another journey with you.

Lord, Kira says she is thankful that you're a forgiving father and you still love her and care for her when she does wrong. Now that she's older and has been given the time to really focus on your words, it brings a whole new meaning to loving people, being with friends and having family

Having Coffee with the Special One

around. Even cooking is more fun when she has the time or takes the time to cook.

Cooking made Kira think about Thanksgiving. She missed the traditional Thanksgiving days with her family, but she didn't go back home for several reasons, some legit and some not. They did other things...but it really made her stop and think.

One day at dinner it was just her and her husband Tim. It turned out to be nice just the two of them, with no tablet or kindle at the dinner table. Kira still must open her mind to the world so she can have an intelligent conversation with him. Sometimes she feels as though he doesn't want to hear what she has to say and it's not an intelligent conversation. They work together so he basically knows how her day went and she knows how his went. They don't see the kids everyday so there are few words to say.

Some couples say that that means they are comfortable with each other and they don't need to talk. But that bugged Kira when she saw couples in restaurants, and they didn't talk to each other. At that time, she and Tim would laugh and crack up with each other. She didn't want to be like those other couples. Yet there she was....

They used to be able to sit for hours talking to each other and she would just listen to him. Kira knows she also quit listening to him. Kira had sort of shut him out too, as she did many others. It's funny when you sit down, think about relationships and see just how much of it could be you. It's not fun to see but it's the truth.

You know God I really do think you have a good sense of humor.

People really think Kira is weird because she laughs at some of the oddest moments, like when Olivia (Kira's mom) cut off the tip of her finger Kira laughed. Kira may seem weird to others but that's because people just didn't know her.

People also thought she was accident prone. She wasn't really accident prone, but a lot of bad things happened to her. Well, some of them were just funny. I guess when you live to tell about it then it becomes funny.

Others don't really understand it: they look at Kira like she is from another planet. To her it makes light of a bad situation, so it doesn't hurt so bad. The funny thing is Kira used to get so hurt when her mom would laugh about things that she would run to Olivia for comfort...and Olivia would laugh. Kira gets it now and she understands where Olivia was coming from: to an adult it's so different than to a child.

Kira must be careful when she is around young kids, like her grandkids. One-time Kris was left at the street corner when they moved to a different house. It wasn't funny at all back then, but now she sort of laughs about it. Kris to this day hasn't forgiven her and draws on it whenever he can. To

Having Coffee with the Special One

her it was funny after they went back and got him ... everything turned out ok. But it wasn't funny at all that they left him. He was young and scared. Why would his mom just drive off and leave him?

Kira doesn't think he will ever forgive her, and she has apologized profusely a hundred times. Now she can understand why it upset him so much. Inside Kira felt so horrible that she broke his little heart. All she could do was try to make him laugh so he didn't hurt so bad. And at the time she thought (adult process) he shouldn't be so upset.

She did go back and get him but that wasn't the point. The point was that she left him. Kira left her young son on the corner. How could she do that? He was so scared and didn't have a way to contact them. He didn't have shoes or a shirt on and it started to rain. He was waiting for her while she got things in the car and they were getting ready to head to the new house.

Kris thought he saw Kira look right at him and then just take off. Geez, can you imagine what that poor child felt at that second?

Kira had no clue. Kira had been having problems starting the car. One of her friends that was helping them move was sitting in the car behind Kira so instead of looking out the back window, she was looking in the side mirror. She was watching the car behind her and drove off. Of course, her son thought that she looked right at him and drove off. Even now she can totally understand why that upset him so much. That was horrible, but how would she have known that? She was so focused on moving and getting the cars full of stuff to the new house. Kira didn't even think it was such a stressful day, but it was. But no excuses; Kris still he had a valid point and it did hurt.

Thankfully, Linda—a neighbor in the complex – took Kris into her apartment while he waited for Kira to go back and pick him up! On one hand that was so scary and on the other it was funny, sort of.

The problem was Kira grew up in a large family. She had several siblings and different times her poor mom had left one of the kids at church or school. That's why Kira thought it was so funny. Her mom always went back to get them. No one was hurt and they were protected cargo. God always watched over them.

Kira can see the humor in it, but she doesn't think Kris can yet find the humor in it. Nor will other mothers, unless they had the misfortune of an incident like it. Then maybe they too would understand this.

Lord, forgive Kira for leaving him but also thank you for making it possible for Kira to be able to pick him up right away when they realized they were missing their child, despite the chaos with moving, so many other vehicles and people helping. "Gosh, talk about a big black hole in the pit of your stomach". Something that's not easy to get over.

Having Coffee with the Special One

Kira can see a big difference in herself, and how she feels, Lord, when she is thanking you and thinking of all the times in her life when you were there. She is appreciative of it. As you say rise above your circumstances and look up to you.

Kira's problems didn't go away, but you were there to help her through them. Kira has the same ones; she just learns how to deal with them differently. Now she doesn't focus on the problems, she focuses on you as you instruct her to do so the problem isn't a big boulder... it's just a stepping-stone.

It takes away the power from the problem. It gives us a closer relationship. Kira keeps it in the place that it really belongs—below you and not above you—and she doesn't allow the problem to make her angry or scared. It's a lot smoother process having you there than the problem. She can see where that makes sense and she's much happier your way that's for sure. Even when she gets herself in a bind and messes up you never stop caring for her or loving her. That's unconditional love.

Kira can speak only for herself, but she knows God when she thinks about a problem and lets it bother her rather than be grateful for what she does have, her life is not as peaceful.

Patty Scott

Like yesterday, she was so out of sorts and out of whack. Kira allowed ungrateful feelings to take hold but remembering to focus on you and that you were there, also that again she's not in control, made it easier and lightened the load. Kira was able to enjoy her grandkids being over for tacos. Yes, she was trying to please her grandkids because it's so fun to do. In some ways, she is trying to make up for what she shorted her own children out on. Or it's just that she truly does enjoy her grandkids and she is going to spoil them because she doesn't have to raise them.

God thank you for the gift of my grandchildren as they bring so much joy and happiness into my life. They were a gift from you!! Kira hopes that one day maybe they too will be to this point in life and be grateful for what they have or had and enjoy these aha moments too.

Kira remembers some of her fun childhood times like days at the beach on the boogie boards.... the play she and Byrne went to when she was in grade school...and the day they played dress up. Those were some of fun childhood days.

In her mind, Kira just had a glimpse of you, Lord, grabbing her hand. We turned and sort of danced and Kira laughed. Even during this trying time, she can feel your love and joy and she can dance with you.

When she really thinks about it, money isn't something that she should allow to control her

Having Coffee with the Special One

happiness. For thirteen years Lord, you have gotten their company through lean times and they are still here. Does the struggle ever really end at any point? Hopefully one day, though, it won't be like that. You tell them not to live off future income, so when they have loans with the bank it takes up their future income. Please help her find a way to stop living like that Lord, your way: hers isn't working out so well. She is beginning to see that this is just the way that some businesses are. Feast or fathom, like a roller coaster.

Dear God, hear my prayer.

As Kira is thinking today: thank you for tearing the walls down brick by brick. You're saving her, Lord, she does need to get rid of the negative thought patterns which she developed when she was working way too much and thinking that things were not turning out the way they should. She hadn't turned to you. There were too many times in her life she allowed negative actions to take hold of her.

She can see what you're talking about there. The disappointments when she was growing up, in her parent's relationship. She just thought that her mom deserved so much better. How she hated the way her dad treated her mom and how he basically ignored the kids——he didn't really have a lot to do with them. That really hurt to know or to think your parents didn't love you.

You know how it was. It wasn't a perfect childhood, but she is learning from it. She threw out some of the memories and some of it she carried on through raising her own kids. It probably had some bearing on how she treated them or didn't treat them. It never went away completely though. Kira always hung on to the hurt and while she didn't think about it daily, it was always in the back of her mind.

Kira didn't truly love her family freely. She could have sat more with them and taken the time to listen to them, or maybe held them just a few more minutes. You know her walls she put up and she put a lot of negativity into her family's lives. She can see now where they picked up on it.

Some of the habits may have been good ones but not all of them. Kira should have let go of it many years ago. On one hand Kira was thankful for it because it helped mold her and it taught her what she didn't want to be like, or want to live like and what she didn't want the kids to have to live through.

Kira didn't want to live in a home of meanness and hurtful things. In some ways she was overly protective, and she didn't put trust in her husband or in you, Lord. Not the way that she should have. Not freely and not with a peaceful mindset, and

Having Coffee with the Special One

sometimes not in her heart which she had protected too much.

Don't take her wrong, it wasn't always in the forefront of her thoughts but is was deep inside and buried in her thoughts. It's important to forgive and you know when the forgiveness is involved it sure helps you look at things in a different light. The problems were still real and they were there, but you stop seeing them as problems and you start seeing the joy and the happiness and the love again...like the fun things Kira and her sisters used to do. The times they would lay on the bunk beds and tell jokes or tease each other at Thanksgiving and take their naps. Those were the memories that you want to hang on to.

The times you stayed out until ten at night and played kick the can or jump rope. The time one of your brothers was throwing darts over the house and one landed in your leg while you were walking your bike; your older brother came out and helped get the dart out of your leg. The love that was shown through these kinds of things, that's what you really want to hang onto. Kira thinks too, that this is what a mom feels like when she watches her child walk out the door to start a new life. You just go through so many different feelings while so many thoughts flash through your mind.

Kira thinks began building walls when her father was alive and causing havoc in the household. At that time, she didn't have the forgiveness in her heart. She used the walls in her mind for protection. Kira knows she was too young to even think about what she was doing, how it was going to affect her life in the future which developed the ways she treated people. Some of it she turned into good. Like Kira had said to others, take what you loved and enjoyed and throw out the rest. But truly throw it out, don't hang on to it.

Kira wanted her kids to be raised in a loving home where they knew their father and would get to spend time with him. Kira did try to keep the faith and you in their lives, but she knows, now, that she didn't really know what all it meant and what a true relationship was with you until later in life. Kira doesn't really think she knew really what all meant, the true meaning of an intimate relationship with God.

You know, Lord, Kira was thankful when her dad died. She knows how horrible that may sound to others, but she really was glad about it, it was such a relief for them all. Kira knew her brothers and sisters and mom would be safe even though you always watched over them and protected them during what he put them through. If he was alive, they constantly had to look over their shoulders and never knew what they would walk into. You finally removed him from their lives in the physical sense. Kira knows that's not one of the nicest things to say, because she still misses thinks of him and wonders about what kind of dad, he could have been but wasn't. She hated the things he did, but she wanted to love him as a person.

Having Coffee with the Special One

It's ironic even though he was so hateful and mean, Kira always longed for him to love her. She always wished she had a dad that she could be proud of. They lived in so much shame and embarrassment from him. She didn't know when or if she did really learn how to separate the action from the person, but she thought that she did. She hated the way he treated her mom, but she thought she always loved him, she just lost her respect for him. Maybe it was just that she loved what she thought a dad should be, her expectations what one should be. It's true, the best way a dad could show a child love would be to love their mother, and the way a man can show his wife that he really loves her is to love their children.

When Kira shows your love and uses it to help others, she doesn't want to be fake or boastful, Lord. She wants it to be compassionate and understanding. She didn't have that in her before and had no clue what compassion was.

She wants to see your beauty, Lord, the gray ugliness isn't fun, and she knows it isn't the way you molded her or made her. Kira is sorry that it was more that she came across as she was blaming you. You didn't create the ugliness, you helped them all get through it and protected them from much more harm. As Kira found later in life, it could have been a lot worse as she met others who did have it a lot worse than she did. It always can be so much worse.

Still today, women must put up with abusive husbands, and husbands must deal with abusive wives. Something so precious as relationships is from the Lord, and the only way the evil can seep in and mess with God's work is to mess with someone you love. That's the only way he can try to hurt you. Jesus that means a lot to you and that's why he messes with it, because he knows it hurts.

A Happier Time......

You recently know Kira and Tim opted to spend a wonderful four days in San Antonio. They stayed at the River Walk. There were lights in all the trees decorated for Christmas. They sat out on the balcony and listened to the children's choirs singing Christmas carols. When the adults floated by on the boat rides, she and Tim were singing along with them.

Ah, the joys of Christmas! It was one of Kira's favorite times of the year, even with all the gift giving and the candy and celebrations, it's the most valuable time of the year. The beauty in the choir's voices...the beauty in the happiness that comes out in people during the holiday season. Most of the time Christmas brings out the good in people, the sharing and the caring. Kira was in awe of the great weekend they had that holiday season. She had to go for a seminar and Tim went along with her, so they could spend some time together.

Having Coffee with the Special One

Lord, thank you for the time together and the time with you.

Kira knew she and Tim hadn't been getting along that great lately. What is it about the longer people stay together when it's so important, they think they run out of things to talk about and can't learn from each other or about each other anymore? Your marriage is probably one of the most important relationships that you'll ever have in your lifetime, yet it's one of the hardest ones to keep fresh and new, and fun. No, it won't be fun all the time, but why lose the fun in it, when you can keep that alive?

You know relationships are some of the most important things in life that God wants us to have, and to nurture and grow. But that's where evil just wants to tear you apart, and ruin what God does in your life and for your relationship. No matter what, just don't let it tear you apart. After all the years Kira has been married, there still isn't another person she would rather be with than Tim, but she just has a really hard time in showing and telling him that. Being with someone day in and day out, can be boring. But Kira wants to keep it fun and exciting, not boring.

Thank you for bringing back the love and the peace between them. Let your light shine upon them and in them. Let them share it with their kids, and they share it with theirs and on down the line. That's one way to keep you alive in Kira, isn't it Lord?

So many times, Kira had noticed where she truly wasn't the one in control. Once she figured that out and accepted it, things became easier. You stop fighting a battle that can't be won, and you realize that you're not really fighting your spouse because they're not the enemy. You won't win, and actually everyone loses if you don't realize that it's not each other that you're fighting.

In Kira's eyes, Lord, you're there, and you're everywhere, we just must let you in. Kira just fought you every step of the way, when you just tried to let her know she wasn't in control.

Kira's attitude was: "I can do it myself", she didn't need anyone telling her what to do, or helping her. She did it all on her own before. But, really did she? How could she ever have felt that way? That she was alone; when God proved every day of her life while growing up that he was there, how could she have ever doubted you?

Now, with each step that she takes, she thinks she is finally learning what it truly means to "let go and let God". There is so much peace in knowing that God will take care of it, he has your back.

All along you have been by her side and guided her but she just wouldn't listen to you or even acknowledge you were there with her. Kira shut you out, out of her marriage, and out of her life. Yet, you have been there every step of the way, you never got mad and left her, and you had to watch the way she felt, and the way she acted. You stood

Having Coffee with the Special One

by and watched her shut you out. Kira's life could have been so much more peaceful if she would have just listened to you. You do allow us free will because you don't want to control us.

Lord, she does recognize now where you have helped her and saved her throughout her life; and she isn't afraid to tell others or share it. Now when she does you know it comes from the heart. When she talks to others, she tries to talk to them, not just tell them as if it's an order, but to share, so that they might listen to what she has to say. She tries not to come on so strong and push others away, rather than bring them close to you. It's a whole different mindset and action.

In the past sometimes Kira would put much more importance on the person or the situation rather than look at it through your eyes. You have been working on her to make her see it through your eyes, so she could see that maybe it wasn't such a powerful monster after all, you'll knock the fizz out of it, and that it might not be so important after all. For example, she allowed her dad and ex-husband to have more power over her and her life than she should have. They too were just human beings and hurting with their own problems. Kira just happened to be the one they took out their anger on. Kira learned that when she would face the facts and bring them to you; they don't have the power over her anymore.

Thank you, Lord, for the freedom from the hurt and the pain, thank you for the gift of forgiveness.

Patty Scott

F reedom has a whole new meaning.

Kira has always been a person who gets claustrophobic. Why couldn't she see how much hanging on to the hurt and pain of the lies and deceitfulness of her dad and ex-husband were harming her? Hanging onto something that really didn't matter anyway.

Kira's ex was someone that she wasn't meant to be with in the first place, but you had a purpose and a reason for allowing it to be as it was. She knows now why it happened and sees the beauty and the gifts from the relationship. It's true they shouldn't have ever been married but it taught her what not to do. She did learn from the mistake. You saved for her someone who really could and would love her despite the way she tried to push him away.

You gave Kira a better life than the one she planned for herself, but even then, she didn't fully appreciate it. She let the past cloud her heart and her vision. Oh, she loved as if there was no tomorrow, but there was always that little nagging in the back of her mind, that maybe it wouldn't last, or she had unfinished business she had to take care of and she wouldn't do it.

Day by day, wall by wall she built them up around her. Now, day by day, wall by wall you're tearing

Having Coffee with the Special One

them down and opening her heart and mind unto you Jesus Christ.

Lord, she is incredibly grateful and thankful for that. It really is a different way that she looks at things and feels things, there is such a difference in the way she looks at Tim, and she doesn't doubt him as much and she really can see and feel the love that he has for her, it isn't like it was before, Kira doesn't even know if she really can explain it, but there e is a big difference in her.

You have opened her eyes unto you "oh Lord,". She will rejoice and be glad in it. Now she knows where all the people who have faith and trust in you have been able to truly let it out and sing your praise. She knows now what it really feels like. The peace of the Lord, surpasses all understanding, keeps our hearts and minds opened unto you "Jesus Christ". Your unfailing love, even at times when we try to keep you away or ignore you. Sometimes she just wouldn't listen. Lord, she can see the areas where she really needed to change and open to you. Kira was struggling with how does she know if it's your will or hers? She now does know the difference. One you feel good about it and the other you don't.

Kira prays that you'll guide her, and she will listen to you. When it comes from the heart it's you and from you. Kira says: thank you Lord, for never leaving her even when she tried to push you away. Yes: Lord, Kira has learned to even thank you for the hard times. It's a way to really know and enjoy the good ones and to know the difference and to really learn that even in the hard times there can be the peace. For the most part too, Kira doesn't rant, and rave anymore, but sometimes, well let's, say sometimes, not so much. Lord, you don't give us the hard life, you discipline us because we are your children, but really you don't give us the hard life, or even give us the easier life, you give us a better way to handle and deal with the life that we have. You show Kira that once she puts her trust in you that she will make it through and hold her hand and walk with her or carry her along the way when she can't. You have been with her every step of the way. As you're taking the time in love and caring and showing her where you didn't leave her.

You fixed Kira when she was broken.

The hard times offer Kira lessons which help her to learn how she can take that experience and help someone else if they face the same thing that she did. So many times, you have shown her that she can use her experience and knowledge to help someone else. A person can be more understanding if they have experienced it for themselves and have more compassion.

Yes, Lord, compassionate. That was something that Kira was lacking. Compassion was not in her makeup. She didn't even really know what compassion was but now she knows it's a kind, soft feeling you have for someone. That you're soft and caring to them....and you show them compassion. Learning compassion has also helped Kira build a better relationship with God.

Having Coffee with the Special One

Yes Lord, Kira says she does likes intimately knowing you. Even though she grew up with you in her life, it really is a different relationship with you now. A deeper more meaningful relationship with you even though while growing up her mom sat with her, reading the daily devotions, praying, and reading Bible verses. (Lord, bless my mom.)

But then, "knowing" you wasn't the same to Kira as it is now.

You're right! You mean more to Kira than she ever let you know....and she's ready to let you be in control!! Ha Ha letting you! Don't you get to enjoy some of the idiotic stuff she does? Yes, she knows you love her even when she says or does stupid stuff.

Yes, Lord, she is aware. Please help her stand back and allow you to do your job and stay out of your way so you can do it. She has been made aware that if she does that, she will give you something to do. But then she will take it back, and it just takes longer for you to get it done.

To Kira it was a normal thing for her to just take care of it, and not ask you for help or even what you thought about the situation. She didn't realize that she was treading in an area where she was trying to be God or doing things instead of praying to you and letting you handle it. Her kids and her husband are prime examples where "she didn't let go and let you". Now she knows that and yes, she continually must remind herself it's not up to her to take care of it or fix it! It's her responsibility to bring it to you and discuss it with you. You're the one who can fix it or show her how to handle it and take care of it.... not Kira. She knows she is a work in progress in this area Lord, and she will learn to back away gracefully and say as she bows, it's all yours, you take care of them, and don't let them hurt each other! "Let go and Let you".

Okay, Kira says you need to enlighten her in this area Lord: **"Don't weigh yourself down with responsibilities that aren't your own"**.

Kira has several ideas that are running through her head. Here you'll need to give her clarity on them. Some she fully understands, some she's not sure of because she doesn't know if she is seeing it correctly. Kira needs your guidance here Lord: she thinks an example came to mind.... maybe this is what you mean?

If someone else makes a mistake don't take the blame or take it on as if she was the one that made it. Kira learned don't make a big deal out of it because it was someone else's fault. Most of all, she had to learn she shouldn't be the blame or be faulted for someone else's actions. Now that makes sense to her. You sure hit the nail on the head, today didn't you?

Having Coffee with the Special One

Kira always thinks she can make things better and resolve the problems of the world. Geez Lord, another area where she was doing stuff that wasn't or shouldn't have been her concern. As you're fully aware of the people and thoughts that are flowing through Kira's head this very moment. Yes, she can see where she is trying to help people, she loves but she needs to step back and let you do it.

She still needs to let go of this house issue that's been weighing on Kira's mind, doesn't she? Lord, that's one of the areas Kira needs to "see" your perspective on the situation, and she needs to know what you want from her, if anything.

To Kira it doesn't make sense to carry the payments out for the remainder of the term. That home in its condition is not worth what it would cost to fix. But Kira also is fully aware that it's not her home. Kira felt like she needed to honor the loan because she made the decision to sign the papers. Please show her what is enormously important here Lord. (You did, you did it Lord,) Kira did "let go and let you". Lord, you took care of the issue, you resolved it. You know Kira just now realized, that didn't you? It just hit Kira, you have resolved this issue, so it was that she needed to just back away, and you would take care of it.

And Lord, on the case with....You know the other thing on her mind. But she can't mention the name.

Kira will need to go over these areas several times so she can put you first Lord. Lord, Kira must learn to know what her responsibility is and what is not. There is such a freedom and relief when she realized the errors and she let go. What freedom to laugh again, to really feel joy! God's peace. Lord, she thanks you and she wants to glorify you. You give her strength. She doesn't or can't conquer the world...(chuckle)... as if she could!

BUT YOU CAN!

Lord, how does she know when it's time to let go and when it's time to dig her heals in and stay strong? How will she know it's your will and not hers?

Kira knows when it comes from the heart that it's from you. Yes, they say never give up! She is just wondering to always know it's you, Kira thinks that she does know the answer, but she was just wanting to ask.

Why did she allow the computer to freak her out today? Or problems we were all having? She finally got online and was able to attend the training course she needed to complete. Why did she let it upset her so much? What happened during the melt down—the outrage—whatever it was Lord? Why does she still do that?

God, Kira loves having this time with you. Why is it when she is away from you, she doesn't always remember or think to say hi or "hey you still there"? You're helping her so much, yet sometimes she overlooks that you're the first one that she

Having Coffee with the Special One

should be seeking or listening to. Kira needs to take a minute to step back, think about it and remember just who you are and who you are to her.

Maybe that would eliminate or lessen the outbursts that she has when she is angry, or when things aren't working the way that she thinks they should be. Yes, it's hard to just sit still and listen. Kira still has it ingrained in her that she needs to keep pushing on and keep busy because there are still things to get done. She has trained herself—or convinced herself—that she is supposed to be constantly doing something.

Geez why can't she just let go of what she was taught as a child or learned as an adolescent? Kira isn't living in that time period anymore and has been away from that for a long time. Let's start a new beginning today. Kira sees that she doesn't have to be constantly busy, and she can take a break and sit back. Lord, please stop letting these stupid things get to her, and her taking out her anger or frustration out on everyone around her.

Kira remembers when she and her siblings were children because there were so many of them her mom would make them go outside and play. Ahhh... Kira sees it... they needed to go outside to play and have fun and to let off some of the steam. Just have fun...play kick the can, or red rover...but get out and play. Plus, she didn't just want us to sit around and do nothing like all the young kids do now. With them playing their electronic games, how much play do they get?

Patty Scott

Kira is getting better about relaxing and playing. Work isn't the only part in life and it's by far not the most important thing in life to do. There are so many better things to do with your time. A job is a means and a way to do God's work and help others, but it isn't your life. That's something Kira needed to put back in its proper place, and she has learned to do that. Now she loves to travel, go places she hasn't ever been... some are only a once-in-a-lifetime opportunity. It's better now, Lord, and Kira has you to thank for showing her she is dependable, and she can take time off and have a life outside of the office. You did that for her, you showed her the way, didn't you?

You're right Lord, usually in December, even though it's one of Kira's favorite time of the year, she normally would be so stressed out and cranky because she used to worry over it was a really slow time of year at work. She would almost let it ruin the joy of Christmas. Kira needed to remember what the true meaning of Christmas was, and that the Christmas season was tended to be joyful and celebrate the birth of our Lord, and Savior Jesus Christ.

Can you imagine just holding that little tiny baby in your arms, and kissing his face? Oh, Kira could only dream, and picture him lying in her lap...holding him....and kissing him. Wow! What an honor that Mary was to be the mother of Jesus but then, look at what you Lord, had to go through as a child. Who are we to complain?

Having Coffee with the Special One

Kira thinks that she waited too long to get up today and spend time with you. She heard Tim stirring around in the bathroom. Kira hates to say this, but Tim is sort of breaking the moment, needing something from her. He will need to wait, for now. Other reasons Kira looks forward to Christmas, is to see the smiles and joy in little kids and to sing all the Christmas songs.

You were born "Lord," baby Jesus, you came to save us from sin, and you give us your love.

Yes, Kira says, she will always need you and want you in her life. Kira sure hopes that she is learning the true meaning of having you in her life and guiding her through her life, so this time she doesn't mess it up so badly.

God, she knows—and can see—where she allowed work to get in the way of relationships and friendships. Kira put too much importance on work and didn't put you first, her family first or nurturing her friendships first. She always had and excuse why she couldn't do something with them.

You know eventually they go away, and it's hard to get it going again. People have moved on and found someone that wanted to spend time with them and would nurture their relationship. Kira has found this out. It's hard for her to take and watch, but she did it... not them. At the time in some ways she couldn't see what she was doing. Kira thought everyone should understand that she was trying to build something for the future, why was that wrong? Now she knows and sees why her thoughts were wrong, and why she needed to fix it, and set things right, with them and with God. You know you can only worship one God and God isn't your job or your work. He is love, he is joy and he is hope. Not work.

You know what's amazing is that you, God, and her family kept loving her and didn't let her go despite that she wasn't properly listening to you or to them. Kira really forgot what was tremendously important didn't she?

"Love, Honor and Cherish". Those words keep popping into her head. They are for relationships: Kira's relationship with you Lord, each family member, and each friend. It means to love and be respectful of each other. Thank you for giving her back the respect she needed for her family...for you...and for her friends. Kira had lost it and now it's coming back.

Thank you, Lord.

Kira thinks that she was just so tired that she had to blame something. Instead of turning to you, she would keep pushing herself. Why is it that the things that are profoundly important are the things that get dumped on? Why is it that sometimes it takes something so devastating to put things back into perspective, and in their proper place. You

Having Coffee with the Special One

know, it doesn't matter where we are or when we do it, but when we call upon your name you're there. You're right beside us every step of the way. Equal partner in a sense, except that you're the Almighty Lord, and Kira is the sheep. What Kira meant was that you walk beside us not ahead of us or behind us. You're the everlasting Lord. You always tell us to grab your right hand and when we do that we are always on your right side. Does that mean we are right with you God?

Lord, there is such peace knowing that you're with us, you love us, and you forgive us for what we do wrong, even when we don't realize we are doing wrong.

That's sort of confusing to Kira too, but Lord, she will just learn to put all her trust in you. You know how she struggled yesterday. There again she was judgmental even while she remembered that she has had to put others off. She has had to remember there are times in people's lives where maybe they truly can't afford what it costs, it's all depending on what you are willing to pay or able to pay. Kira has to learn the right way to handle this, and act when she is faced with someone that can't pay for the service that they need, and that she is in the same boat as they are and there are just times when there isn't enough money to go around for everyone. She has got to learn how to set boundaries, so that this doesn't happen. For their sake and hers. Forgive her for not doing it properly, not handling it better than she does.

Patty Scott

Help her to learn the proper way to handle and use a fair price for the job that's done. God you know this is an area where she is struggling. Kira knows she still has something to learn there and she needs to open her heart and mind unto you Jesus Christ. Kira remembers the times where, in her life, she didn't have plenty and there wasn't enough to go around for what she owed people. It was due partly because she made bad choices, was around the wrong people, and that was just the way it happened. There isn't a time in someone's life when if they lost a job or things just weren't going well, that they could pay what they owe if the same amount of money isn't coming in as hoped for or expected.

There were times Kira had an extremely low opinion of herself and she didn't know or realize her own worth. You know there is a difference between being worthy of something or deserving it. Lord, she never has deserved what they have or what you have blessed them with, but you do show them that they are worthy of your love, your grace, and your forgiveness.

Even in all their trials and struggles Lord, they always had a roof over their heads, food on the table to nourish them and clothing on their backs. You always did provide for what they needed. Kira remembers how she felt when they lived in the apartment complex in Colorado, when they lost

Having Coffee with the Special One

their home (by the way she does know that she probably messed up on that one too.)

Her negative and bad way of thinking didn't allow her to trust you or let you in, did it? She didn't know if that guy that came to the door was sent by you or not but she didn't even listen to you or him, and she didn't talk to you about it or ask what your thoughts were. She just turned the guy away. She was so angry at the world at that time. She was so mad that she felt like she had been used and abused by someone she didn't even know yet. Kira had put trust into them.

Now that didn't make sense at all. Why would she do that and not trust you Lord? Why wouldn't she go to you and talk to you about what was happening? Kira was wallowing in self-pity. She wasn't listening even though she was praying to you and asking for your help. Kira just wouldn't listen, and now she knows, that maybe if she would have just sat back and let you handle it, things might have turned out differently. The problem was still there, but at least she would have handled it differently, like maybe ask the guy a few more questions, and see if he would have liked to see the house. Hey maybe he wasn't all that interested but at least she wouldn't have just shut the door on the opportunity right off the bat.

Another thing she has learned since then too, is you don't put so much importance on what others think of you. But because of Kira's background and her profession, she thought she should have been able to handle her finances better than that. She has learned now: she wasn't always the one that was in control.

Kira felt lower than dirt at the time, but again now as she remembers, no one can pay their bills when there is no money coming in, and you can't always fight dishonesty. Kira was mad at the mortgage company, the guy that closed on the loan; she just couldn't understand why or how she fell into the predicament that she was in. By the way too, she hates to admit it, but she was glad that he was held accountable for his actions, even though it was several years later as she had learned, but at least he was held accountable.

Kira is reminded of it at times even still, but at least now, she can see how she can use it to help others, and has been able to, so that made it all worth it, but she still wouldn't ever want to go through that again, and doesn't wish it on anyone either, even if she disliked the person strongly. ,

That's also what you have taught her Lord, that even in bad things that happened you have turned it into something beautiful and good. Kira has got to hang on to that and know that it's true, you made something beautiful out of a bad situation and made it good. Gave her strength and courage and went on anyway, even in the same industry, they tried to black ball her out of , for something that she really didn't have a lot of control over, maybe in all honesty this really was the best way for it to turn out, look at what she gained from it,

Having Coffee with the Special One

and how she has healed from it. You forgave her in this area; you healed her, she was able to help others as she said, and more than one other person, several others. In several different ways, but you were there the whole time, you showed her the way to help them.

The shame, the pain and the anger are gone, and the embarrassment, you know when you talk about the skeletons in the closet, they can't hurt you any longer. Suddenly one day it just becomes non important, and you don't even really think about it. It no longer has control over you or how you think.

Thank you, Jesus, Kira now looks at it as a blessing Lord. Look at what you showed her and taught her, look who Kira was able to help after she had to go through that. When you can help someone else, you really get a different perspective on it, and you learn why it happened was to help others.

Kira learned a lot and even now as you're talking, she can see what she did wrong, but you have given her peace about it. She did hang on to it for too long, but in the long run it helped her to remember that you carried her through it all. You gave her the answers even though they may not have been the ones she expected or was hoping for. Not that Kira even really knew what she was looking for, she just wanted relief. This has helped to teach Kira not to allow anyone person define who she is, because they don't get to do that.

Kira watches herself so that she keeps her integrity in check. Now she makes better choices. It comes to Kira that there isn't a person or company on this planet who would be able to pay bills or take care of their responsibilities if they didn't have money coming in. No one can. Kira is more compassionate about it too; she tries to help them keep face even despite what is happening to them. Why do we put so much importance on this, is it our integrity or what exactly?

That's why people work for what they want, but maybe at times we want a little more than we should have, and we let it get out of hand. Maybe we just don't think about where we are heading, and it gets away from us.

God always provides for what we need, and you do the rest if you want more. But remember that more isn't always better. Keep God always in your decisions and prayers, don't leave him out because that's not what he wants. God wants to be a part of it and in it, in the decision making, and really it always turns out better than you can even dream sometimes.

Kira has also had to realize and remember the abilities that she has all come from you. She can't start thinking again that she is doing it all on her own, or that she's alone in this. What you have brought her through over the past oh gosh, forever, when she looks back, she sees that you have been by her side all the way. It's almost embarrassing because she just didn't see it at the time: Kira

Having Coffee with the Special One

didn't see that you were always with her. How could she not see that, or even realize what she was doing with the way that she was thinking?

You gave her the ability, the knowledge, the ways to find what she needed to know and the answers when she needed them. There have been times in the past where she can see now, where you were there, and you brought people into her life. She just hopes that she can help them. This is the case even with family members. Everyone knows when it comes to your kids, it breaks your hearts when they are in trouble and you want to help but you can't do it for them, as you won't for us. But you do and will fight our battles for us when we can no longer do it, or we have done all that we can do.

Kira knows at times you tell her to do what she can do, and you'll do the rest. That's a promise that she and others can hold on to...you aren't going to tell her something that's not the truth, or that you have no intention of ever completing what you told her you would do for her.

You're fully aware that there are so many things that are happening in her days that remind her where she has been and how far you have carried her along the way. Kira wants to learn to look at each one of her experiences as a blessing and thank you for the experience so she would know how to handle it if it came along again and how to help someone else. To share your love and help other people. Kira must stay humble; remember she's been there and to ask you to enter here and be with her so she can discover what is right and what is your will.

In ways Lord, she didn't want to bring work into this, but Kira thinks she has a lot to share and must at times, because of the difficulties she's been having and the confusion in her head.

Kira read something...it must have been from what the pastor sent over. She is going to have to read it again. Something about shame or embarrassment. Kira has been embarrassed and yes, she guesses shamed. She knows they are human, and they aren't perfect, but yes, she strives to be perfect because she thought that she had to. Even her oldest son said something on that order, and that Kira had pushed him too. Kira was so much harder on him because she thought they had to be perfect: what a misconception. She has had trouble with that before, but she does remember the pastor saying they don't have to be perfect.

She got to feeling again that she had to be perfect, didn't she? Kira was allowing other people and what they said to her, affect her. How many times will she need to hear that before she will replace all the other crap with the good stuff? Kira was getting embarrassed for reasons she shouldn't have let bother her. Hopefully, she will find that balance. "She guesses this is where she falls under the category as a people pleaser".

Ok let's work on this area, Lord. Obviously, Kira needs help in this area, because in her mind she

Having Coffee with the Special One

never had thought that at all. In her mind she used to think that she didn't really care what others thought of her, so what changed in her? Was it because she started her own practice, and thought she had to deal with some of the stuff, that she was faced with? Why did it change the demands on her time? She isn't sure, but something changed, and she doesn't even know when it did.

Something just came to mind, Lord. Kira needed help in friends (of which things have changed tremendously here too, thank you by the way.)

Help her to really appreciate the ones that she has, they really do care about her, and she really does enjoy being around them, and doing things with them, they mean a lot to her. Lord, why was this area so hard for Kira, was it trust issues again? Please cleanse her heart and mind, help her to know the ones who really care and let go of the ones that don't. She knows in the past she picked the wrong ones, so she must allow the right ones in. It's true some people will like you for who you know, what you know or what can they get from you. But in general, most people are good, and they just want to be friends. They enjoy the friendship too. She just must be able to weed out the bad ones, and don't assume anything.

Lord, Kira knows that it was that she didn't basically trust people, she doesn't know how many times she had been told you know one day you're going to have to learn how to trust someone. Kira didn't want to get hurt so she had built up the walls. But she also knew that they didn't want to get hurt either.

Kira remembers when Coletta told her "when you want a friend let me know" ... that still sticks with Kira. The Bible study group she used to go to weekly keeps inviting her to come back, but she shied away for several stupid reasons!

Lord, cleanse her heart and help her learn how to be better in this area and not let things that people say upset her so much. It isn't about them, it's about you building a closer relationship to you!

Do not be afraid for I am with you says the Lord. In every area of life, you're there. Ask in my name "you shall receive" and "your joy will be complete".

Kira misses the inner circle of friend she had while growing up. It was always the four of them: Norma, Chandy, Coletta and Kira. Two were strong-willed children and two were milder, softer, and gentler. Looking back, Kira knew that all four of them needed your love and your guidance. Yet as they grew up Norma and Coletta moved away, while Chandy and Kira were still in the same area. Funny though, even though Chandy and Kira were in the same area, they don't get together as much as they used to. Kira thought, guess time just slips away too quickly and neither one realizes that it's slipping away.

Having Coffee with the Special One

Yes, you know Kira's inner thoughts here and she doesn't have to mention everything, but she does have an attitude that "She can do it herself" doesn't she? Kira knows that she has convinced herself of that and she has said it more than once. She must remember she can't do it by herself, and really, she doesn't want to either, because it gets lonely when you think you're alone. All that Kira does is with you and your guidance Jesus Christ. She has come to know and believe that it has made things so much better. Even when Coletta and Norma come back to visit it's so much fun, and entertaining, because they still enjoy each other and pick up where they left off the last time, they saw each other.

You've made it possible for Kira to see what she has done in her life and can see that you Lord, do and will stay with her always and all that we do. We do to glorify you oh Lord, ...

Ahh!! It's Kira's attitude that needs to change. She needs to remember that she has you, so it's ok not to lean on people! But she can't start thinking again like she did in the past, and that she doesn't need anyone, that she does it all alone. That was so wrong of her, because Kira has you, and with you on her side then who can be against her?

Put her faith and trust in you not other people or things, or even her own ability, because that will fail her. Kira has been shown that lately too many times. There is so much to learn...this is going to be a long journey. But that's ok, because we have time, you take the time.

Yes, Lord, you have filled the emptiness that she has felt...you filled that void in her... you were what she was missing all along. Kira was feeling like something was missing, there was this hole in her heart. She was bringing "it" to you, but she wasn't really bringing you into her life or building the relationship that you were wanting.

What is it with her? Why wasn't she having this intimacy with you or spending the time with you that was necessary to build this loving deep relationship with you.?

Kira really wasn't listening to you or paying attention to you knocking on her heart, or her mind. She was blocking it out and kept talking because she didn't wait for you to answer.

Yes: Kira has let her defenses down because she does feel vulnerable right now. And, yes, it was uncomfortable, at first. She also feels that her walls were falling but she was still trying to hang on to them for protection. She had them built up for so many years, so no they were sort of like a security blanket. "False protection false security" right! That's where she keeps you out too, right? When she does that she needs to focus on you and you only, so the fear and insecurity will subside and eventually go away, and she will finally feel and enjoy the peace that you give her so freely.

Having Coffee with the Special One

Trust in the Lord, with all my heart, lean not on my own understanding muses Kira. Ask in Jesus' name, and my dreams will be complete. Until now you haven't asked, so ask and your joy will be complete. That means something, and until Kira got to this point, she really didn't understand what she was missing, and how much more it means to her now.

Yes Lord, by building this close relationship with you Kira has realized that she can say that her life is so much better when you're with her and a part of her everyday life.

Not that you, Lord, weren't there before, but Kira is more willingly acknowledging you and giving you the credit for being with her. That's the difference. Why does did Kira allow things to get in in between you, Lord? Kira knows from what she had been going through with the cleansing of her heart, body and soul that she has really learned to appreciate you and feel the love and the care you put into her life.

You know it's like when Kira felt so in love with her husband; she feels it came from you, too. It's a very powerful way of showing your love, and our love for you. The presence and the love you have for Kira, it's like no other. It's as powerful as when you love your child or husband. It just dawned on Kira that she had missed out on that type of love so much of you in her life. How could she have allowed life and other things to get in the way?

Kira enjoys your relationship and the care from you. Kira thinks if she didn't stray away and she hadn't become complacent with your presence, maybe she wouldn't have realized the magnitude and the difference your relationship is now versus how it was in the past. Maybe that's why Kira forgot the importance of your being with her. Kira thinks sometimes that she did take you for granted, and she hopes she has learned now not to do that? Kira doesn't like people doing that to her, so how could she have so easily done it to you. Kira must make sure that she doesn't do it to you again.

Knock and the door will be opened. Seek and you shall find. Ask and you shall be given. All if we ask in your name, Jesus Christ. Do not be afraid for I am with you says the Lord.

Kira has learned no one is ever alone when we allow you to come into our lives. Kira knows that all the trials and tribulations she is going through right now, but Lord, she can't get through them alone. She can't do it without you in her life, helping her. There are times when she gets so overwhelmed and anxious. Kira finally figured out that she was allowing anxiety to win and take over. She didn't realize what it was at the time, but since then Kira has realized that it was anxiety. There were too many things going on and she didn't know how to handle them. Kira was so shaky inside—it felt like fear set in—and she was so frustrated.

Having Coffee with the Special One

Kira felt like no one listened to her and she felt so alone.

Lord, you knew exactly what Kira was going through and you tried to tell her, but she was so wrapped up in the misery. All Kira could think was she must haven't wanted to listen to you, or she didn't like what you were saying to her. She was allowing her misery to have a power-hold on her instead of asking and allowing the peace of your presence in.

You know Kira does at times chuckle at herself and you're right, Lord, one day she will be able to laugh at her idiotic things that she does. She is glad about that because that's one of the things Kira loves about your forgiveness. She gets to laugh about things when they are all over and done with, you got her through it. Kira hopes you'll join her when it happens and laugh with her.

Kira was feeling like she had the burdens of the world on her shoulders and yes, you're right Lord, she is not strong enough to carry the burdens of the world. Really, Kira doesn't want the responsibility of the world on her shoulders, so help her to learn when it's something she should take care of and when she should walk away. Let God and let you. Oh yea!

Lord, you told Kira to bring her problems and burdens to you so the two of you could discuss it. Kira would get your answer, but she had to remember that maybe it wouldn't be the answer she was looking for or thought that it should be...but you would always answer!

As with any child, they aren't going to get everything they want and Lord, you won't always say yes to what we ask for because you know more than we do. What we ask for now could be bad down the road, or what we ask for may not really be what we wanted in the first place. Or Lord, you have something better in mind, so that's why we need to relax and put our trust in you.

Hey Kira says she remembers you told her that, so isn't that a step in the right direction?

Kira sure knows that since she let go of her kids so you could help them things have gotten better in some areas, and in other areas, well, they are still a work in progress. Why would she expect anything different? Kira sure has had freedom from the burden of worrying about them, and she can see where you're helping them for as much as they will allow you to.

After all, look at how old Kira is, and she is learning still. Kira is just now understanding some things that maybe she should have learned a long ago, especially since she has been a Christian for all her life. But nothing like she is now. Your word and the songs, and the teachings mean so much more to her. Kira isn't just going through motions; she really thinks about what the words mean and the songs' verses.

Having Coffee with the Special One

Kira is noticing the freedom you're giving her. She soaks in the peace that surpasses all understanding and keeps her heart and mind open to you, Jesus Christ. Thank you for all you do for us, Lord, it really is a lot that you do.

Remember when Kira was a young teenager, she had such a free spirit. So did her daughter when she was young. Kira loves that free spirit you gave her, but she hopes that she will keep you alive in her and not allow her to fall back on fear which ruins what you have worked so hard to accomplish within her. Kira doesn't want to be that way again. She wants to laugh, to sing, and to enjoy you in her life. You open her to love, laughter and joy, so why would she want to squash that now?

The next few months Kira had a lot of challenges and deadlines facing her, so she knows she can't do it without you. Kira hasn't had the time to finish training, so she is going to really depend on your help to get her through these challenges, especially with the new work that's sitting on her desk. Please Lord, help Kira get it done and help her stay true, the best that she can with what she has.

Kira hopes and prays, Lord, with each step of this journey that the two of you, are one. She doesn't forget you're the one and she allows you to guide and lead her in the way you want her to go. You have transformed her into a better person. Kira doesn't want to fight it anymore. She doesn't want to fight the world anymore either. Kira just wants to take it one day at a time, one case at a time, do what she can and depend on you to do the rest. Kira wants to do and be what you want of her to be and know it's your will. She wants to let people see that you're in her through her words and her work. Lord, let the light shine in her and through her. Kira likes the glow in her smile and the sparkle in her eyes that you have given her. She knows that that comes from you and within, it's not from anything else.

"The power of forgiveness". It shows in Kira every day: how much forgiveness has helped her, and that the trials in our lives are opportunities to open to you. All need to remember, Lord: you're there for them and you're with them. Look at Kira during the struggles in her marriage, in her relationship with

her kids, with her staff and her friends, you have guided her. You let Kira know when she needs to do something and when she didn't. Let go and let God!

Lord, thank you!

Each day Kira sees where you have helped her. As you said, you're not going to make all of the problems go away, but you're going to help me get through them, and you have done as you promised Kira. You have helped her get through them and

Having Coffee with the Special One

learn how to handle it if it arises where she needs help again.

Yes, at times Kira did rush at things and try to hurry them up. Yes, she will wait on you and when she did, she was happy with the results. She felt much more love in her relationships because she had gotten her respect back for those in the relationships. Now those people were treating her differently too. There were several things she wants to do and yes, she convinced herself that she had to get them done, but she learned those too will be taken care of. She had to stop and smell the roses.... all things will be done according to your will.

Kira also knows when it comes from you it comes from the heart.

Lord, Kira doesn't think she can ever say that enough. Hopefully, she will really get it and understand that it was the way it was. Kira wants to write books, as you know. She wants to make sure it's not her that's putting it off, letting life get in the way and slow her down. What you have taught her needs to be shared, because others need to know that you'll do the same for them as you have done for her.

Is that the correct way to think?

Kira wants to make sure it comes from the heart and it just isn't her hopes and dreams. She wants to make sure that's really where you're leading her and directing her, and she has to remember too, that it's your timeframe not hers. Yet, she still wants to make sure that she isn't dragging her feet on something that you really want done.

Kira saw an ad on a social media site, which said something like "when God wants something done there is nothing you can do to stop it, and when he doesn't, you also can't force it."

That was something to remember.

Kira had gotten into a habit of putting herself on deadlines and time frames which took the fun out of doing what she loved doing. Also, sometimes she would overextend herself. Her reality how long something may take to complete something and complete it well, was another area she needs work on.

She has learned to really appreciate and hang on to the joy in what you do for her. Kira also needs to realize, understand, and accept that you know what is best for her. Kira must stop losing herself and learn to hang on to what you give her, the peace, and the joy.

At times she feels like a whirlwind is going through her, and she can't stop it. She wants too many things done in a short amount of time. You can't enjoy doing something when you're always in a rush to get them done. She had to learn how to enjoy and cherish each accomplishment. She had to learn not to short-change herself or the joy she

Having Coffee with the Special One

could receive in accomplishing what she set out to do.

Kira needs your help to keep her focused on you Lord, so the anxiety doesn't creep up on her.

Kira has realized other areas where she was wrong. When things at home became hard for her to handle, and she didn't want to constantly battle and fight with family members, she used her work as a haven or a refuge instead of bringing you in closer to her. Kira became a workaholic to hide away and not put up with arguing and unhappiness, which was caused mostly by the kids growing up and leaving the nest.

You know the empty nest syndrome: you just feel a loss when your kids move out, and you wonder what the heck you're going to do with the rest of your life. You haven't learned completely how to let go of them, but also know that you still have them.

Kira is sorry Lord, why didn't she think to take it to you, and why didn't she develop a better relationship with you? You know and she knows that she isn't perfect, but really that had nothing to do with it. Why was she so mad at you that she wouldn't trust you or talk to you?

Was it part of the move to Texas too? You know it takes her so long to feel at home somewhere after they move.

Or was it that she had to move and leave her children, in a state that wasn't close to her, so she could be with them if they needed her? It sure wasn't something that Kira had expected because whoever thinks that you'll get transferred and leave your children in another state? As a parent, you're prepared to have them leave you when they finish school... but not you leave them. She knows that was part of it but didn't know how to handle that either.

Kira realized that she won't ever be perfect, but she knew that you loved her anyway. You didn't give up on her and you didn't run away and leave her when she was going through this.

She was the one that pushed you out or wouldn't let you in. Hmm, she wonders why? Was it her self-sufficient attitude that stopped her? God, she does remember so many times those words coming out of her mouth. Geez! She can and will get through all things but not without you.

You're the one that makes Kira strong and gives her the courage to get through.

Kira just can't take credit for it. She must make sure that she doesn't profess that it's her. Kira must admit it's you...it's you that's helping and guiding her. She can do all things through Christ who strengthens her.

Having Coffee with the Special One

Lord, she is more than willing now that she has learned and has finally realized the magnitude and errors in the way that she was thinking, to turn it all over to you. Kira didn't want to be alone in life and she didn't want to grow old before her time. Kira feels like she has so much to give still and man she just loves the joy and the renewal in life you have given her.

She can't remember when the last time was that she felt so free; free from the burdens she must deal with on a day-to-day basis. She is finally learning, after all these sixty years, she doesn't want to carry the weight of the world on her shoulders, as she said earlier.

You're right Lord: the problems don't go away. She just doesn't dwell on them as much and she doesn't allow them to control her. Just because we are Christians and we believe it doesn't mean we won't struggle and have problems; it just means that you're there for us and with us to get us through our struggles. Kira was told that by one of her sons and she read it somewhere too, so it really makes sense to her.

She knows she still has a lot of work to do and has several areas that she needs to be cleansed. Kira knows that the two of you're on a journey and Lord, she is very excited to see what is in her "life bucket". She wonders what you have planned for some of the resolutions to other issues that she has. It's kind of like a movie, and she wants to know the ending, but in this case, she isn't in any hurry because she doesn't want to rush life any longer. It goes too fast as it is, and then one day it will be gone.

Kira doesn't want to be a worn-out old nag! She must remember to always put her trust in you and yes, wait on your time frame and schedule. Kira thinks that she finally gets it, but she chuckles as she knows it's a bad habit of hers. Kira wanted results now, she didn't want to wait, and she didn't realize there are just some things in life that you don't get total control over. In fact, that maybe none of it really is in your control anyway, so why stress about it? Why let trying to control things take away your joy or consume your precious time!

Kira will continue to pray, but she has realized that she can't be in a hurry for a resolution. She's also learned that God won't always make you rich, but he will help you become a better money manager. That's what he was giving Kira. The Lord helped her manage her money better, and he also blessed her with some fabulous sales to make her dollar stretch further. It's amazing how such little things, have shown her a lot. Giving on a continual and consistent basis does help and guide her. Donating is a blessing where you can give to another in need. Blessings don't always mean more, sometimes it just means you can manage things better.

You're our guide; you keep us out of trouble. You give us the strength and endurance to get through it. Blessings don't always mean that you're going to receive money. Was that just a problem in

Having Coffee with the Special One

Kira's thought process or was it just one that she had realized recently?

Yes, Kira knows that she was a strong-willed child and yes, she can be very stubborn.

Kira needs to remember to watch out for when it's you and try to back off where she isn't supposed to be the strong-willed one. Yes, she must admit though that being strong-willed is one of the qualities in her that she likes. In her mind, Kira used it so people wouldn't run all over her. She kept people at arm's length, or away from her.

Apparently, Kira missed the value in and the point of being strong-willed in the first place. Kira can see where a person needs to have neediness in themselves and she understands it's one of the ways she learned the need for you. She needs to start to lean on you instead of herself. Kira had to learn that's why you, Lord, are here for us during a time of need.

Everyone can depend on you, Lord.

Dear God, I can see where you're doing a lot for my life and you're working on my behalf.

Kira thanks God as she thinks about a couple of things that are going on in her life, and where she really needs God's help.

She knows that at times she has a fleeting moment of hesitation or an urgency flash through her, where she wants it to be over. But Kira knows she must wait on you.

In Kira's mind five or six years is a long time to get a resolution, but in so many ways—mostly for God—five or six years is nothing. If you look at things in the proper perspective and in the overall scheme of things, five to six years is nothing. Kira needed to quit thinking of it in time frame and keep moving and pushing forward. She had to lean on God, and not let the problem hold her back from moving forward.

God, you have been in Kira's life since she was a child, so you know she has gone through both good and bad times. Even at her age, when Kira thought you weren't there, you have shown her still that you were there and have been there always. You were there even when Kira was doing things that you shouldn't have had to watch. Even how hard it was, Kira wanted to share the moments with you, and have you told her how wrong what she did, was. It's hard to swallow at times, to have to sit and listen to what you have done wrong, and even make it known. However, in all fairness, you must be able to talk about it and share it, or what was the purpose?

Having Coffee with the Special One

Lord, Kira knows she just doesn't want to let you down. When something needs to be done, she knows it will happen when it's supposed to, and she is ready for what you have in store for her. You know it's starting to make sense to her. When you told her that all things would fall into place, well she believes that has started to happen. To Kira everything seems to be falling into place, but that doesn't mean there won't be any hiccups along the way...but things are starting to fall into place. She doesn't want to feel like she is the one that's dragging her feet, and she has realized that's just not so. Kira needs to remember it's your will...not her.

You know she thinks that it's soaking in finally.

Lord, she really does enjoy this time with you and the time you're giving to her. Kira knows that she still has some healing to do, and a lot of it will be done through her writings. You're showing her day by day how you're helping her and you're giving her the answers. Now she knows what you meant when you said some of them would just work themselves out, and they have.

Jesus, you have almost given a resolution to every one of the issues that were bugging her. You didn't really make them go away, but you showed her how to deal with them. She needs to give her body time to heal and know that it's you that will do the healing.

Patty Scott

Lord, Kira says she does really thank you for Sheila, and the rest of her staff. They really did help her. Kira had to learn again to let go and let God. There are so many circumstances in life where you must learn this lesson, because it happens a lot. As Kira looks at things it probably happens more times than not.

There was something there Lord, that Kira couldn't quite put her fingers on that kept bugging her. But she also knew that if there was something bugging her, well it would come to pass too because you would provide a good resolution—Thank You.

You were telling Kira something, but she just wasn't sure what you were trying to tell her. Kira just waited, and when it eventually it came to surface, it was that Sheila just didn't want to be where she was, and had no desire, to change. Which was ok because that's just the way it is at times. Kira had to learn people's limits, what they did or didn't want from a job, and that maybe some just didn't want to advance or the huge responsibility that comes with some positions. That's not a bad thing, it's just you need to watch and see it, so you don't push them too hard, or put them in a position that neither one of you are happy with.

We can't miss the opportunities that you may have for us in life, but if it's what you want for us, then

Having Coffee with the Special One

we also can't stop it. Look at where Kira is today; that's because of where you lead her all her life. Funny thing was it wasn't that opportunities just kept falling into her lap. She had to complete a lot of prep work and training to get where she is today. You opened the doors for her, and she was always getting jobs in the accounting world. Now she has her own tax practice, all thanks to you.

Isn't it funny how hindsight works? You can see the road you took to get where you are, but you can't see the road ahead where you're going, that's a total surprise, from God. Kira knows it was you Lord, and you gave her what she needed to do the job. It was a gift from you, for Kira to be able to learn and retain all the knowledge that she needed to put it all together. She still remembers the day you pounded on her heart and said it's time, it's time for you to go out on your own.

Kira just allowed it to become too much of her life and she didn't keep you first in her life where you belong, and she didn't keep family first. You had to teach and show her again, what really is important and where each thing belongs in the priority list of life. You're first and above all else then Family then job. Not the other way around. Kira is sorry for abusing your gifts to her.

Every job you put in her path and you got her, you lead her to them. She learned so much. The opportunities she had at the time, she didn't understand that it was all for her to learn, at the time that she was going through them, but then you shed light on them, and you showed her, when she looked back it was all a part of your plan, and it all worked out how you wanted it to. That's why when she took the exams it didn't work out in the other states, you waited until Kira and Tim moved to Texas to bless her with it, because it was time for her to succeed.

When things went wrong in life or in her jobs, Kira saw it as personal failures. In her mind, because it wasn't going the way she thought it should and Kira didn't have the vision, yet that God had planned for her. Now she can see the difference Lord. Now when Kira looks at it all as opportunities, she is thankful for the opportunities. Kira sees all the blessings in it and her experiences and realizes why things went the way that they did. It was all for a higher purpose, and along with the training and knowledge to use for what she is doing today!

God Had A Plan.

Once she realized that it didn't hurt and, she delighted in the experiences she had because she learned so much!

Kira met some great people along the way, and built some lasting relationships, and gained respect from the professional community, she really got a lot of different opportunities. Kira started changing her attitude and stopped looking at things with a negative attitude and looked at the

Having Coffee with the Special One

blessings and it all turned out for the best and to glorify you Lord!

You do give us a better life than the one we plan for ourselves. Kira hung on and it paid off, she didn't lose the love she wanted to have, and she didn't lose the relationships with her children or the people she worked for in the past that were good to her. She is a better person for it now too. Kira has even gotten to where there is excitement in her again, and when she looks at the past as an opportunity, then she sees them as blessings. Kira will still stumble and fall but Lord, she does see the blessings and she is really opening to them now! A work in progress, she is still in training, you know one baby step at a time.

Yes Lord, she does feel the warmth and security of you taking care of her life. Kira knows that you're there, just waiting for the chance to help her or take care of her again and this time there is a difference how she will respond to your help. You want what is good for her and you make sure that she gets it.

In Kira's eyes she does try to live by faith because she goes around like a horse with blinders on in this world. But she gets the tendency where she forgets to discuss all things with you Christ. She is sorry and she thanks you for what she is going through right now! She won't lie, she doesn't comprehend all of it, but she knows you'll do what is best on her behalf and send her the answers eventually. It's because she feels the love and the warmth from you Lord. She feels so protected with you present in her life, and she has learned that she can trust you above all things.

Kira takes it you're letting her know she is doing what you have intended for her, so she doesn't have to feel bad because she just wants to be with you at this time. Kira wanted to be healed inside and out! That's why she was hurt in the wreck so you and her could have this time and she would allow you to come in and cleanse her. Who knows what would have happened besides you if this didn't happen?

Thank you for explaining what it means to be "Holy" Lord. Kira was struggling there, as you know. You know all things; nothing can be hidden from you. Kira just had to get to the point to where she could bring them to you, no matter how bad she thought they were. Or how wrong she had been in the past. The way she thought, her thoughts were misconstrued. In some of the ways she looked at religion, in which has nothing to do with Faith, or a relationship with you. That's something we don't always learn until we are older, or as Kira knows, that was something new to her having a real relationship with you has nothing to do with religion.

Lord, Kira does want to spend this time with you and heal.

Having Coffee with the Special One

Kira really doesn't mind not working but Lord, she does have responsibilities. In one way she doesn't care about those responsibilities and she doesn't worry about them. But as you know, at times she gets anxious, and doesn't know how long it will all last. Kira must be able to share her experiences with people, so they know you're real, and you're there. You save us!

Lord, Kira knows that she has needed this time with you for a long time. In fact, it's long overdue. You had to tell Kira to let you in her heart and soul and she does thank you for that.

It's funny how she used to wonder how elderly people could just sit still, and not do a lot. She didn't realize the awesomeness in it. She didn't appreciate or ever know how to sit and relax and enjoy the presence of you and the peace that you would give her. Now she knows and she thanks you for this time Lord! For her to learn too how important it really is, and what it means.

Kira says thank you again for cleansing her, you have brought her a long way Lord! Through the forgiveness process you opened, you tore down her walls so you could have this time together. Kira could spend time with you now without any walls or barriers up which she used to erect to stop you from coming in. You opened her heart and you're letting love in again. Forgiveness is for the one that forgives, and Jesus will forgive you when you forgive others. You must forgive others so you can be forgiven.

Patty Scott

You have carried Kira through so many times of strife and pain. You hung on to her, so she didn't fall.

Lord, all she had to do was to open and take the time to listen to you and what you wanted to tell her. To show her that you have always been with her. It wasn't fair to you, or to Kira, or her family or her husband, when she hung on to her walls and kept you out. She learned that through the process of keeping you out she was keeping out love for her family and love for you. Kira has learned that now, she realizes that anger just keeps people at bay and closes off her world. Stops her from enjoying peace, and happiness. And, it's only herself that she can blame...no one else.

Lord, you have carried Kira through some immensely powerful processes. Spending this time with you is teaching Kira how to absolutely love, honor and cherish you, and worship you and your holy name as we are supposed to and as the Bible teaches us to.

Lord, Kira does enjoy this holy time with you.

Thank you for letting her know she doesn't have to be "goody goody", to be able to understand you. You know that she was confused there, Kira opened herself unto you, Jesus Christ, so she can have your love and peace in her. Now that she has, she is a kinder, gentler person. She is more giving, and she

Having Coffee with the Special One

doesn't feel that brick wall in her. You softened her, you don't make her weak, you give her strength and there is a difference. You know how scared she was, because of the stupid wife's tales, she had thought up in her head, what would happen if she let go and gave it all to you. She had some misconceived notions and had to get through them. You know Lord, that her confidence in her ability to do what she is doing has been shaken.

She knows why now Lord, she needed to turn her attention back to you. Kira needed to put you back into her life, at the head of it. You did prepare her for these moments. You let her know of your presence in her and she knew something was happening. She could feel you moving and cleansing her. She could feel that something was happening in her life, but Kira just didn't know or understand the full magnitude of it.

Before the wreck, most of the benefits Kira got from you was love and peace. God, you healed her on the emotional level that she needed. You gave her strength, you're the only one with your Spirit who could heal that part of Kira and fill that hole in her. Kira opened unto you Jesus Christ. Now she can comprehend what that means to do that, to open to you Lord. It means Kira will listen to you, put you in place where you belong, replace all the bad stuff with you, and let you guide her. It doesn't mean that she is dying or giving up. It means that she is your child, Lord.

Kira will mess up and she needs your guidance...but she is yours. Kira has come to understand why this quiet time with you is so important; She needed and wanted the Holy Spirit in her. It flutters around singing within her: let the Lord, shine in her. This is how you truly learn that you're one of God's children, and you really get to know him on a deeper, more personal level; and build an intimate relationship with him which is what he wants from us. He wants a relationship with us as bad as we need and want him in our lives.

Lord, Kira could just see the Spirit in Eve's eyes...the sparkle and glow of the Spirit in her face. She is truly a gift from you Lord. Please watch over her and protect her.

She is such a sweetheart! It isn't just because she is one of Kira's granddaughters either, Lord, it's because she just sparkles and shines with pure joy. Lord, there is something incredibly special about her, and the way her face just shines, and the excitement she shows in life.

Kira is finding out that the crud she deals with on a day-to-day basis really doesn't mean a lot, it just helps her occupy her time and keeps her out of trouble. But it also gives her an opportunity to allow you to shine through her. She had to stop being embarrassed by what she has gone through

Having Coffee with the Special One

and be thankful for it because you have been with her and brought her a long way, Lord.

Even though she listened to you, she still had her family and other people kept telling her to slow down. Her pastor told her at communion that she needed to get some sleep when she was overworking herself. Kira's kids saying that she wasn't listening to them—which didn't make sense in her mind.

She didn't understand at the time, but now she does Lord. She wants to have a meaning in her life, and she wants her life to stand for you, Lord. You give her a sense of purpose, and a reason to keep on pushing forward and not give up.

Now she understands what all the fuss was about, what her husband and kids and others were trying to tell her. As you're aware of too, it takes her a long time—sometimes—to get to what she should have learned years ago. Kira knows that you'll continue to show her the way; you'll open her heart and mind unto you. You'll keep her from going down that wrong path again. Now she can have a decent relationship with her family because she is no longer worn out. She no longer puts her company first, and she takes time when necessary for her family. She learned the hard way...which for some reason is how she almost always had to learn things.

The hard way.

Patty Scott

Lord, Kira still thinks that you have a great sense of humor. She knows it's not funny when she doesn't abide with you as she is supposed to, but it's funny how you get our attention sometimes.

Lord, Kira doesn't care what other people thinks about her relationship with you. In her relationship with you, she can laugh and talk with you like she would anyone close to her. But she also knows, Lord, that she would put you down with the rest of her relationships. Kira saw you as an equal before but guesses that's best way to describe the error in her feelings with you.

She is not the Alpha and Omega, you are, Lord. Kira does think that you're her friend and you sit by her; you talk to her, not at her; and you listen to what she has to say to you. You can't sit on the steps anymore like you did in the past, but you can still sit with her in her car, or in her room. She still has glimpses of your presence and sees that sparkle in your eyes, and your smile. You know it's funny, Kira can see the sparkle in your eyes, and the smile on your face but she can't really see your face or remember what it looks like if she did get to see it.

Lord, when you tell Kira that she caters to other expectations, what exactly does she need to do so that doesn't happen? She looks at herself as a peacemaker. Is that what you mean, it's not up to

Having Coffee with the Special One

her to make peace or is it that she jumps so quickly to take care of things?

She knows with Tim she sometimes feels like she must jump through hoops around him and she knows that has got to stop. Kira felt like she must walk on eggs. It isn't always like that, but at times it just drives her crazy. Kira gets so frustrated with him at times. Kira loves him dearly, yet he drives her crazy.

Lord, help her in this area. Help her to see things through your eyes, and not let this get to her so much.

Kira feels and thinks he is an extremely negative person. Lord, is there really something there that she may be missing? Is there a point he is trying to make? She really tries to blow it off but sometimes he just wears her out. If there is really something wrong, then it needs to have some light shed on it. As it turns out that's exactly what happened. Tim was in so much pain because of the pinched nerves in his back, that it was getting hard for him to deal with it. Since Kira couldn't feel the pain he was in, she couldn't understand why it was causing him problems. You helped her get through this through guidance and allowing her to talk it through with you, Lord.

So here is something else that Kira wasn't aware of or didn't realize. You're telling Kira, if she is understanding you correctly, that even if she says that she wants to be in Heaven it doesn't mean you'll take her away from earth today!

Kira understands that she has no control over her destiny. But because you're the all-knowing of our inner thoughts Jesus, Kira had been afraid to complete certain things such as completing her legal will because she feared by signing it would end her life on earth. She felt that signing her will was the ultimate statement that she was ready to enter Heaven. Her intellectual side tells her that's a dumb idea. But Kira must admit that's only partly why she hasn't done a will. She also thinks things will change in her life before she dies so she really doesn't know what to put into the will. Heck she could sell everything she has, or something could happen in her life that would take whatever she has. So, in her mind, there was no point to it.

Yes, Lord, another dumb thing on her part, but Kira wants people in her life to know how much she cares or cared about them....which in her mind is dumb of her too as she sits here and thinks about it. If you want them to know how much you care about them why doesn't she show them and let them know while she is alive?

Geez! What a goof she has been, as her son and attorney pointed out to her on two occasions. If you want someone to know you love and care for them, then show them while you can. Don't wait to hurt them or make them wait...because by then, it's too late.

Having Coffee with the Special One

You give us times of trials and tribulations to allow us to keep you close in our hearts and in our minds. Kira will joke and tell people you're not done with her yet because in her mind she has had a lot of trials and tribulations especially since she has gone to the edge financially with you in hopes of one day having something for retirement. In some ways it's not smart for all the concern that Kira has put into it because tomorrow it could all change, even today it could.

When she looks back, Lord, she can see where you have always been with her and provided what she wanted and needed so why is it a concern? She guesses she does have to try to save up for it right? But she shouldn't make it her focus, as a lot of things in life or worry about it. Because you have always promised that you would take care of us, you watch over and feed birds, why wouldn't you watch over and give us food?

May the Holy Spirit and the power of hope be with you always. God will not leave you. He will help you and guide you through your days. God doesn't lie. You're with us always and we don't have to go through life alone! Delegate to others where their expertise is and always bring it to God and discuss it. Let God guide you in life. We don't know what we don't know.

Patty Scott

We overflow with the love, the joy, and the peace that you give us in blessings. The result is to be in eternal life with you in Heaven. Like a child we will dance in the rain. Your angels will dance with us, with their glowing wings. As you're aware Lord, Kira is out of sorts today, seems like it must happen once and a while. Not sure why, Kira guesses she's not opening to you as she should be, and she feels off a bit.

Kira asks: Why am I so stubborn about going to doctors? She knows one reason: Kira doesn't want to hear if something is seriously wrong. She thinks you'll tell her when something is wrong—which has been proven to be truth in the past—and you'll let her know in your subtle—or not so subtle—way as you did when she was hurt.

You had it come through the minister at church in a sermon. She was so out of whack! You watched over her and protected her. God if it wasn't for you, she wouldn't have gotten the proper care she needed. Kira is still amazed at being able to walk around and travel and do what she did with a broken neck. You got her the right doctor for the surgery and you're healing her. Lord, Kira is just in awe of what you have done and are doing. You saved her.

You're the silver lining around the dark clouds.

Having Coffee with the Special One

Lord, Kira remembers the day they were driving west on I-20 and when she looked up into the clouds, she could see the silver lining. Kira could see your glory shining through the clouds, the light at the end of the tunnel. She knew you were present and with her. Things are really going to be ok. You let her know she would be ok. You were preparing her for that day so she would get through it. You were working in her for several years.

Months prior she knew that, and while she had the feeling you were preparing her for something. she just didn't know what it was or when it was going to happen. Never in Kira's wildest dreams would she have thought it was going to be an accident to put her in the shape she ended up being in. But she only left you one choice.

She was so involved with work that she let it run her life. Something had to be done so that she would stop making it the priority in her life and the problems she was having in general. Kira was so overwhelmed, you had to remove her so you could work for her benefit and you could work through others, on her behalf. Even Sheila thought the same way, you had to remove Kira.

She was so lost in the trees that she couldn't see through the forest, as she was often reminded from one of her co-workers. Kira doesn't know how many times Lea said that to her before it even hit her what he was saying. She didn't understand what it meant; now she thinks that she does. Kira was allowing for everything to bog her down. She was really taking things very seriously and wasn't using common sense or depending on you God for your guidance or peace. You know this can really mess with a person's life when they won't listen to what you're trying to tell them.

Who or what was Kira allowing to control her life? She forgot that God was in control, not her, Lord. She did let go of your peace and she forgot, didn't she?

Kira wasn't using good judgment or even making good decisions. Kira really lost who she was and what she stood for. She knew you must stand for something, or you'll fall for anything. But Kira felt so unimportant and felt like she was drowning.

God, you really have helped her. You have shown her even when she did not want to see or admit where she went wrong. You still forgave her and stood by her side even when you may not have agreed with her. You didn't give up on her, even when she was wrong. Kira prayed: Thank you Lord, for forgiving me. She really has needed to be healed, Lord.

There were things in her life that she still feels she didn't fully heal over. She didn't really heal from the shock of Tim and his actions when he moved out. And Kira didn't really rest from overworking when she lived in California and then when she moved to Texas.

Having Coffee with the Special One

Man, Kira thought, this has been going on for a long time. This is a perfect example doing things in your time, Lord. Kira has needed to turn over to you for several years and look how long it took! But you still stood by her and didn't let her sink completely. Kira needs to be able to get this point across.

Is how she was would be the proper terminology (flitting around) Lord? She really feels like you're bringing her into the joy! She has been so lost for so long and she finally sees you changing her path. Leading her straight.

Lord, she has been allowing so many other things in life control her and her judgments and decisions. Kira lost herself. She forgot what really meant something to her and what she stood for.

God, Kira was allowing and making things important that shouldn't have had any bearing on her life of decisions. She has been allowing too many things stress her out! You're giving her clarity, Lord, and you're showing her where she has gone wrong in her thinking and in her actions. Kira took on too many responsibilities and tried to do it alone!

Lord, Kira says, she didn't even consult with you when she made the decisions to buy the practices. She didn't even think to ask you what your thoughts were on it; she just went and did it. Thank you for freeing her from and forgiving her for not asking for your advice and help.

Lord, Kira doesn't have the power or the strength to do it alone. She doesn't want to do it alone either!

"I can do all things through Jesus Christ which strengthens me", doesn't mean she needs to take on the problems of the world! Thank you for making things smoother, allowing us to be in the business that we feel good in, and bringing the people into our lives that want the same things in life.

Jesus, thank you for showing Kira that she needs to just listen at times to others' problems, but she doesn't need to take them on. You're giving her peace. Please help her to hang on to that peace. Your peace and your face are shining down on her, oh Lord!

Why did she take on this Lord? She has made this error in life more than once! When she went to work when she was a teenager, taking care of her siblings, why did she think that was her own responsibility to do that? Kira worried about so many things that were not in her control or even something she could control. She hung on to her kids instead of letting them go and letting them grow. She wouldn't allow or want them to fall. There is freedom and peace of letting go.

Speaking of which: Lord, Kira is hoping to be able to go spend Michael's birthday with him. Will you make a way for them and let her enjoy it? Lord, she needs to make time in her life for her kids.

Having Coffee with the Special One

Help her to find the balance in life. Keep you first and foremost in her life. As for her and her house she will serve the Lord.

It just hit Kira, we are supposed to get up off our butts and get outside so we can enjoy the fresh air, look at the skies and see the beauty that you have given us and the air we breathe. You created the stars, the clouds, the sun, and the moon. We are supposed to enjoy the beauty. You did it for us to enjoy and to thank you. You created it all for us to have you all around us. We just need to pay attention and do as you ask. We can see you everywhere. We don't allow the clouds to block our views. Kira bets you had fun creating the world, watching, and seeing how it all turned out, and being proud of the work you accomplished. Kira means, look at the beauty all around us, who else could do that?

It's too bad we don't fully enjoy what you really have given us. Why is it that it takes us until we are old, to really slow down and appreciate what you give to us? You know this world could be all black and no color, yet you give us beauty. Along with the freedom from a child dancing, like Eve's eyes the other day.

Lord, she just glows with your love. Eve is an angel sent from Heaven, and she has brought so much joy into Kira and Tims' lives. Whenever Kira thinks of her, she can just hear her voice and how she is so excited when she talks and shares things with them. Watch over her and protect her please.

Kira wants you to watch over and protect each grandchild. By the way, she knows you saved Derk. Thank you.

The joys in life that you give us and bless us with.

Help Kira get the most out of having them in her life. Please help her take the time for them and make them a part of her life.

Help Kira show just how important they are to her. She still thinks about how special she felt to her grandmother: she wants the same for them, for them to feel special to her. They will grow up all too fast. Marcus, Raven, Lee, Eve, Kristoph, Riss, Lang and Derk.

Lord, you have blessed Kira and Tim with wonderful grandkids. Now a great grandchild, thank you for the blessings. Kira really does love them.

In all that we do it has to come from the heart.

You give Kira meaning Lord.

You make her life worth something. When it comes from you, you give her a purpose.

Having Coffee with the Special One

Kira is really learning what she does in life it really does mean something when she brings you into what she is doing and thinks about what you would do, when she gives it all that she has and she shows your love and your glory in the work that she does. When it's more than just going through the motions, you give it true meaning.

Prior to spending time with you and building a relationship with you, Kira had started feeling like she was just an assembly line, punching in numbers. Her work had lost the zest and the zeal. The reason that Kira had started in the field in the first place, which was to help others, she felt she had lost that too. She didn't want to work in this field just to put out fires…she wanted to continue to help people.

It seemed like she was fighting losing battles. Everyday something would pop up and she would look up and say really, Lord, now what? She lost sight of her purpose and forgot that it wasn't her goals. It was what you wanted from her, and what you wanted her to do.

Kira found out that tax accounting was a pretty tough field to be in, but when she was under the gun with deadlines, if she would just sit back and take deep breaths and let you in, then it all fell into place. Something so simple yet so difficult to remember. She guesses this is what you're talking about when you tell her that she is like a horse with blinders on because at times she just waltzes in and tears into her work, and forgets to ask you to come into her life.

More and more this is even where the common table prayer comes into play. Come Lord, Jesus, be our guest.

You're asking the Lord, to come into the moment and asking him to be there with you. Amazingly simple to do, yet so easily forgotten. Kira is seeing more and more where if she just lets you in, you'll make everything fall into place, and she will do what is required.

Even yesterday, the morning was hectic as ever, but then suddenly, a sense of peace that surpassed all understanding, came over her. What happened next? The rest of the day was successful, with no more delays even with two or three more items put on her plate. Well, Lord, it all worked out and Kira accomplished what she needed to do.

Why is this still so hard for Kira? Why can't she remember that all she must do is talk to you and you'll help her? Kira really can feel your love and your help. She knows that there is no way that she could have done it on her own, you just put it all in place and helped Kira get it done.

Kira had gotten to the point to where she wasn't building relationships with the people that she

Having Coffee with the Special One

worked with, and that was becoming part of the problem too with her business. In Kira's mind she thought that was being professional and that was how she was supposed to be. Yet that wasn't working for her, and Lord, that wasn't how she wanted it to be either,

Kira looks back and when she first started her business, she made everyone on her team all feel like they were a part in her life, and that they mattered. Then Kira got so busy she forgot that the true purpose of a business was to build relationships—not walls—and talk to people. Ask how they are doing, ask about their families, act like you care about them, and show that you really do.

That's what God wants from her. He wants Kira to build the relationship with her team. When she understands that, then it will all fall into place, and Kira will have a better time doing her work. Building those relationships will help bring back the enjoyment in work. What Kira can sit and work on a financial, or a tax return, and really put her thought into it without interruptions, (sort of lose herself in it) then that's what she loves. This is what she was trained to do... and then work becomes fun again.

Oh, Kira knows, she must do a reality check. She realizes that there are just going to be interruptions. But that's something Kira still needs your help on Lord, so when she has the interruptions, she gladly handles them without feeling it all has to be "today". She learned to take the time that's needed to really get to know the people you work with, and take the time to let them you know you do really care about them. Try not to let your pride get in the way.

A few years ago, Kira's oldest son Kris had told her that she needed to get over herself. At the time he said that she had no clue what he was talking about. Later she found out, she had put too much importance on herself as a person, and not what she was doing. You know be of service not to be served.

That's another area where she really needed your help. Kira has this "all or none" personality that she either cares a lot about herself or she doesn't think about herself at all. Kira had lost herself in people and yes, she lost herself in her work. Now that Kira isn't in it anymore, she can see where she was more like a robot and jumping through hoops. Now you, Lord, have given her meaning and her work meaning. The purpose why we do things in life, is now at the forefront of Kira's mind.

Lord, you're not taking away the problems, you're showing her the way to get through the problems and helping her with her true meaning in life. Now Kira could see that you were there every day and she would talk to you... but she wouldn't take the time to listen to you.

You know now Kira looks back on it and she was running herself into the ground physically and

Having Coffee with the Special One

emotionally. She had let the wrong ones be in control—or anyway in Kira's head that was what was happening—rather than her stepping back and allowing you to be the one in the driver's seat.

God, it goes so much smoother when she listens to you, lets you be her guide and lets you be at the control boards. Kira has found that she gets much better results and it's much more fun and efficient than when she tries to go it alone.

You know it's funny looking back now after all these years, seeing the changes in herself, and in the way, Kira handles things. It's amazing how much she has changed, and how much love is being let in. The way she used to be and think, and the way Kira is now, you complete her. You give her the fulfillment in the emotional area of her life where no one else can fill that spot or fill the empty hole in her heart that was there. Why would Kira want or chose to live that way, when with you there is such a peace, that you just don't get anywhere else.

Kira asks: How could she continually go to church, listen to the sermons, and not truly grasp the meaning? She's learned that's the difference in truly listening to you or merely being there.

Today Kira wanted to just go back to bed and sleep just a little longer. (Chuckle)

Patty Scott

Nope you wouldn't let her go back to sleep. Kira's mind was racing, but this time, it was filled with songs and praises. The words from one of the songs she loved kept running through her mind. But that happens so often now with Kira. She hears in her mind wonderful songs of the great artists that sing to help others, and share their stories, through their music.

God you have so many ways of helping others and using ordinary people to do great things. Kira had to drag herself out of bed. But she is always glad when she does because really, it's fun to sit and talk with you.

Kira is getting used to this now. She knows that there is a purpose, and it's for yours not hers. You give her the words that you want her to say, and you tell her what you want her to know that day. You want to spend time with Kira as she wants to with you. And you're just so persistent...Kira knows you're going to get her out of bed no matter what. You even allow Kira a glimpse of your smile and laughter in your eyes too.

It's a pleasure for Kira to be with you Lord. You make her whole and complete.

A while back when Kira was making her way to bed, she noticed the flicker of joy in her and it dawned on her Lord: she said she thinks she is going to make it.

Having Coffee with the Special One

Kira felt alive and she had the warm bubbling feeling in her—it was peace—and she really felt excited, God. Kira realized that you're healing her; you're working in her and for her.

Kira notices and enjoys the wonder of your glory. The blue skies are bright; the sunrises are full of color and beauty. Even on cloudy days there is beauty. Kira likes to look at the clouds and see what kind of object she can make them out to be. Sometimes she sees angel wings, and sometimes she sees the bodies of angels blowing trumpets.

When she was standing outside her office one day with Sheila and Lydia, she saw those angels in the sky. It's amazing when you give that to Kira because she knows you're watching over her, and she sees that you're showing her that you care.

Oh hey! On another note Kira remembered one night when she was looking at the moon. She saw a face in the moon, and it was laughing! The face looked like the Wizard of Oz. She wasn't kidding. Kira thought it was funny, and she loved it.

Lord, thank you for everything you do for Kira. Like the phone call with her oldest son yesterday which was so fun! He made Kira laugh so hard that she was about to fall out of her chair, and she had tears running down her face. It's so wonderful to really laugh like that again. Kris just knew what to say and how to say it, to keep Kira laughing.

Patty Scott

God, Kira is just so happy you kept her alive! It's great to be alive again, mentally and physically!

This Christmas season is extra special to her because she's alive. Christmas has always been one of Kira's favorite times of the year because you were born. Even with the stress of getting everything ready for Christmas and finding "that right gift" for everyone, she hadn't lost sight that it's all for you Lord, Kira just really loves Christmas time! Mary did you know....

Kira still can't imagine why someone would really choose not to have you in their life. But that wasn't fair for her to think like that because she didn't have you at the top and before her family where you were supposed to be.

Kira doesn't know how many times in her life, she could really account for your presence but she is learning more and more each day and seeing that you were always there even in the times she didn't pay attention to you. She hopes she is saying this right, you're always with her. But there are times when you really stood out Kira's life and times when you didn't. Kira has learned during this journey that you're always there... it's us that's not in tune to you. We don't let you shine through...and when we feel that you're far away from us, that's a way of us holding you, Lord, at bay.

Having Coffee with the Special One

Like when Kira's dad was alive, you protected Kira, her mother, and the rest of her family. Her life could have been so much worse when he was around, but you saved her mother so many times. In all he did—and you know what he did—you kept her there with the family even when she was not safe from her father.

The whole point of this is, that Jesus, you were there for them. Kira still wonders, how could she separate herself from you when she knew darn good and well, you were true. You watched over her and protected her.

Kira learned too, that being a Christian doesn't mean a life without challenges or bad things. It just means you'll be there for her and carry her when she can't do it on their own. You don't want her to do it on her own, you want her to want you and admit that she needs you. That's why at times she needs a reality check, one to remember who you really are and two, to grow closer to you and learn to live in dependence of you.

Kira can understand why now Lord: she knows and sees what you really were meaning. She was drowning; she was so overwhelmed. Kira tried to make a go at it alone, but Kira has learned too that she can't allow life to break or take her spirit from her! And yet it happens at times.

Kira loves the spirit you have given to her Lord. She had forgotten that you're there; she forgets to lean on you. Her and her independent ways! She has learned that you don't want her to be a push over—that's not what you're asking of her—but she has to learn not to depend on herself, and to stop thinking, she has done it all on her own. The way Kira used to talk and the way she acted, who did Kira really think that she was? Kira, has learned there is such a difference in your power and her heroes who are quite small and meaning less, compared to you.

Geez: Kira hopes one day she will learn it – "get it" — and it will stick with her. Ha! When she continues to have the same problems year after year or day after day, you would think something would go off in Kira's head like a light bulb going off. Sometimes it takes her so long to understand, it just doesn't make sense at times. Kira is a smart person, yet at times, she doesn't seem to have a brain in her head at all.

Kira forgot to look at it as an opportunity to get to know you. When she was young, she was like a sponge and she looked forward to new, challenging things in her life. Now, she doesn't as much. Is it "because of age "or is it time to do it differently? Kira beats herself up so much because she can't or didn't understand how to look at things in a different way.

When did she start taking such a negative approach at life?

Lord, you're going to have to teach her when to dig her heels in and when not to. Kira needs to learn

Having Coffee with the Special One

to do what she can then let you do the rest. Thank you for opening her heart and mind so Kira can see that there could be a different way. Kira struggles between being selfish and being too giving. She just must find that balance in life. Lord, honestly can a person be too giving.

It seems that the more you give the more you must continue to give. But Kira knew she also had to set boundaries. It really isn't all about us and how we want to feel, but still, surely there are areas, where we should learn when not to continue to give.

Thank you also for giving Kira the answer, Lord. Kira is learning to pick and choose, and has realized too, it isn't between her and the person she gives to it's between them and you. She is to give what is right, then move on and pray about it on the way. There is still so much work in her that needs to be transformed or changed.

Ha Ha. Lord, you're going to be with Kira for a long time. Kira asks, do you have the time? (Chuckle) Kira sure has a lot to learn and she guesses when she stops learning, well, that could be a different story. Kira thought she knew it all. Now she guesses that's also where maturity and wisdom come into play in life: you learn that you don't really know anything, and there is a lot to learn.

Patty Scott

There are so many times, when Kira will ask you: Dear Lord, please open her heart and mind unto you Jesus Christ; and show her what all you're doing in this time of difficulty.

There are so many things going on that Kira is dealing with, but you know, and she remembers, that you're not going to make all of her problems go away. You're going to help Kira through them, and some of them are going to work themselves out. Kira can see that she must let go, and let you, and some problems, well they just don't matter. Kira does see some of it and she does see new opportunities coming her way, which have come to truth.

Kira needs to look at this to put things in a better perspective.

Lord, she was enjoying the slow down and being able to breath and take time to relax and have fun. Thank you Lord, Kira really did enjoy the time you gave her to spend with her family so she could build a better relationship with them and let them know how much they really do mean to her. She even found time to be with friends, as that's important too. But most importantly, Kira has gotten to spend time with you, of which is the most important relationship that needed to be mended.

Having Coffee with the Special One

Kira has noticed the changes in her that she hadn't had before. Kira didn't know what compassion was or understand it: now she does. She knows that caring about people is not so bad, and it's ok to do so. When they don't feel good, don't do it for them, but try to be understanding, instead of so hardnosed about it. It's almost like Kira had hardened so bad, she was sort of like a drill sergeant. It slowly creeps up on you and you don't even realize it's happening, or for the major parts, you don't know you subconsciously shut others out. The little things, well they keep adding up and then, one day you don't know how to let go and the change is so........ subtle.

Kira knows she's tired of worrying about everything: it just sucks the life out of you, and it uses too much of your energy. Worrying is not fun, and it's not productive. If it's meant to be then it happens and there isn't anything you can do to change it, and if it's not meant to happen, well then, it's not.

As Kira told you last night, when she was talking to you that she needed to let go and give it over to you. Kira likes being the bubbly person that you created her to be. That's who she wants to be. Kira wants to keep your joy and peace inside of her, and she wants to be that little girl again who dances in the rain and laughs. It's so much more fun.

Dear God, Kira prays that she is grateful that you have given her slow days and she really does look for the opportunity to a day or two where she will have nothing to do, little to do. This gives her time to just breathe you in. Kira needs to make the most of those days.

There was a year that Sheila and Lydia were so excited about the office Christmas party. they were planning so many games for the kids and they put together such a nice program, they could get their faces painted, or make stick Santa's, it was all so cute and fun to see them Lord,. Thank you for this time for them.

They did work very hard during most of the year, Kira just still can't quite relax like she should at this time of year, she guesses too, it's a place where she needs to understand the true meaning of working like you don't need the money, December is just a very hard time of year for business and time off to spend with our families, why can't they make the funds last?

Every year it's like this, not much work, or the kind that's difficult on the clients, and us, because they try to take the joy out of Christmas. "Do not be afraid for I am with you".

Kira knows Lord, because even with all the setbacks she has gone through, and the change in the company, when she was hurt, they learned to cut expenses so the bottom line, was damaged too much. Kira still believes Lord, that she gained so

Having Coffee with the Special One

much more than what she lost! What you have given her was so fun and nice to get back only better! (Smile), money comes and goes, but life, well life you don't get back once you lose it, so chose life, and living......

If Kira didn't have all that pain she had, maybe she wouldn't have learned to feel again. You know how she had been asking you why she felt like her body was numb? Well she can feel again so that pain was for a reason! She can feel again; she still doesn't understand in some ways why she had to get so bad before she realized she really had something wrong with her and she needed help!

There is the key isn't it Lord, she always thought she could do it herself, she could do it on her own, and she didn't need anyone! Kira must learn that didn't she? She had to learn, that she wasn't alone, and she needed to feel again, she had hardened her heart so much, that's why she was like she was numb.

Oh boy.... now we get to address the clutter that Kira has in her life.

Basically, she has worked on some of it. Kira saw how horrible her bedroom was at the other house, how much she neglected to clean it and the dust built up. She doesn't think she ever let her house get that bad before. Her office had another pile of files and cases to be completed setting on her floor. It's almost like a barricade to keep out of her space.

Lord, when she worked for other people, she never got that bad!

Kira has got to develop a way that she can work on cases and where she doesn't get buried in all the paperwork. You know she can't see through the trees in the forest. Kira's problem is in her mind if it's out of sight it's out of mind, so she leaves everything in front of her face. But Kira can't finish one thing before she has to start on another, and she gets lost.

Kira needs to find a workable system for her. Sometimes the piles get so big and there is "so much" paperwork which seems is affecting her ADD. Could it still be an effect from being put on steroids during her accident recovery?

Kira was just having such a hard time staying focused while she was being pulled from one direction to another. This was a real struggle for Kira. She had so many cases going at the same time and she forgot to just sit back and take one at a time. Kira had to remember to do one thing at time because it was hard for her to find her balance when she didn't do that.

Even Sheila's office was getting to look like hers. Kira was sure that was hard for Sheila because she was organized in a different manner than Kira.

Having Coffee with the Special One

By the way, thank you Jesus for getting us through those rough times. Kira is so glad that that it all worked out for the best, and you helped them so much. Kira knows it was you sitting in the seat, she saw you.

Sometimes during life, it's the little things that just keep piling up. Some tasks will just take a few moments to finish but Kira would let it bog her down. You know if your heart isn't in it, sometimes, it makes it even more difficult to finish the task at hand.

Thank you, Lord, for giving her heart back. Thank you for teaching her proper order and giving her the ability to meet the deadlines she had to meet.

Sometimes she saves work for the no brainer days when she doesn't want to have to think too hard or at all. In the meantime, she would let them pile up, and she had no one to blame but herself. She needs to take care of them and get them resolved so she can file them away in the done box.

In the case of her house, well, that's just her being made aware of how much she neglected to be home and when she was home it wasn't to clean her house. Kira didn't have the energy or even the desire to clean it. Cleaning her house wasn't what she wanted to do on the time she had off, when it was such little time. Kira hopes she doesn't get like that again.

Patty Scott

Oh yeh! And her dresser drawers...Kira must dig and go through each drawer to try to find a matching set of socks! Yes, she keeps saying she'll get to it! Kira wastes so much time looking for stuff! Geez! she needed to get her mind back and her energy. Kira needed to stop and take the time. This is where her life was a mess, she had neglected it for so much time.

For a while there Kira was also just sick and tired of feeling like it was all left up to her and her husband. If they could just figure it out and if she didn't let some stupid stuff get in the way of your relationship!! Yes, it was petty on her part. Kira was sorry and asked for your forgiveness.

Kira can her mother say, "she cut her nose off to spite her face sometimes". Now she understands what that means...she gets it. Anger doesn't do anything good for anyone, neither does exhaustion.

Sometimes Kira thinks that she needs to teach a lesson but in fact it was her that needed to learn. She realized it kind of slaps you in the face, when you really take a look at your life and what you have done to it and if you own up to it, that it was you at fault in the first place. Kira has learned that you don't pay meanness with meanness and you don't ever want to get in a game of trying to show someone where they erred. All that does is bite you in the butt and backfires. You just don't want to get into that game.

Having Coffee with the Special One

Kira needs to learn how to properly vocalize her concerns and problems before they get so bad!! Communication is one of the most important things in relationships. You need to listen to who you're talking to and really hear their words. Don't assume what you think they are saying to you, but what they really are saying to you. Kira really has a problem with listening: she wants to think she knows what they are going to say,

Please help her in this area—help her to stop and listen, not only to you Lord, but to others too.

Thank you also for teaching Kira how to delegate and let someone else do things she normally would take on herself. Helping them learn how to do the work properly. Showing her that when others are there with unique skills, utilize their talents.

This is where the team in teamwork comes into place. If they have a problem doing something, guide them and instruct them, but don't do it for them because they won't learn how to do it themselves. And always remember and keep it in your mind, that no one does it on their own. It's God who helps them and guides them. Do what you can and leave the rest up to God.

Pray—that's always important too—and thank God for what he does help you with, and when he does help you. Then you really can focus on what really is important to get done, and get it done in a happier way.

Patty Scott

Kira thinks she is finally, understanding too where she has allowed to let cases just eat up her thoughts. She would just dwell on them and let them control her mind. She would just get so lost in her mind, and her thoughts.

Now that she is more aware of that too, Jesus, she prays for your continued help in this area. Kira hopes she stays more aware of the problem as she now sees this is where she made a lot of bad choices and let it take over her mind. Things like this can sure get out of hand can't it? Especially when we are weak and not looking out for it. Just one more way, where evil lurks, and messes with us, when we are low, or not aware.

What a way to zap someone's energy.

Something else you've taught Kira is that you can care about someone, but you can't care for them. She has learned that she was given a job to do for her standard of living, it was not for her to make it her life. That's why they call it a job. It's great to work at something you love doing, but it's not okay to let it become your love in life.

Kira had to learn, to put that in the proper perspective too. When Kira and Tim were first married, one of her main complaints was that Tim had put more of his time and life into his job than in their family. Yet now she turned around and did

Having Coffee with the Special One

the very same thing when she buried herself in her work. She couldn't understand why he got so upset with her, when that's how he was. So how was that ok for her to do? How could she justify that in her mind?

Jesus, thank you for showing her that there was more to her, than just work, and she was and is a caring person. Thank you for waking up the creative side in her again and giving her new life. With better meaning, and so, so much more love, letting it come through.

You have given her a newfound "Freedom" Kira didn't allow herself in the past. Anyway, for a long time she hadn't felt that "Freedom".

Why did Kira do things to where she feels like she is being punished or she puts herself through the torture and punishment. What is it with her Lord, she forgets that she is worthy of your love and that it's healed over time with your help?

Kira still needs help in remembering to stop in the middle of the day, or every so often, to say thank you and say Hey! I know you're there, thank you for that.

She isn't sure how many times, but Kira needs to be reminded that time is not something you get back. It's something you need to cherish when you have it and utilize it in the best way possible. Money and material items can always be replaced, you can't be! Maybe too, she means more to others than she has fully realized but is realizing that now.

Learning how important it is to take the time to be close to you, Lord, and really get to know you, your love, and your forgiveness is important to Kira. To allow you in her heart and mind, Lord, why does she forget this wonderful grace you give unto her when she lets you. For it's by your grace that she is saved, and yours alone. There isn't anything she did to earn it. You gave it to her freely.

Kira knows now that that's what gives her a new meaning. She would much rather feel your peace and warmth rather than the rat's nest she created in herself. The frustration and uneasiness she allowed to move into her.

God: Kira loves knowing that you're with her and in her. Thank you, Lord, Kira knows it's not reality, but she could bask in your warmth more than she is. But if she did, that's all she would do, and she must go to work to function in life.

Here is another thing that Kira learned: Don't ever state that God needs to knock you in the head to get your attention, because he will. (Chuckle)

Lord, there is a person that Kira is working with (you know who it is) that she has no control over. She knows you don't control, that you give people

Having Coffee with the Special One

free will and allow them to make their own choices. But Kira is asking for your help, so the person doesn't cheat or harm others that are involved. How is it intended to be?

These are times when Kira can't have or doesn't want the responsibility on her shoulders and can't or doesn't want the control either. Sometimes she wonders really, why do you send these things to her? In the end she realizes why you do, and she realizes that you do help her with them.

Kira is so grateful and thankful to you that she is not money driven, and she can see where being that way does get a person into trouble. We all need money to pay our bills and make a living, but there is more to life than just striving for money, or material things. Kira sees where it's easy, to be on the edge at times and could see where it could have affected her too, maybe she was on the edge, she doesn't know if she went over or not, she's pretty sure she didn't but it was a challenging, lesson to learn, for both? Thank you so much for your guidance and love.

She never looked at things that way, Lord. Here you had the power to save yourself or get out of the brutal beating that was inflicted upon you or carrying the cross as you did.

Lord, you could have walked away but you didn't! You did it for us. To die on the cross, to save us from sin. Wow!! Lord, you gave Kira a whole different perspective on how to look at things.

Sometimes she just must face what is ahead of her and remember the reason she is there in the first place. You get the opportunity to do something to save us from sin and you could guide us and lead us in the right direction. Nothing as powerful as you but in a sense of others. You could have walked away unscathed. This is where the part in the Lord's prayer means something too: Lead us not into temptation. That's for us, not for you, as my sister Dawn pointed out. Again, I never thought about that but now it means a whole lot to me: we are asking you to not let us be tempted and fall for the wrong things.

Lord, Kira does hope and pray that she does let your light shine through her. She hopes she will let all people that are around her see you and know you are.

God. Let you shine in her—and through her—how you want her to do it. Let your glorious light and joy shine in her and let her flow with your peace.

When she sits here with you each day, she feels so safe and protected. There are some cruel people in this world, but they are of this world, and not in you.

Kira believes that you'll make her path for her. Lord, direct her and keep her on your path that you want her to go. Yes, she does feel like there are roadblocks that have been in her way: you know... sometimes two steps forward and three steps back.

Having Coffee with the Special One

Kira is trying so hard to stop trying to control her life and let you.

God, Kira knows you have a better path laid out for her and it's getting easier and easier for her to relinquish control to you. She has learned while taking time with you each day that she Trusts you more and more, and she is not afraid anymore. Kira knows that just as she is sitting there now: you have showed her that she can trust you with her life.

Yet, Kira doesn't always want to admit it, but she is still a little confused as you're well aware. She is fearful that she will do something wrong, yet you have told her to not be afraid for you're with her. And, it's not for what Kira does or doesn't do that concerns you, or why you show her love. You know and are aware that she is on the right path, the one that you're leading her through. Bumpy as it may be at times Jesus, it's still your path.

Kira has relinquished control; she is letting you lead the way. Yes: Kira knows there is not a whole lot she can do but to wait on you Lord! You know too, that if she didn't wait on you, she would mess the whole thing up, and probably, make it take even longer. Kira is just going to have to concede which might just be one of the things in her life that there won't be a resolution.

She knows it's time for her to open her heart unto you, Jesus Christ, and know that you have her back. You promise to take care of her, and you'll do it. You always did in the past why wouldn't she think you would do it for her now? If she just thinks you're going to take care of it, maybe she needs to make sure she isn't taking you for granted?

You're the truth and the light. You know what is in everyone's heart.

Holy Spirit, please watch over and protect Kira from ever taking your for granted. Please always have her ask in your name, and always say thank you for all that you do for her.

Every day is a miracle Lord. Just that you wake her up each morning that's a miracle because if you wanted to you could just take her out. But instead you keep her around. You keep her alive and you show her where all your miracles are in her life.

It's a miracle she has her children; you know you didn't have to let her have them, yet you did. You watched over them and protected them, especially when she did stupid stuff, like dropping them when they were small, or leaving one somewhere, just because she got in a hurry and forgot one. You watched over them.

The awe of a child, a newborn baby.

The air we breathe.

Having Coffee with the Special One

The earth we live on.

There is so much that's from you. It's all from you.

Who else could have given it all to us?

Yet at times we take it for granted. Some days we just don't think about it. How do you not get upset with us?

Kira knows you're the Almighty but still sometimes, we mess up!

She is at awe of what all you do for her and her family. Kira wonders why it takes her so long to realize; that all she must do is sit down and talk to you. She means to sit and just have a conversation with you. You're a great mentor.

Kira knows she can learn a lot from you; you're the best teacher. Then why is it so easy to sometimes forget or not take the time to just invite you in her day or talk to you and see how you're doing. Not take so long to do it.

God, thank you for forgiving her life and keeping her safe in all she does every day of her life.

Jesus, even in the times, when there is nothing, she could have done to prevent what was happening, thank you for caring for the others that day.

You know that Kira has got to stop talking about that day. She knows she shouldn't even mention anything about that day. But, Lord, you did so much for them all. You watched over and protected every one of them. They all walked away and were breathing. What more could we ask for? Thank you, Lord.

Thank you for your healing hands on her and getting her through it. Some days it's hard and other days Kira knows that she is getting better. You know how they say that broken bones are better than bruises, and bruises are better than verbal abuse. But bruises take a long time to heal, and so does emotional stress. You never know when it might sneak up on you, and sometimes, you don't even know that it's bugging the heck out of you. You're taking the time with Kira to heal her inside and out.

It's the little things in life that mean so much. But, really are they little things?

You know saving Kira's life, well, to her that's a pretty big thing. And the thing is you have done it more than once.

She can remember when there were times, that she didn't want to be here anymore. Since then she has really felt horrible that those words ever came out of her mouth, or even for a split-second feeling like that was an awful feeling. Kira hopes she doesn't ever go down that path again. Her mouth can really get her into trouble if she doesn't watch out.

Having Coffee with the Special One

Hopefully now, she can help someone that may go through the same thing and let them know life is better at the end of the tunnel. Yes, there is an end to the tunnel, and a silver lining at the edge of every cloud. Just hang on and don't let go.

Kira used to tease about some things and say, "hop on baby we're going for a ride". Well, now Kira feels the churning in her life and knows there were going to be some major changes in her and her life.

Meanwhile she will enjoy the Holidays and talk about some of her favorite ones....

Christmas and Easter are two of Kira's favorite times of the year. Christmas especially because it's so exciting to hear all the Christmas songs and listen to the voices of the people singing them, spreading the Word. You know, Lord, life has a new meaning to Kira.

She really listens to the words and in church when they sing the hymns, she can feel the songs flow through her. She can tell by her voice, that the words in the songs have taken on a whole new meaning and she knows what that meaning is. Singing is one way that she can worship and praise the Lord, for all that he has done for her.

When Kira reads the Lord's prayer, she has realized that she really wasn't into it as much in the past. There may even have been times when she didn't even say it, or maybe not even lip sync it.

Patty Scott

Kira had to have a clean heart before she could say that prayer again. She had to let go of the hurt and anger, because did you know Lord, that it blocks the true meaning of what you're praying?

Did you know that you don't really feel, what you're hearing or reading unless you open your heart and mind unto Jesus Christ? If you don't forgive others, then how can you expect to be forgiven, Kira didn't even think about how that all goes hand in hand.

Kira has noticed each day how she is changing within and out. This all has meaning, and there is a higher purpose, but it's not all about her. She is paying attention not blocking out your words. Kira has come to realize that when she tried to block out the pain in or from the world, she also blocked out the joy and the blessings. Kira always thought she was right, and she could justify how she acted and talked to others. Kira felt so bad that it got to the point where she didn't even think how she could go to you, talk with you and get help. Kira realized that all she needed to do was to ask you in.

Jesus loves me this I know for the Bible tells me so.

I am weak but you're strong. Kira needs to depend on you and stand strong with you. You're her strength.

Praise God from whom all blessings flow, praise him all creatures here and below, praise Father, Son and Holy Ghost. Praise him above yea Heavenly host.

Having Coffee with the Special One

Kira saw that she had unconditional love from you. Really, how many relationships in life truly have that?

Even as she tries to love unconditionally, she sometimes puts conditions on it, even subconsciously. What if something doesn't go her way, she gets upset. Ha Ha guess the world doesn't revolve around her. (Chuckle)

Lord, Kira is starting to laugh at her own shortcomings. You told her that one day she would be able to and you know you were right, it's nice to be able to do so. Jesus, Kira knows that you're there to help and guide her. Kira is so thankful that she asked you into her life and you're clearing it up!!

She knows you have been there all along, but she also knows you won't force her to be what you want her to be and you won't force your will on her. Kira must invite you in and ask you to take over. Thanks for cleaning up her mess that she left for you. Kira thought she had to be strong and she forgot that she really could depend on you.

Lord, Kira doesn't know if she will totally understand the magnitude of your power and the relationship that you two are building. She doesn't even know if that's important for her to understand completely, but she knows that the relationship in itself is.

Kira will continue to grow in your love and praise your Holy name. She has come a long way, and she's not turning back now.

Kira is starting to go to concerts, finding more ways to be with others and enjoy friendships, and going to church activities and seeing what she had been missing in her life.

As Kira looks back and reflects on her life, she can really see where you haven't left her alone. You're filling her with what she was missing, and that's life. It's so much fun going to the concerts and listening to peoples' beautiful voices which are gifts from you. No matter if there are over 30 people in a choir or just 10, they sing so beautifully like there is no tomorrow! Kira knows they put a lot of time and work into these programs for all to enjoy. Thank you for opening this door up to her and for her.

Thank you for Kira being able to be a part of the fellowship, getting to sing the songs along with them and being around great people. It was a very friendly and welcoming atmosphere where she could be with people from all around the world in one place under one roof.

Having Coffee with the Special One

United we stand. Kira is really learning what that really means, and what it means to have one nation under God.

During the last few years, Kira felt so many roadblocks in her life. Were they placed there for a purpose? To stop Kira in her tracks, make her stop and take time out for important things?

You know, when you work all the time there are things in life that you miss out on. You miss out on what really is important, and you forget.

Kira doesn't always connect the dots in the ways that you may choose to get her attention. She also doesn't always think that it just maybe you that's putting the roadblocks up so that Kira will just stop.

At first Kira took it as a bad thing, but now she is accepting that it's from you and part of your guidance and your help. Now she is looking at the blocks as hey, maybe she needs to stop and do something else. Even at times maybe it's for her to look at the blocks as a great time for her to relax, take it slow and take it easy. Maybe she isn't supposed to be pushing as hard as she does.

Like on her birthday, everything was going wrong: the computers weren't working, everything was locking up and she had a deadline to meet. She sat back and said, you know maybe this means, I really am supposed to take my birthday off, even though she had a deadline to meet.

It just seemed like nothing was getting done any way and it sure would have prevented a lot of stress and frustration. She should have just gotten out of her chair, shut down the computer and gone home. Tomorrow would have been a new and different day. Your bringing so much joy to her life after all these years, she really should stop and celebrate the day you gave birth and life to her through her parents.

Another thing you have created in Kira is a new willingness to accept gifts, help from other people and help from you Lord, even without the skeptical side of her wondering what do they want from her? Isn't it horrible, that she would even think this way, but she did? Kira wanted to know what the ulterior motive was or might be? Good thing that you taught her Lord, to accept these as blessings from you freely! A new change in her due to your love for her, taking time with her and letting her know that she really can trust you because you'll do what it best for her.

Back to Kira's birthday....

Even though that day was one she should have just gone home, the next day went smooth as silk. Lord, you helped her get done what she had to get done with time to spare which was so cool! Jesus, Kira

Having Coffee with the Special One

realizes she has got to stop letting anxiety get the best of her.

Kira thinks she will follow your lead because you have taught her how she knows it's you and your will, not hers. People and others used to say the hard way was your way but when Kira doesn't fight as much and she allows you to be in control instead of her, well, it does seem to go smoother. God it's your peace that surpasses all understanding. It's your loving arms wrapped around her.

Kira hopes that on this journey with you she can learn how to share what she has received with others, and tell them so that they believe that you really do care about them and you do want a friendship with them. There are so many people in this world that need you. Kira is just in awe as she sees how you're with so many, how you watch over them and protect them.

Kira can see why it takes time Lord; she understands that now!

Geez how selfish of her at times. She just never looked at it that way! We all need your time and attention!! No, you don't ever let go of us. All things are given unto us by you in your time!

Kira will try to be more understanding. You also told her that you wait on things because you're giving them a chance to stand up and do what is right. You're trying to let them do it on their own, and sometimes, some are just so stubborn. I mean really look how long it took Kira to truly forgive, and yet she expects things to happen overnight, when she asks you. That doesn't seem right or fair, does it?

Yet you haven't let her go. God, I really am glad, that you're giving me another chance to make things right and to correct the wrong that I have done.

I never really understood what others already knew, Kira really wonders at times, why does it take her so long to get it, get what all along she could have had if she would have just taken the time that she needed to take. No, we don't really want to look back all the time, but it's interesting to reflect on where you have come from. Well, you have come a long way baby, and that makes sense to Kira now.

Life is a journey not a destination.

Kira gets impatient at times and she when she does get impatient, she forgets that you're there for her.

She doesn't mean to do that Lord, and she is sorry for it. Kira has got to try to get you engraved in her brain, so during the times she doesn't put you first or think of you first, something will go off in her

Having Coffee with the Special One

mind. "Ring the bell" and ask you or thank you for being there with her. You do have a way of spinning her mind back to you. Lord, you're her best friend, so she has got to keep you where you belong in her life, at the head of it. You need to be the first she talks to when she needs to discuss something.

Kira really got complacent and sort of took you for granted. She really wasn't sure what to call it when she did that. Kira hated to say it, but in some ways, she was allowing money to drive her. Kira doesn't love money, but she was driven by trying to make sure it was brought in so she could keep the people that she had on staff and keep them paid. She just wasn't keeping you first.

How many times have you told her that you would take care of her, that she didn't have to worry …? yet she wouldn't listen? Kira also wouldn't let go and let you.

She knew you always took care of the birds, they never had to worry about food, or where they were going to nest or sleep. Kira knew the birds always had food and a place to nest, so why wouldn't you, Lord, take care of her.

Kira can't remember off the top of her head the Bible verse, but it does stick in her mind at times. Do not be afraid for I am with you says the Lord, Kira never looked at things in the way you God: would look at things, how tiny and unimportant that some of it was, yet it had over run her.

You have taken so much time with her and nourishing her. If Kira wasn't one of your children, then you wouldn't have taken so much time and care into her. Yes: you went to such an extreme measure to get her attention but hey you've made it a fun ride of getting through, you have made it all worth it. God, Kira got to enjoy being with her grandchildren when they went over to her house every day to spend time with her.

Kira is still in awe how her kids were there to help her and take care of her!! They all put their differences aside and took care of Kira. She didn't know if it should be called better care, but they had a lot more compassion for Kira than Kira ever showed or had in the past. She didn't even really learn about compassion until in the past few years!! That has got to be something they picked up from Tim, because he was so much better than Kira at times of illness or when they really needed some...well...compassion.

Hmmmm...again, thank you Lord, as you have taught Kira to be more compassionate. And you showed her that her children really loved her too!! You have blessed Kira with some great kids!! Kira is so glad to be able to look at them differently and oh she loves them, thank you so much!! Kira is going to rejoice in you Lord.

You, Lord, come first over other people or things in her life. You're worth every second! Kira hopes that she doesn't forget this...ever....

Having Coffee with the Special One

Lord, Kira has noticed a really big change in herself. She wishes or hopes that others notice it too, because it's a big change in her.

Kira has learned that even in lean times, you're near. She's also learned to live on the edge with you as you have asked her to, and you didn't let her fall. You keep telling her don't give up! You know there are times when she feels like she can't do it for one more second, that she just wants it all to go away But you just lift her spirits, guide her and show her she can get through this...just don't give up because you do not know just how close it's to being finished. It's just around the corner. You have come too far to give up now..........

Even though December is one of Kira's favorite times of the year because of your birth, they also normally have had to get an additional short-term loan, but you have made it possible for them not to have to go to the bank for a loan currently. Lord, thank you for the miracle of getting the work in and being able to receive payment for the work they have had to keep them going! She knows and realizes that it's feast or famine, but Lord, you always pull through for them. Lord, Kira truly feels that she is blessed by you watching over them. Thank you.

Kira knows one day she is going to break down and cry if she would just give herself that pleasure—so she could cleanse her soul with tears of joy knowing that you care so much for her and about her.

You know Kira can remember that day as if it was yesterday: she was sitting at her boss' desk, getting reprimanded. She hadn't been working at the time as she normally did, and her boss wanted to know why. Kira didn't want to tell him, and it just came flooding out of her including the tears just fell like a waterfall. She was so mad at herself because Kira had a problem with women that did stuff like that to their bosses. Crying just to get something that they wanted, and Kira didn't want to be like that. Funny thing was there wasn't anything she wanted either, so she shouldn't have felt that way. But any way, that was the day Kira swore she wouldn't ever do that again: she wouldn't break down and cry like that especially in front of her boss.

Was that ever wrong of her to do that! She shouldn't have done that to herself. What she should have done was ask him if she could be excused, gone to the restroom, cleaned her face, pulled herself together and gone back into his office to finish the butt chewing. But that's not the way it went.

You know it's really good for your emotional health to cry. You clean yourself out, and God gave you tears so you could cry. Kira has got to work on this as she can't continue to do this to herself.

Having Coffee with the Special One

Kira is learning, Lord, that she either must let go or get someone else in her office help with the workload. Kira's body still can't deal with the stress and pressure of audits. Plus, why do they pick one of the most important months of the year?

Really Kira knows the answer why. She just can't believe that they get to ruin or alter her fun time for Christmas and celebrations. That's the only time during the year income tax returns aren't due, but they need something to generate revenue during the off season even though the season is short.

Lord, Kira's body really was hurting. She didn't think that she was ever going to get back to where she didn't hurt every single day. Kira must learn to hang on and bring you in when she has a difficult time dealing with stress.

Whisper your name because there is so much power in your name. All Kira must do is say Jesus, and you'll be there. Not only does the Bible tell her that but in several Christian songs, they sing, just say Jesus.

Lord, in your mercy hear my prayer, help us today and be with us, we need to get it done so the staff and I can enjoy the party that Sheila and Lydia have planned for her team and for all of their kids.

They took so much time and planning into it so that the kids would have such a great time.

They look forward to that oh Lord! Help them to enjoy! Kira cannot let the audit and workload before the holidays intimidate her Lord!!

Funny, as Kira goes over this again, she realizes that it has been several years in a row that someone was being challenged and it had to be resolved.

Jesus in these situations Kira needs to hang on to you and your power!! Yes, Lord, we get to—she gets to—celebrate the birth of you! Christmas is about you and for you! You're our shepherd that watches over us even as a baby!! You saved her so that she can be in Heaven with you! She could live out the rest of her days glorifying you! Enjoying your presence and being with you.

And Kira knows she is alive!! You saved her!

Lord, Kira has needed this walk with you, this time with you.

Each day she is realizing more and more just how important it really is. Lord, you have been on the journey for a long time as she gets closer and closer to you. You have brought Kira a long way, Lord!

Having Coffee with the Special One

Kira has always believed in you. She just didn't think her trust and faith was where it should be and as strong as it is now!

Lord, thank you for reminding her that you're the true one that she can trust! Somehow, she really forgot that or let her judgment be clouded. Kira has learned to be thankful for so many things, even the challenges that she was faced with and still is, with family friends and work. You have showed her all she had to do was ask you and let you in. She thinks that she has said it before and she will say it again, that the problems don't go away but you help her through them, and some of them do end up taking care of themselves. All Kira had to do was to let you in and do it in your name.

God, you helped her to forgive others and to forgive herself. When you said that she had to get away from the negativity you were talking about her, and the way she thought. Kira couldn't change anyone, but she could change herself and the way she treated others. Kira had to stop blaming people for her own shortcomings and idiosyncrasies.

Kira genuinely loved her husband, she just needed to learn to respect him and trust again. Neither one of them was sin free, this is where in the Bible you say to look at the log in your own eye before you talk about others. Kira didn't even realize that was what she was doing to everyone around her, she just thought so much of herself, that just wasn't like her. When and where did she fall into that black hole? Now she has learned that there are different ways to do things and others have their own ways, and somewhere you come together in the middle.

Kira has started to show love for her work again, but she stops, and lets it go so she can show others they are more important. Kira has learned to turn it off, but as others had asked her in the past, could she turn it off? She had so many times let her work become more important than Tim and she is terribly sorry for that.

Instead of talking with you about its Lord, she means really allowing you to help her. You have forgiven her!! She needs to keep this peace in her today and all to follow, each day you show her that that's what is important and through time you have shown her, that some of the junk doesn't really matter, it's all in how she was looking at it. After all it's just temporary, it doesn't last a lifetime.

Things change, people change, and some things just go away and getting to enjoy the ones that are loved the most!!

The peace of the Lord, that surpasses all understanding; keep your hearts and minds open unto Jesus Christ.

Trust in the Lord, with all your heart!

Having Coffee with the Special One

Today is the day you were born Lord! A beautiful baby!

You'll be with us now and forever into eternity. You bless us each day.

Some of the thoughts going through Kira is when we open ourselves to you fully Lord, it doesn't mean that we must be naive but that we are accepting, right? So that we don't push you away or try to keep you out. Kira was holding you at a distance too, wasn't she?

You're healing of her and your presence in her. You have made her feel alive again!

Kira is happy and thankful to be there today especially Lord, to celebrate the day of your birth! You bring so much joy into her life, she has opened her home and her heart to others. Enjoying what others must share and what they bring to the friendships, instead of trying to control everything. Others help in sharing and bringing joy and laughter. Kira must remember it's not all about her, it's all about your purpose and what you want, not what she wants. Your relationships are what's important, everything else is just stuff.

Kira never really looked at it that way!

She doesn't think that she really thought about what all you gave up being there with her. You were in Heaven immersed in all the laughter and joy of pure children and angels. Your beauty that was given to us is all around us despite it being a sin-filled world. At times, Kira forgets to appreciate what you do for her on a second-by-second basis.

Just enjoying the beautiful sunrises, or the sunsets each day.

Lord, Kira is sorry.

It seemed Kira did take you for granted and she learned she could be selfish at times. Now Kira is beginning to understand a lot more, and you're showing her, it's not just others it was her too, she was no different. That's hard to have to face, but she had to face it too. Kira just had to realize that it was her, and now with your mercy and care, she can be forgiven, and let go.

Kira still has so many questions: you have turned the light bulb on in her mind.

You really do know what it's like to be poor and to see what people feel inside. But even if they don't have money, they have you. Olivia—Kira's mother—used to tell her when they were growing up how rich they were in your love for them.

One thing keeps popping into her mind: when people including herself think of blessings, why do so many ties it to financial wealth? Even though at

Having Coffee with the Special One

times financial success could be a part in it, it really doesn't have to do with money. Blessings are the fact that you can be happy and at peace, even when you may be struggling financially. It isn't money that brings you happiness, it's the fact that we have God in our hearts, and we are filled with the Holy Spirit. That's what we are supposed to learn in life, and we are successful when we can face that we need him in our lives, and let him in.

That's what true success is: not that money. Money is a tool that everyone needs and wants, but it isn't what is important in life. Now that Kira has realized that, she has learned that it doesn't matter how much money you have in the bank or your pocket. But when you depend on God all things will be taken care of, no matter what, and you can still be happy.

She didn't think she ever really had a love for money, but she let it be the focus too much because she had employees to care for and a business to keep afloat. Then it dawned on her: money isn't hers in the first place. Kira is just a steward of the money that God has placed with Kira to manage. The way Kira sees it, God has wanted her to live on the edge with him, and that's what she has done. Kira has been living on the edge with God, and in turn he has fulfilled every promise he made to Kira, and more.

Kira's business is still on the edge, but she isn't worried or afraid anymore. Kira knows that whatever happens is what God wants to happen and she is staying open to every opportunity. He is opening new doors and bringing in more opportunities. Kira now realizes that if she hadn't lost some of the work, then she wouldn't have had the room to let them in. You see it all works out for the greater good.

Kira though we don't understand it at times when it's happening, and maybe we're not supposed to all the time. So just sit back and watch, and see what God does in your life. It's amazing how he turns something horrible into something great.

Funny how when your youth and your adulthood can sort of tie together at times. You'll learn something at a young age, but through time, you sort of forget it, and yet when it comes back, it starts to make sense to you.

When Kira and her family were growing up, they had so much more than others, and it wasn't money. Kira's mother often read devotions to them. Kira remembers sitting on the floor listening to her read daily devotions...sharing your love, Lord, with us. You know you did come back to earth in a humble way.

Lord, you could have been one of those ruling, bossy beings but you knew better. You wanted us to worship you and follow you, not despise or hate you.

Having Coffee with the Special One

Hmm... Kira never looked at it that way, as you well know. Yes, she knows that she can at times categorize you with all men on earth. You know how she feels at those times.

Thank you for helping her change her attitude there, Lord. That was a dangerous way for her to think; yet you forgave her, and you still love her. Did you sort of chuckle at times how dumb she was and still is?

You know, Kira sure is glad that you take the time to really know what is in someone's heart, and you don't act irrationally. You could have done away with Kira a long time ago, yet you stayed with her, and kept loving her no matter what. Jesus, I really do enjoy talking to you and spending time with you.

Thank you for taking this time with me, letting me really share my feelings and tell you all about what was on my mind. Kira can picture you sitting right next to her. Even there are times when she is in her car and you're there too. You even let her see the sparkle in your eyes at times. They are just small glimpses at times, but they are glimpses, and lasting ones.

Lord, thank you for what you have done for Bryne and Raven. You have protected them and their home, in so many ways, and you have helped them, thank you.

Kira can see where you're doing so much within her family shell, she is so grateful and thankful for what you have done and what you're doing. You have given them a strong foundation, and that foundation will hold up to anything that tries to destroy it. You're our protector and our shield; you get us all through it.

It isn't you that wavers in our lives; it's us that bounces around with our faith and our belief. When we stray away from you or don't really sit and enjoy your presence, it makes Kira feel as though you're not there. That's not you; it's her. When she doesn't take the time to really listen; you don't forsake them. Yes, Kira beats herself up a lot!! When she makes mistakes or feels that she isn't living up to your expectations.

Hmmm, it just hit Kira that you have told her several times, that it's not on merit that you love her. It's by faith and trust. Why hasn't she realized she doesn't have to perform for you to love her, and that all she has to do is just trust you and believe in you. Kira needs to remember she wasn't put on earth to please people; it's to praise you Lord, and your holy name. You sure know how to be direct and to the point. In the Bible you don't mince words. Lord, you tell us like it is, and you don't sugar coat it or hesitate to say what needs to be said.

Thank you for being so straight forward with her and letting her know when she is wrong. There never are excuses for Kira no matter what. It

Having Coffee with the Special One

doesn't matter how others are treating her, she is to follow what you say not how others make her feel. Kira should hang on to your steadfast love for her.

Despite all her faults you continue to care about her and love her; and she loves being loved. Kira thinks that all everyone wants is to feel loved. Kira tells people that if they really want to know her, to know her is to love her. She should use that in helping her stay close to you because she does love you Lord, she needs to listen to you to truly get to know you.

Kira was really having a difficult time several years ago, until you changed things and she had the time to really sit down and talk to you.

She was in a place where she thought she was so alone. Kira didn't even think about it even though she was talking to you and praying to you. She wasn't inviting you into her life and letting you stay. Kira wasn't paying attention to what you were telling her. She was the one who wasn't living in love she was the one who hung on to the negative. She wouldn't let go. Instead, Kira got into the game of tit for tat!!

Why Lord?

Kira much prefers the feeling of love. It's much warmer, and she is much calmer. Kira didn't realize that how in the past she felt so warm and peaceful, it was your love for her!! All those times it was always when she was staying close to you.

When Tim and Kira were close and their relationship was good, it was when they were close to you. That's why he treated her so tenderly and lovingly when they lived back home in Windy City: they both were so close to you Lord.

Fear, love, and trust in God, above all things that whosoever believes will not perish but have everlasting life.

When a couple forgets about their love, things start falling apart! They start losing each other. Their love needs to rejuvenate. As their relationship with you Lord, they always need to replenish and renew their feelings and keep them alive!!

Kira's journey with you Lord!! As Kira has learned that at times there are growing stages, each one goes through growing pains. They just need to remember, that it's ok to change, and change is good. But don't forget to hang on to the love that you do have for each other.

Lord, Kira needs to spend as much time as she can with you and has learned also how important your time together was for her.

Having Coffee with the Special One

You keep saying you have a plan for her, and she believes you. It sounds like it's going to be very exciting. She doesn't want to lose sight of you again Lord, Kira wants you to be involved with it. (By the way, is it just her, or are there a lot of "God sightings"?)

Kira is noticing more and more movies being made that talk about you and the main purpose of them is to show how the world will end and the steps up to that point. Are there more out there or is she just noticing them more now? For some reason, there is such a strong spiritual warfare going on within her. Is that too, because she is growing closer to you and the evil is trying to ruin what you have done in her life? Holy Spirit keep her close, don't let her go.

Kira has come to believe that spending time with you is a luxury that she can't afford not to do.

Yes, Lord, Kira was that way before and she hopes she continues to take the time with you. She hopes she can give back unto you for what you give to her. You know Kira became aware of during the last few years is she wanted to pick her friends and people who believe in you.

Kira wants to make sure she is around people who don't suck the life out of her. She had a bad habit of picking the wrong people to be around when she was younger. Kira realized that in some ways, she was taking from others, and not giving back when they were so kind to her. She just didn't do anything: she didn't appreciate it and she didn't say thank you to let them know she appreciated the kindness.

No one wants to be taken advantage of, but Kira also needs to make sure she doesn't take them for granted or take advantage of them either.

Yes Lord, when Kira works without you, she gets drained and she feels as though the life is just sucked out of her.

Oh Lord, thank you for showing Kira the way to the light at the end of the tunnel. Giving her this time to heal and grow in your love, and showing her the way, the way to do things with you.

How can we get this across, to share with others so they know, they see and feel the difference of what life is with you in their hearts and minds? Kira would like to share with others so they can remember what it's like in your presence.

Yes, Kira is one of those people—isn't she God—who waits until she is drowning to cry out for you rather than enjoy and trust in you every day? She lets time get away from her and she allowed other things to become priority. Kira says she is sorry, and you've told her what? A hundred times to keep her priorities in her life straight.

Having Coffee with the Special One

In the past when Kira stayed close to you, she was able to do more in less time. (A light bulb went off) Kira was wondering how she worked so well for others and yet it was a struggle for her to work for herself. When Kira remembers that she is working for you, Lord, even though she has her own business she is still working for you. Kira guesses maybe this needs to be put on her wall to remind her each day, that it's for you, not for her or others... but for you Lord. You're the purpose!! When she has the peace in her, Kira should realize that it's you in her, and you're helping her see the way. Kira isn't being lazy...she is at peace.

Kira says: Thank you for showing me that you do take care of the things I talk to you, Lord, about and showing that it's in your time not mine.

Kira can see now where she talked to you about family matters a few years ago and there is change now... all thanks to you, Lord. Another thing that maybe Kira should put on her wall so it's in her face every day: it's all done in your timing, not hers.

Yes, there still are unfinished issues, but they aren't eating at Kira like they were, thanks to you, Lord. Yes, they still pop their ugly head up once and a while, but she knows you got it, you have her back, Lord. It will either just go away, or it will get resolved...eventually.

When you say you want to use us as an example, Lord, Kira is finally getting the understanding of that too. For others to see you in her, she must act accordingly. Yes, sometimes she still fails, and blows up, but for the most part Kira hopes that she is walking in your light and showing others that you're there, and you care Lord.

You came down to earth to be human for our benefit. To live amongst us so you could learn about us and utterly understand our needs. Or, you could not wait to learn about us, Lord, because you're the Almighty. What Kira means is you lived in a humble presence so we would follow you, of which no other (idol) or person has done something like that for everyone on this Earth.

Why is it so hard for some people to believe?

Here Kira thought everyone would be saved and has found that not all will be saved. Some will turn away, and that's their choice. There is good and evil; that's how the world is. We must have each although that wasn't the intention in the beginning. And, for all of us to know what is right and what is wrong, then there must be both.

You speak the truth, Lord. You don't use mean things to get our attention. You don't want us to live in fear.

Yet Kira thinks the government at times wants people to be poor and needy, thoughtless, and not

Having Coffee with the Special One

be able to think for themselves, and to put their trust in the government versus you, Lord.

The media is always pulling peoples' heartstrings to get their attention. You use or should Kira say that you turn bad situations into good. Last night Kira was wondering why some people really say they don't believe in you. She has a hard time of understanding how they can say that because she grew up with you. While her homelife wasn't the best at times growing up, Kira's mom still held steadfast faith in you and love for you, Lord.

It just dawned on Kira, too, she doesn't think her mom ever turned away from you, or if she did it wasn't apparent to Kira. Kira could see the wonderful things you did for all of them daily even though at times in her life she was a strayed child. Now she can see your glory every day, and sometimes has small glimpses where she could have missed it if she wasn't paying attention. Kira probably would have seen a lot more if she wasn't like a horse with blinders on, as you bring to her attention quite often.

You know Lord, even with Kira believing in you all those years, she in some ways was like others too. Kira would get so wrapped up in her problems, that she just wouldn't think about you. She forgot you were the one in control, not her, and when she jumped in with both feet without you, well you saw the mess she was in!

Patty Scott

Thank you, Lord, for guiding Kira and allowing her to see and understand where she had been wrong. Even though it wasn't something someone wants to be faced with— what you're doing wrong—you helped Kira understand what the heck was going on! Lord, you explained things to her, you didn't order her around, like she was a minion of yours, you really put thought and care into it.

Lord, Kira is telling you she had fun again yesterday shopping. She knows that's not a thing that guys like to do, but she knows you were there with her.

Kira hoped you enjoyed being with there too while she shopped. Lord, you helped her find the three dresses right away and the coat. The coat is so pretty. It's a green wool with black leather on it. Very fitting, and light weight but warm. Kira doesn't like coats that weigh her down, but she wants warmth.

Thank you, Lord. And you helped her not spend a whole lot of money...and you got Kira in and out of the store in no time!

Kira always tells friends that she isn't rich. She is just blessed because she can find great items, at great prices, because you, Lord, show her all the good sales. The sales lady at the jewelry store was nice and friendly to Kira. Kira probably should

Having Coffee with the Special One

have visited with her a little longer and the sales lady really acted like she wanted to visit more with Kira and hear more about what Kira had to say....even though Kira wasn't buying anything. Kira felt it was genuine kindness, not that the lady was a salesperson wanting to sell something.

Kira still has skeptical thoughts going through her head. Lord, she has got to relax more ...we're working on that too aren't we still Lord?

Kira thinks she will always be someone that needs your spirit in her because she's not going to be perfect, and she will always need to be cleansed, just like when things like this happens.

Today on the drive home from work, Kira was thinking about the battles she had been going through for the past five years. She also has come to realize that some of the battles are in her mind just going to be unfinished.

She knows that you're doing everything that you can do. And that's okay with Kira. She isn't going to push. Right now, what she wanted to do more than anything is find time to visit her friend Max—which is Pam's nickname—in Alabama.

Pam was a shy and timid white-haired, 5-foot 4-inch, blue-eyed pretty girl. Pam and Kira had been friends since they were in junior high school, then

Patty Scott

Pam got married and moved away as soon as she graduated from high school. Kira found out yesterday that Pam had died. Pam hadn't been feeling really good for about a week and was taken to the hospital. She was there for a few days and sent was sent home. They told Pam she'd be okay, but then after a couple more days she couldn't hardly walk. Pam was taken back to the hospital, and then her heart gave out. It just stopped pumping.

This was so hard for Kira to handle because so many times, Lord, you put Pam on Kira's heart, and she would forget to call her. Kira would send Pam a card, and let Pam know she was thinking of her, but she didn't call. Just think Kira could have talked to Pam one or two more times, and maybe she would have squeezed in a trip to go see her. But Kira thinks it just wasn't meant to be now Kira and Pam were not going to sit on the porch, have a couple glasses of wine and laugh about old times.

So many memories, so much laughter and so much orneriness. Mostly on Kira's side, not Pam's, because she was just so good. Pam was the one though that talked Kira into smoking because back then it was the cool thing to do. Not so much now, but hey it was ok back when they were kids. She hosted Kira's wedding shower when Kira was getting married for the first time, to Pam's cousin Nevan. It was awesome. Kira still remembers what the bouquet of flowers looked like: they were made from the ribbons and bows from the gifts and a paper plate. Long pink ribbon hanging down, with

Having Coffee with the Special One

blue and green and yellow and white bows and ribbons.

There were a lot of people that Pam and Kira worked with at the drive in, and family and other friends at the shower. It was a joyous day for them all. The shower was at Pam's house, and Pam's mom was a big part in it too. Kira will miss their long telephone talks. They wouldn't talk for months then out of the blue Pam would call. After Nevan passed, Kira and Pam talked for over five hours and talked about some of the fun times that had.

To have a friend like Kira had in Pam, and Pam had in Kira, are the type of friendships you don't come by every day. Pam was such a recluse in so many ways, while Kira was a little more outgoing. Yet they hit it off in the very beginning and stayed friends for all those years. No matter what happened or what was happening in their lives, even if it was a year before they talked to each other, it didn't seem it had been that long.

One month they talked several times; then didn't talk again for a while. Kira had a hard time thinking why they didn't stay in closer contact. But, when you both work, live in other states, and are raising kids, well time just slipped away from them. Time is something you don't get back either, no matter what you do. You can't stop it from moving forward and you can't go back and change anything.

Patty Scott

This is another thing that Kira has had to learn too: we are to live in your presence, Lord, and that's why life is a present. Each moment of our life is a gift to us, and Kira is starting to see how precious it really is. In a split second, you or a beloved family member or friend could be gone. Kira has lost a lot of people that she cared about in the past year, and sometimes, it just got too overwhelming. Kira likes weddings and baby showers much more than she likes funerals, and viewings.

You know Lord, you mentioned something a while back that it's not up to Kira to decide how or when you bless someone, and you're right!

It's not up to her and she wants to thank you for the lean times in her life and the sad times, when she had to face the losses of loved ones. Kira really is learning how to appreciate the finer times more. But why does it seem like the good times don't last as long as the trials and tribulations that you must go through?

Kira knows that that's not how it is because every day of your life is blessed. Just to be able to get up out of bed, and enjoy a new day, that's a blessing. It just seems when there are issues that don't have a resolution they seem to last forever, and they just don't go away. But exciting and fun times, well they last, but it just doesn't seem like they last as long as the trials. Is it just because Kira has conditioned

Having Coffee with the Special One

herself and she isn't focusing on you as you tell her do in her daily studies? If you don't go through the rough times it's hard to really appreciate the good times, and sometimes, maybe they are taken for granted.

Thank you, Lord, for helping Kira see things in a different light and to look at it in a better way. One of the things too is, Kira didn't really like being poor as you're fully aware. Really, it was only financially poor because you fulfilled her life with what she needed and much more. Kira had so much love from family and friends, it was just the financial part that was the struggle. It's too bad she couldn't see then what she really had. Lord, why is it, that sometimes, we don't see what we really have until it's gone?

Kira has heard of so many others saying things like that, yet, here she is. She didn't learn to really appreciate what she had, while her kids were young. Man, just think she could have rolled on the floor with them a little more, or taken her daughter out for lunch a little more, or do something just to spend time with her...instead of staying so busy really doing nothing that mattered, or made a difference.

The other day one of Kira's granddaughters asked her what her mommy and grandma did to build memories when her mom was younger. Well there were some good memories, but for the most part, it wasn't like what Kira did with her grandchildren at all. Kira was almost always stressed out, and worried too much. How can Kira say that she had you in her life, yet she let life get to her and take away a lot of the good times she could have had Kira can't blame anyone but herself for that, because she worried too much about crap that didn't really matter.

They always had food (even though they may not have liked what they had to eat.) They always had nice clothes and a roof over their head. It may not have always been in a home, or where she wanted to live, but none the less, they always had a home. They had your love, Lord, for them and your protection. Things could have been so much worse.

When Kira was growing up and living with her siblings and in her parents' home, Olivia, Kira's mom always made sure through your love and guidance, Lord, that they had a home. They may have moved a lot, but they always had a home, and heck in Kira's mind they were always nice homes. They weren't like the homes that are built these days, but they were nice.

Kira was always around several people who had a lot of money; some were born with it and some made it their own way. Kira doesn't think that some of the ones that are born with it really know how to appreciate it, because they don't know what it's like to be without money, what it's like to be out of work or wonder where the next meal is going to come from. Even Kira forgot that at times, but you can't forget who you are and where you come from.

Having Coffee with the Special One

It's too important and a very important part of your life journey.

Kira is a people watcher. One time she read somewhere, and someone said to her, you better watch what you do and how you act because you don't know who is watching you. Until that day, Kira never really thought about it that much, but it made perfect sense to her. You don't know who you may run across, work close to, or go to church with, and who may be watching you or see you as a mentor and in which case what you say could mean the world to them.

So always try to be on your best behavior. Think if God sat down by you today, what would you want him to see? Even, though there is nothing that you can hide from him, what would you want him to see? Kira does catch herself doing or saying things at times and starts to chuckle because nothing was as bad as it seemed at the time, and she got them through it all. Now Kira can see how they struggled when their kids were young, but boy did, they share a lot of laughter!

It was how Kira looked at things, wasn't it Lord,? How she let things get to her when she shouldn't have. Kira should have just enjoyed what she had? Now Kira sees what some of the important things were that she missed. So much of the enjoyment with her kids she never shared and now they're grown up and all she gets to keep are the memories.

Overall, Lord, Kira feels that they really had a great time! Like when they lived in Fort Collins and Raelee was four or five years old. Raelee danced around the kitchen and sang don't mess with my tutu. Such a little girl, full of spunk... short blonde hair and sparkling blue eyes. She was such a cutie pie.

Lord, Kira hopes that she has learned that she can depend on you always and in everything.

Why was it that she either felt unworthy of your time and love or she didn't want to bother you? Kira hadn't quite figured that out yet why, for her, it was hard for her to really ask you for something. She can't quite put her finger on it! Was it because of her "I can do it myself" attitude? Or was it how she had lost respect for men and she didn't completely want to trust you?

Kira isn't quite sure but whatever the barrier was in her she is sorry, and she thanks you for putting that aside in her. Now she doesn't feel that way at all. There isn't the hesitation or the mistrust of you in her. Kira thinks that's what the problem was: she just didn't trust you or anyone else for that matter. But, you, Lord, you're the important one.... you're the one Kira should have known that she could trust. Is this something that we only learn once we have gone through what all Kira went through... you know, the forgiveness process. That's what started all of this and the accident:

Having Coffee with the Special One

you, Lord, are saving Kira and getting her through it.

Kira knows she had a rotten attitude about some things. There weren't too many men in her life that earned her respect, but it was so wrong of Kira to even think you were anything like them. You're the powerful Almighty, you don't have to live up to her expectations.

Lord, Kira is so sorry. She's sorry for lowering your importance. How could she put you on the same playing ground as men? Thank you very much for your forgiveness. Kira guesses that she had to go through this, so that she could learn what she was doing, and thinking was wrong.

You know, Lord, she really is noticing the freedom she has from you lifting the burdens in life away from her or her turning them over to you. She is feeling so free and uplifted!! She feels good! Kira is excited about life again!! There is joy in her heart again, but she must admit that she is scared she's going to mess up again! She doesn't want to, and she hopes she doesn't Lord. Kira feels the spirit in her... really...and she feels good and is so happy to be alive!! Now that Kira is enjoying your peace that you have given her—and which she has needed it for so long—how could she squash you like she did?

Patty Scott

Yes, Kira thinks at times Lord, that she is guilty of self-sufficiency!!

At times Kira had that attitude and remembers saying to others "I can do it myself". Kira was where she shouldn't have been? How does Kira stop that when she tells herself: we can do all things through Christ who strengthens me? Kira guesses it's the way that she thinks things through and it's her thought process at the time?

She needs to make herself more aware or be more aware of this, so she doesn't fall into the wrong thought process again. Really, it's like being trapped, and you can't get out. Not only did Kira have to say it, but she truly must believe that it's you are working in her and through her.

You're showing her that she is the tool in a way to get you out into the world. People must know when they are around Kira that it's your spirit in her that's shining. So, you're telling her that even the small steps that Kira takes in the direction of trusting you more and depending on you more is ok. It's ok that it has taken her 60 years to really understand some of this and see where Kira has been wrong in a lot of her ways?

Honestly at the time she didn't see anything wrong with her attitude. Kira used it as self-preservation.

Having Coffee with the Special One

There it is, Lord. You're right: she wasn't completely trusting you.

Lord, you're the one who really matters and what you see in her. It isn't anyone else who can do what you do or see what you see. We weren't put on this earth to make others happy, it's nice if we do but it really isn't that important. It's you that's important....

Lord, can she use this as an example, so Kira knows if she is understanding properly?

Where Kira gets confused at times, is knowing if it's her will she is trying to push through, or is she trusting you? The minister said that to know it's from you, it comes from the heart. Kira knows right away if it's something from you because it jumps out at her and grabs her.

Kira's shopping was another area of life where she needed to curtail it: was it a want or a need? When they moved into the new home, she wanted some different lamps, and when she walked into the store two jumped right out at her. Nothing else in the store seemed to get her attention, but again, is that her will or was it really something from you?

Kira still has them, and still loves them, so she is thinking it was from you. They are incredibly unique, and she hasn't seen them anywhere else.

Kira still thinks that they from you because she doesn't like things that everyone else may have. Kira doesn't want to keep up with the Joneses, as they say.

Thank you for today, Lord, and please stay in my day asks Kira.

Lord, you know what Kira needs to get done and she needs your guidance and help in it. Kira has figured out that as long as she is doing what she does in her industry—tax accounting—then she is always going to need you to guide her, keep her in your will, and help her with the work.

Thank you, Lord, for taking this time with me and spending the days with me, as you have been for all this time, and doing it also in the future.

Lord, Kira may say this a hundred times, but she really is enjoying this time with you.

You have been helping Kira with her quilts and picking out the perfect pieces for the right people. That's a gift from you, Lord, and she knows it. The perfect piece and the perfect color scheme.

What a friend we have in Jesus, all our sins and griefs to bear. What a privilege to carry everything to God in prayer. There is no other like you.

Having Coffee with the Special One

Kira never knew what joy a relationship with you having would bring to her life. You have showed her more than she could ever imagine, and you have helped her to heal. She is glad you're the Almighty and you have time for her. As Kira has said a hundred times, Lord, you have so many that you love and care about, yet none of us go without you. It's just another way to show, the more love you give the more love you get.

You know Lord, now that Kira's head is clear and she is taking time with you, she is able or willing to really think about situations that have happened, and getting a clearer understanding of why they happened. Kira sees areas where she still needs work on and help with.

Kira believes this is an ongoing process and she will always need your help and guidance. Again, life is a journey not a destination. If she understands correctly it's supposed to be this way so Kira can always recognize that she has you in her life to help her and to completely lean on. Kira doesn't have to feel dumb or let her pride get in the way for needing you or even wanting you. Kira thinks in some respects she's finally getting it.

Show love, get love. Show compassion, get compassion.

Patty Scott

Kira thinks that she had forgotten her true self, Lord. And, she's right. Kira has spent so much of her time and life taking care of others that Kira has forgotten who she is.

Kira wants to be true to you and to herself, without being selfish and forgetting others around her, but find that balance. You know Kira didn't like it when you told her she had to stop being a people-pleaser. Kira didn't realize that was what she had become, but putting all the stuff at work above you, well she can see it. Kira knew she needed to put you back in your proper place in her life, and she had to put her family above her work. That's probably what her co-worker was talking about, when he asked Kira if she could turn it off. At the time he said it, Kira didn't quite know how to take it, or what he meant by that. Now, she understands what he meant. Yes, now Kira can shut it off. There are times when family members make Kira feel like she isn't good enough, and that she isn't trying her hardest. Why do they push her?

As you're aware, Kira doesn't need to be pushed, she does all that she can do, Lord, Is Kira looking at this the wrong way? Sometimes, Kira feels that it comes at times when they want something from her, and they try to manipulate her into giving them what they want. Help her see what is important at those times, and look at it the way

Having Coffee with the Special One

you would, so she doesn't overthink it, or react incorrectly.

God, Kira doesn't know if she gets totally off track with them or she's not reading them properly or what the deal is. Frankly, she doesn't even really want to think about it anymore because everything you do, Lord, works out in the end, and well, it all belongs to you anyway. So, Kira will just pull you closer in her life, and what will be will be. At times Kira feels like she is the last person on their minds, so why let this get to her. Enough of this and let's get onto the good stuff.

Kira thanks you for showing her that she forgot who and what she was. Thank you, Lord, for showing her the way. Kira hopes and prays that she doesn't stray away again.

Even this morning, when she was thinking about the home you helped them get when they moved to Texas in 1997, it was such a blessing to them. She loves that home, but now it's time to let it go. One thing Kira knows is that she has got to invite you into that home, and let it be loved and feel love again. There was a lot of joy and happiness in that home, but there also were a lot of arguments, and heated discussions.

Holy Spirit please enter that home and let everyone know you're the boss of that house, no one else.

Don't let sadness overrun the love and joy in that home. She even realizes she didn't do the praying she should have, and Kira didn't invite you in like she should have. That's sad, as Kira always felt that that their home was a blessing from you, Lord,

Here is a perfect example of Christians letting others down, and even not showing God the love you should be or the Glory that he deserves.

Hmmm. You do so much for us, and yet we fall short. Jesus, Kira really does hope that the person that buys it, feels the warmth and happiness from your love. The happiness of all the birthdays that were shared in that home, the grandkids swimming in the pool, and the happy times. Because there were a lot of happy times....

Also thank you for the gorgeous sunrise and sunset yesterday. Kira finally took the time, to look at them! The skies were so clear, and the colors were awesome in the morning! Kira loves the unique way the clouds look in the sunset and the way sun shines through the middle of them: the yellows, the pinks, and the purples!

Kira had been missing out on those two items when she was working so much! Go to work when it was dark and come home when it was dark. Lord, she missed out on so much! She only has herself to blame. Kira remembers waking up and pushing herself to get up and go into the office. Kira would say like that old commercial, time to make the donuts. Kira was burying herself in her work because she didn't want to deal with the what she had to face each day.

Having Coffee with the Special One

Tim and Kira were going through a rough patch in their marriage. It was so hard, and she couldn't understand what was going on. Tim was so unhappy, and Kira just added fuel to the fire when she worked so much. How could they work things out if she wasn't around to try to talk about it? There were things Kira didn't know or understand that he was going through, because Tim wasn't one that would share much, or talk about it. Or maybe Kira just didn't listen to him and what he was saying.

Lord, why didn't Kira see what the real problem was? Some of it was just so stupid and she let things affect her way too much! Kira took a lot of it personal, and really most of it didn't have anything to do with her in the first place. It was what happened to Tim and it was hard for him to talk to her about it. It was his deal, not hers. Kira is sorry that she didn't handle it all properly, and she should have been more caring to him, and more respectful! Kira should have pulled herself out of the equation and realized she had taken it to heart and was letting her feelings get in the way. Sometimes, that's how arguments started: Kira allowed her heart to get in the way and didn't think or speak the proper way.

Funny when you forgive, and let it go, you really see how silly you were, and how you overreacted. Well, you don't forget, but you do forgive, and let it go.

Patty Scott

Lord, thank you so much for all your help in letting Kira look at others in a better way. Also, thank you, Lord, for helping her listen. You know she doesn't know what others are going through and that was so wrong of Kira to judge other people on how they act, especially when she has no clue why they could be acting the way that they do.

You have showed Kira several times, how she was wrong about someone, and thank you for helping her build a better relationship with them. She understands more now that sometimes they have been able to open what happened in the past, and why they act like they do. It surely helps to understand more, and Kira is finding that she does have compassion, but you had to show her she did.

Kira wishes that she could share some of their stories, but she doesn't have permission to do so. Just know that God is working in both their lives, and he is helping them heal.

Jesus thank you for that……..

This has helped Kira enjoy her work again, and really, help her to start to enjoy life again. Now Kira isn't working the long hours anymore, and she has a life again. Lord, you have helped with her personal relationships, and have shown her how to have a happy balance with work and the rest of her life. You have really lightened the load she was

Having Coffee with the Special One

carrying. Lord, you did exactly what you told her you were going to do: you weren't taking away all her problems, but you were showing her the way through them. You showed her how she was taking more on than she could handle, and she wasn't letting it go and letting you help her.

Since she backed away her kids were seeming to be more in sync with their spouses and they seemed to be happier. Or was it that she now was letting them go so they could grow up? Kira has learned to listen to them, but not act on what they say; and she has learned to let them get through it on their own and be there just listen to them. Kira is glad that you, Lord, helped her realize that she needed to let go and turn them over to you!

Jesus they're not there yet, but Kira knows that you have a plan. She will step out, and let you do what you want to do. It's between you and them, not Kira and them. Anyway, Kira realized that she was probably part of the problem because she involved herself too much and tried to help too much. She had to let them do for themselves.

How could Kira ask you to help her when it was her that was causing the problem? Kira didn't think it was right to ask you for help, when she wouldn't listen to your answer. Or she would hold on too tight and she wouldn't let you help her.

Letting go has been such a blessing to them and to Kira! Lord, she hopes it has also been praising to you! Glory to God, glory to God in the highest!

Patty Scott

You know it's funny in some ways, how things have circled around, the time it has taken to finish something, and the changes that have been made in the you, Lord, and Kira started talking about. Jesus, there are changes every day, and some of the same old problems that just won't have a resolution. As you have told Kira several times, you're helping her learn to deal with them, and some well, some, you just have to sit back and see what will happen.

Let go and let God! Immensely powerful, meaningful words.

We can't grow and flourish in peace, faith and life without you Lord, that's a sad way to live. Even in tough times our lives (Kira's life) is great! You have showed her your way to get through them. Why is Kira so stubborn and hardheaded to where it took her so long to figure things out?

Lord, she has needed you every second of her life, but she tries to do it on her own at times. Like a famous crooner once said in one of his songs "I'll do it my way" (chuckle.) Kira is so glad that she can laugh with you, and you do have a sense of humor.

God you're healing her heart, her mind, body and soul. You both know how much damage has been done to her body. You even know more than her because you can see it all, she can't. Kira thanks you for every little crook and cranny in her that you're fixing. Kira understands now why she had to go through it, and she really does thank you for

Having Coffee with the Special One

the time and the lessons. She hopes she doesn't have to go through them again, but Kira is grateful of you taking her hand and sometimes, dragging her through them.

Thank you, Jesus......................

Lord, even when Kira is all shaky inside like she gets at times, she needs to remember that you'll give her your peace.

Kira is so thankful to you, Lord, that you have given her these private moments to go over with you what she needed to change in herself and in her life, and so she could get to the place in life that you wanted her. God, she does want your peace in her.

It's you that heals Kira on an emotional level, isn't it? It's not anyone else, because no one else could see what her problem was, or what is inside of her. Kira was wrong when she told Nevan that he filled the void. It was the forgiveness and it was you, Lord. All the junk inside of Kira pushed you out. She had to make room in her heart to let you back in so she could be whole again. Kira had suffocated your spirit. She had to set you free and let go of the past.

Lord, you're the only one that can fill that void and the hole in someone's heart. She is sorry she didn't give you the full credit for it. Thank you for directing Kira, showing her, it was you and showing her what you needed to get out of her. Only you could lift the burden in Kira and show her how she was slowly smothering you out.

As good and joyful as she felt afterward, Kira couldn't understand why it took her so long to get it, to let go. Kira knows in all honesty she thinks it happened when you wanted it to, because she knows for as powerful as it was to deal with all the pent up feelings and deciphering, "oh my gosh Lord,", Kira just didn't know how to put it into words how strong and mighty that cleansing was!

Lord, Kira knows she wouldn't have been able to handle that on her own. No way no how! Kira knows you were right there with her. The power of forgiveness! Kira was just so overwhelmed with joy, love, and release. "Gosh," Kira just didn't know, it was like a whirlwind going through her! She was so confused, yet Kira felt the release and the freedom, excitement, and joy all because you taught her to forgive and to ask for forgiveness.

Jesus, help Kira get the message out to others. She knows she isn't the only one in this world that needed to forgive someone. Sometimes, people just don't know how to forgive someone that has done you wrong? How do you let go of the hurt and the pain, that it has caused you to hang on to? These are questions that others have asked, as Kira

Having Coffee with the Special One

knows she even asked some of the same questions. Well in all honesty how can you not?

A person is only hurting themselves when they won't forgive someone. It's true as much as she hates to realize and face it, Kira was only hurting herself, and her relationship with God and others.

You promise to stay with Kira and pour yourself into her. She will hold you to that promise, Lord.

Yes, Lord, she's really going to need you in the future as you already know. Even when Kira doesn't think so, she has always needed you.

You know how Kira was disgusted with women who were needy. Well guess what? She won't be anymore, now that you have made her understand what it really means.

Lord, Kira is sorry for looking at that the wrong way. Kira guesses she needs to look at things better and in a different light. Kira won't be so—what's the saying—so quick to push you away? In her life, Kira has realized she needs you, even more than she would have admitted in the past.

Jesus, Kira is walking on the edge with you, as you have asked her to do. Thank you for not letting her fall. Thank you for helping in every aspect of Kira's life, her family, her work and even Jesus, in building a better relationship with you. Thank you for your time.

Kira is a risk taker, so living on the edge with you, really falls into the type of personality she has. You know Kira just goes through life on a whim, and now she sees you would help her. Lord, you know Kira: she will try almost everything at least once. If it doesn't go well then, Kira will do something different, but sometimes, she needs to learn when to let go, and sooner than she does at times. You always get Kira through even when she makes the wrong decisions. Lord, you show Kira a better way, even after she forgot to let you in!

For the next few months, it will be our busy tax season, so please don't leave Kira. She really needs you, Lord, because as you know she isn't fully back to herself yet. Kira still has a hard time with handling stress. She needs your strength, your wisdom and help in making good choices.

Lord, teach her to delegate, and get rid of the clutter so Kira can do what is important. That's something ongoing really, so please continue to help Kira during everyday of her life with this. Help Kira to make the right choices, when doing the kind of work, she does. Help Kira be with the proper people and let go of the ones that aren't a good fit and take care of the ones that are.

Help Kira to stay focused and joyful and help her keep your peace which is what she was missing.

Having Coffee with the Special One

Thank you, again Lord, for giving Kira peace. She really has and is enjoying this time with you. It's great to feel the warmth of your love. Talk about someone having the world on their shoulders. You, Lord, are the one that really does. We only see a small glimpse of it in our lives. That's why Kira asked: how do you do it? She knows you're the Almighty because you're you.

God by the way, Kira really doesn't want your job, even though at times, she acted like she took it on. You're right: it isn't something she can handle. Kira doesn't know why she even would want to or try to take over. That's not smart of her, is it? You really don't give us a burden we can't bare; we just feel like it at times and Kira knows that she has felt that way at times. You really have taken her to the edge in more ways than one.

"Do not be afraid for I am with you" says the Lord.

Good morning Lord.

Kira does pray that she opens her heart and mind unto you, Jesus Christ.

You know when Kira met with her old high school friend Kaley for lunch the other day, they shared how you have helped them and what you've done for them. But Kira also finally admitted out loud that she did not completely trust you in the past.

Patty Scott

You tell her to seek your face with an open mind, Lord. You have made her life so good; you have led her to where she is today.

Kira is going to trust you Lord; you have shown her that she could trust you. Lord, you promised her that you won't harm her.... you tell her that. Kira believes that Lord because you're the most powerful Almighty God. You could hurt her if you wanted to, but you have no desire to do so. Why would you want to? Kira is enjoying this journey you're taking her on.

Kira is enjoying and seeing the changes in herself... and knows it's all for the good. She has really started to even like herself and who she is again. Kira loves the smile you have always blessed her with, the deep laugh that she has and yes even her weird sense of humor. As you said Kira is noticing the cleansing you have done in her and she is opening her heart up to you and to others. To give love and get love again, what a joyful thing.

Finally, Kira realized that she was shutting down—slowly—and pushing everyone away. She thought it was self-protection and preservation. Guess she was wrong. You're the only one who does know her and understands her completely, Lord, Kira is aware you have a plan for her. She isn't sure at this time what it is, but Kira does know it's something worth waiting to see what it is and listening to you. In the meantime, Kira will still plug along at what she is doing until you make it truly clear to her what you want from her.

Having Coffee with the Special One

(Sigh.) Kira is tired of going through life the hard way, but God she doesn't want the easy road either. She just wants it to be your way. Oh, don't get Kira wrong, she is fully aware that she will face challenges and have issues, but she is going to take them to you and talk with you about them. Kira isn't going to do it without you anymore.

Please help Kira remember to ask you, Lord, and talk to you first.

Lord, Kira has learned to really put her trust in you.

Trust in the Lord, with all your heart, lean not on your own understanding, until now you haven't asked in my name, ask and you shall receive.

Remember, it's what the Lord, wants.

Kira can see where her mind needed to be transformed and can see where you have done the transformation. She knows you work diligently in her mind every morning, because she knows you're taking out the junk she doesn't need and showing her what is important to keep. It was Kira that needed to get rid of the negative thoughts and let the positive ones take over. While she thought it was someone else, when you told her to let her negative thoughts go, Kira didn't realize she was the problem. Again, you made Kira aware that it was her way of thinking that was damaging to her.

Patty Scott

You told Kira to get rid of the negative surroundings, wow! It was her negative surroundings in her heart and mind. Kira has done a lot of it, but some are still around her.

Kira muses she really needs to clean out the clutter in her office; she has got to take a day and clean it.

Kira seeks you and your small miracles—ok, some of the miracles are large ones! —each day.

Yesterday Kira had a great time dancing to the music at the bank! The music just grabbed her, and she couldn't stop dancing. Lord, she can't remember when she really felt like that last! It was fun and funny! Can you believe she did something like that! Right there in the bank lobby! Everyone laughed and enjoyed it and they didn't stop her!! (ha, ha, ha) It was fun!

Last night was fun too when Kira went to play dominos and celebrate New Year with her friends. God, you gave Kira a very blessed ending and new beginning into the New Year. They had a much better year at the office than Kira could have imagined, and you helped her get through it. They were starting the New Year off in the black instead of the red! Kira has you to thank for that, Lord. You gave her (blessed her) with some great clients and mentors.

Having Coffee with the Special One

God, she is so blessed to have met and befriended them. They have helped Kira and her team in so many ways. You know who they are. Please stay with them also Lord. They really trust you! Just watching how they handle their business and help others is an inspiration to all of us.

Lord, you're putting music and songs back into Kira's heart again. What happy stuff!! Thanking you for helping get Kira to where she is today.

Man!! Kira was so scared too, and you have watched over and protected her. You have healed her deepest, darkest fears and you're still with her. You didn't leave her. You showed her the way.

Lord, you know the attacks that are coming my way, and the people that are trying to hurt Kira. Compared to what you went through when you were beaten with whips, had vinegar placed in your wounds and then hung on the cross ... well, what Kira is going through is nothing.

Lord, you went through so much to save us all from sin.

Whenever Kira starts being concerned what other people say about her, she really isn't going to care anymore. Instead, Kira is going to remember Lord, it only matters what our relationships are like and that you died on the cross to save her.

You promise to never leave her side.

It just really doesn't matter what people say.
An ah ha moment. Do not be afraid for I am with you says the Lord, the peace, and the protection we get from you when you wrap your loving arms around us.

You know Lord, there were times in her life when Kira would remember your words. She would say them, but she really wasn't letting them sink in. Now she has a totally different perspective and understanding of these words.

With God on our side who can be against us?

You know Lord, that Kira needs to break down and cry. She needs to cleanse her soul. Kira knows that she needs too. You say that tears cleanse the soul. Is she really that damaged that she doesn't feel enough or care enough to be able to cry?

Kira read somewhere one time that if sad or emotional movies or when little kids get hurt that she cries, why can't she open her heart for the tears she needs to shed. She does remember the day and where she was when she shut the door on tears and crying.

It was when she worked in Denver at the CPA firm and Tim had lost his job. Kira was being

Having Coffee with the Special One

reprimanded from her boss because she just wasn't into work—or it may have been when Kira told her boss she was going to go to work somewhere else—anyway, the tears just started flooding.

Kira shouldn't have ever broken down in front of her boss, but she couldn't stop the tears! She swore that she wouldn't ever do that again and that hardened her heart. Kira knows she did that Lord, and she is sorry.

She should have told herself this is not the time or place for this and stepped out to the restroom. Kira shouldn't have stopped herself from feeling.

Kira does feel cleansed when she will let herself cry, but she just won't do it often enough because she doesn't have the time or the place.

Lord, you're helping in this area, because the tears of joy are coming back. That's a start.

People don't have power and control over our testing. You do Lord. But others can put blocks in our way or try to stop us. Kira must remember that when it's your will Lord, nothing can stop it!!

Not even Kira!

Do not be afraid for I am with you says the Lord.

No one can hurt us if we don't let them!! Don't let someone define you or who you are. Kira could have gone the other way, right Lord?

Kira could have fallen into the sinking ship feeling but she didn't. Now look at the blessing you have bestowed on her, her family, her friends, and the business. God, this is the best they have done and the best ending of a year for her business. Kira is learning to do things your way!

Wow! What a difference you've made in her life. Each year gets better. Lord, you're taking them back to where they can breathe. Thank you, Jesus! All along you have been by Kira's side, carried her, and walked with her. Like the footprints in the sand, you didn't leave Kira, her family or her business team for one second. You promised you would be with her always and you haven't broken that promise to her.

Look at where they were in 1987 and 1989 mentally and physically!! Kira did not depend on you properly and she did not trust you Lord. She thought there was a lesson for someone to learn back then. Kira had an "oh poor me" attitude, not a grateful attitude.

Lord, Kira is sorry because now she sees the difference you make in the world. Kira was mad at the world and was looking at it as not being fair. Kira let her bad judgment and decision cloud her mind, not your peace and joy!

Having Coffee with the Special One

God, Kira is really understanding why they must go through the turmoil they go through. They must learn what their lives are like without you and what they are like with you, Lord. There is a big difference! Kira guesses it just takes some of the kids a little longer to grow up.

Kira does chuckle at times to see where she was and where she is today, Lord. Now she really does appreciate the good times and having you in her life! It puts a whole new meaning and light on it. We all must suffer to really realize your love for us and your forgiveness.

Kira didn't truly trust you in the past, did she Lord? You have shown her many times that she didn't put her trust in you, and now it's not fun to have to face? Kira says she is sorry.

All things in life can be replaced but time can't be stopped! Smell the roses and take the time that's needed with God.

The Lord, he gives you so much more than he takes from you. He wants our love, our trust, and our praise, and that's not much to ask of us.

Patty Scott

Look at what Kira constantly asks of you Lord. It's so easy to do when we freely give you our time and attention.

Kira gets so much more joy from it than anything because you give us much more than you ask from us. Why does she let joy slip away from her life and in life?

Kira forgot her purpose in life and why she's here in the first place. She forgot that she is here to honor and glorify you Lord, not for life to trample over her.

Basking in your warmth and love for her is like lying out and basking in the sun. You give Kira warmth and peace because you let the sunshine in. Your love shines in her. Please let it keep flowing, Lord. It's so much better than anger. Now she understands what it truly means to "let go and let God" ...so many things show her this.

Each step Kira takes you're opening her eyes unto you, Lord, Kira is seeing things in a different light. Kira isn't fighting you or the world anymore because she has learned to choose her battles and which ones to fight. It takes too much energy to try to fight them all! Kira doesn't want to fight them all. She'd rather be with you so she can fully and completely understand what battles she has to handle on her.

Having Coffee with the Special One

Kira doesn't want to cheat you out of your time together or her awareness of you Lord. She likes the warmth of your love and the tenderness you show her. You'll let her see what your will is for her so Kira knows she is doing your will. Right, she does know you have let her see the silver lining on the dark clouds!

God, it was beautiful that day and Kira did see the silver lining in the dark clouds! It was awesome! She was driving with Tim west on the Interstate when she looked up and saw the dark clouds. The silver edging and the brightness of the light around the dark clouds! Kira can't recall ever seeing anything like it before!! Maybe Kira wasn't open to you or it before, but she knows how it's there!

Thanks be to God.

You always know how much Kira needs you in her life Lord, better than she knows herself at times. As she grows stronger in her faith and belief in you Lord, Kira has realized that she didn't fully have faith and belief like she does now.

The other day Sheila said to Kira that she doesn't trust anyone. Several times in her life people have told her she has to trust someone. Even the attorney in Denver who was helping with a mortgage company that closed on a loan told her that. (By the way Lord, Kira thanks you for that experience, too, blessings came out of that.) She did learn a lot there but what Kira is trying to say is she didn't truly or fully trust you then.

Lord, Jesus, Kira does trust you now and she believes that you'll prevail. She knows you don't lie to her. You're not out to hurt her and anything and everything in her life is a blessing from you. Kira hopes in some way, which she thinks that she has been able to, is to help someone else if they must go through what she has had to. Use her experiences to help someone else. It makes it worth it doesn't it?

In the song Kira was listening to yesterday it said you died on the cross to save us from sin, and it was worth it to you to do that for us. You say that we were worth it. Kira personally wouldn't want to go through that much, but no one ever really wants to go through pain and suffering. But, Lord, Jesus, Kira is glad you have given her these experiences which helps her understand that the blessings do come from you, and the difference when it is a blessing.

It's all worth it when you can help someone else. Lord, Kira knows she is not the Almighty God. You are!

What Kira is trying to say is that something good comes out of something bad! It doesn't mean Kira wants to go through it again, but she does want to use it to help others.

Having Coffee with the Special One

Kira is so glad that she has really learned to trust you, Jesus. Fully, completely, and whole-heartedly.

When she is with you, you restore her energy, her spirit, her desires to go on and her strength. We have come a long way (chuckle.)

God, Kira is so glad you have a sense of humor and you brought her here to be a child of yours. No matter how this turns out, Lord, she knows you're there! But she truly and honestly believes it's going to be a great turn out Lord. Kira is trusting you. Kira isn't going to let the negative take over her, that was where she went wrong in the past, she let it swallow her up. She believed in you, she had faith, but she didn't listen to you, she went it on her own.

Lord, when she looks back over the past, she can see it wasn't you who did her wrong, it was the way she was looking at things and the bad choices that she made. Kira is still a firm believer that everything happens for a reason and good always comes out of bad. But she also sees things in a brighter perspective now.

Oh yes! No, she isn't mad at you anymore either. Kira can see where she was wrong how could she blame you. People must be held accountable for their actions, why do we blame God? You give us freedom and free we will only be blamed for our own actions, like we can't blame ourselves for someone else's actions either, they must be held accountable for them.

You allow us the room to make mistakes man, but sometimes this just bites, Lord, you know sometimes we bite our noses off to spite our face. Kira is glad she finally realized it, or it finally really soaked in that it's hard to have a great relationship when one of the persons involved isn't around.

Kira just expected the same respect from Tim as she gave him. Kira guesses she should have voiced it rather than keeping it in her head. You know God, that's also another thing is you walk beside us; you clear our paths so we can find our way. She guesses in some ways that's why men hold doors open for woman! Another place to where she wouldn't let Tim be a man and help her! She can do it herself. She didn't need a man to take care of her!! If she only knew then what she knows now!!

She doesn't want to be the head of the house anymore either Lord. Both hats are more than she wants to wear. Kira wants to be the woman, the one who gets to take care of the home, and the things that are important in the family life. Kira is learning to enjoy it Lord, too bad she couldn't have realized that when she was raising her kids, she just felt like she wasn't useful. Now that's such a wrong way for her to think especially now she knows just how important it was to be at home and spend time with the kids, but of course it's too late

Having Coffee with the Special One

for that, they are grown and out on their own with families of their own. You made Kira a woman for a reason, right?

You do know that in the past she hadn't ever felt that there was anyone she could depend on and she also knows in some ways, that's her own fault. When she wouldn't allow anyone to help her or take care of her, she trained them to stay away. Yes, she knows that here everyone at one time or another will let someone down, there is no way you can do all and be everywhere to help who is in need, but that's where you come in to place too isn't it, we talk to you about it, and you can help them or get someone who can to them.

It isn't supposed to be all on one person's shoulders, and Kira has got to realize that you can't read another person's mind, she has no idea what they think or what they feel. That's what probably caused most of the friction in her relationships is she thought she knew what they were thinking and acted according, when there is no way that she could have known. Yes!

Lord, now Kira can laugh at her idiotic ideas and beliefs and you'll love her anyway. Even in the cold and rain yesterday when she had to be out in it, she enjoyed being out and she felt you with her all day. It was fun to be out and about again, she always hated being cooped up and sick, because she wasn't one that liked to be confined, that's how she feels when she has been sick for a few days or had to stay inside, guess that's why her mom couldn't ever keep her down thank you for spending the day with her.

No one can ruin your plan for Kira or take her happiness unless she lets them and she's not going to this time. She can't allow anyone to ruin what you have done in her life for her and with her. She can't let them take it away this time, she must rise above it as you tell her so often, keep focused on you and rise above the circumstances.

Lord, she thinks that she has gotten rid of most of it in her life, but every once in a while it rears its ugly head and she doesn't catch it before it explodes, but she is aware of it and knows she can't let it get the best of her. This is where you have taught her to go over the boulders that are in her roadway, climb higher and stand tall.

Being on this journey with you, well Lord, all Kira can say is Wow! It has been nothing like she has ever known before and she has found through help in her le Bible studies, and taking this time with you, that she really can have a personal relationship with you.

One that's sort of like others yet nothing at all like it, does that make sense?

Kira wouldn't have ever dreamed that this is what you really wanted from her, as far as she can remember it sure wasn't anything that was taught in church unless she really wasn't listening, but she doesn't ever remember anyone else talking about

Having Coffee with the Special One

having a personal relationship with you. But now it's funny, she has run across more than one study book, in the years, and they have talked about it's very important to you that we do this. It means a lot to you, that we will take the time and really share our lives with you, it's sort of like building a relationship with someone you love and want to be married to, except Kira thinks it's much deeper than that, she thinks you're the soul mate that everyone talks about, and you're her soul mate, who else could know her inside and out as you do?

Kira can't even think of anyone taking the time to get to know her inside and out like you do. She doesn't even think that humans would be able to comprehend what it means to do this. It's something that's from you, you make it possible for her to do this. This is something that there is no way she could do it without you. You're the major part the other half of the friendship.

You ask nothing of her, except for her to love you, trust you and believe in you. Worship you, and ask for your help, that's not much for all of what you give to her, what you help her with and how your answer all of her prayers, even eventually, the ones that go on for a while, she knows you'll get to them when you can. She sees it happening already, through the years, the people she has prayed for, you're helping them, some have major changes in their lives, and some well they are still taking baby steps, as you have asked her to do.

Patty Scott

God, all of this is from you and because of you, you have lifted the dark clouds! You're why people don't have power and control over her destiny, they may be able to withhold what is rightfully hers, but they don't have any sort of control how she will live her life or react to the way they have treated her.

This is where Kira learns what really matters and it's you God, and it's your plans. You'll carry her burdens. Kira can go to you with all of them, she can give them all over to you. God is watching over her, protecting her, and keeping her from harm. She sees a flash of all the negative things that have been going on in her life and she sees the walls of protection God that you have built around. She has even seen the arrows and the shield, you have stopped others from harming her, you have kept them away from her. Nothing can stay in the way of the Lord; he has cleared the path for her.

This has been a long road but God it was worth every step of the way to be with you! My trust in you and faith in you Lord, has overcome it all and been restored and renewed in me!! Kira looks forward to the path ahead of her and if she stumbles along the way she knows you'll be there, Lord, to hold her tight and keep her from stumbling. You'll be right by her side. You'll guide her, and you'll carry Kira when she needs you to, no matter what! With you on her side who can be against her?

Having Coffee with the Special One

God doesn't lie...people do. Or they tell you what they think you want to hear at times. They won't always tell you the truth. Just because you tell the truth doesn't mean that someone else will.

Lord, this may be a little off track. You know how Kira's mind works and she is sorry. Kira was getting so overwhelmed there for a while because she was losing so many people that she had grown close to Lewis, Roger, Marilyn, Royline, Cheryl, and now Pam. So many people that she cared about. Kira knows they are now with you in Heaven and in a better place, but that doesn't stop the hurt and the sadness of losing them all.

Kira was glad the losses had slowed down some. She knows being in business and working with the public opens her up to seeing it more often. It just got to where there were so many people crossing over. The hurt and the pain those families were enduring for the loss of their loved ones. Lord, you're aware that Kira is one of those people who can really feel someone's pain and sadness. It's almost like it's her own pain and sorrow.

Lord, Kira can only imagine what you felt on the cross, taking on our burdens and our pain. You have a million times more strength than Kira does. Yet you bear all the pain from us because you're the Almighty, the most powerful.

Lord, Kira is glad you think saving us was worth it, and that we are worthy of it.

You made all things that everyone gets to enjoy: the air they breathe, the moon and the stars, and when the sun goes down and comes up. There are times when Kira didn't even really appreciate what you had created for everyone.

It could have been a whole different way for them if people had listened to you and believed in you. Kira guesses there was a time when she was just as bad. Kira's life could have been much happier if she really would have listened to you. But would Kira have really learned then to love you and trust you if she hadn't gone through what she's been through in her life, Lord?

Lord, it has built Kira character. It has given her endurance as she has learned how to get through some of the toughest obstacles. You have taught Kira so much and she has found that it isn't punishment (at times she felt like she was being punished) as she has had to learn things. Lord, you've shown Kira that there's always a reason for allowing something to happen, even if the person doesn't understand it at the time why it's happening. Kira is so glad that she can learn to turn to you and Lord, she really trusts you!

It was a month after Kira turned sixty years old when she finally took the time to sit down with you, Lord, and learn from you. What Kira learned was that she can truly— or does truly—trust you!

Having Coffee with the Special One

The thing is Lord, when Kira took the time to go through the purpose-driven life, she wondered why she didn't realize at that time that's what was missing in her relationship with you. It's interesting what you divulge to her and when you do it. Maybe that was because of what she was going through at that time in her life. Lord, you know the battles Kira was fighting and what happened, and you were teaching her then that you were the purpose in her life and the world doesn't evolve around her or her problems. You taught Kira that you are and were the reason that she was there in the first place.

That brought you, Lord, and Kira closer together, but nothing like it's now. Even though that lesson was especially important at the time—and still is and still sticks with Kira—this time, it's so much different than that lesson.

Just goes to show again you open us to what you want us to see and for us to understand that life is a journey with you, not a destination. Kira wouldn't have ever thought that this would have been possible before taking this one-on-one time with you. All the fear and burdens she has carried she could have just let you take them on and let them go. Kira could have just let go!

Kira guesses Kris was right in a way. Was she hanging on to it all as a child with a security blanket? You know at times, Jesus, Kris is wiser than it seems he should be for his age. You, Lord, made him so much older in mind, than he was in age.

Lord, you have helped her truly get rid of the guilt, that Kira shouldn't have been carrying anyway. It's such a freedom, to let go and let you, each day you teach this to her. You have blessed Kira with everything that she has, and who she is today. It's funny just yesterday, you let her share again with Kolt how you blessed her with such a great mind. Kira is so thankful for that Lord, and she is so thankful, that you did give her good long-term memory. During the past at times Kira thought in some way it was a curse, because she could remember so much from the past, but she made it an event or memory bigger and more important than it was. Now it has become extremely useful for her, and Kira is grateful for that, thank you Jesus.

This is funny too: Kira was carrying around guilt for others not having what you have given her. Lord, you have showed her and told her that it isn't up to her, how or where or when you bless others. Some need more than she does—like one of her neighbors—more than she did, and then some don't need as much as Kira needed. It's all your decision, not hers.

You have given Kira relief in this area too, she had always felt that anyone could have what she has if they just applied themselves, which is also true, but it all boils down to, is if that's what you want them to have. She doesn't feel guilty anymore,

Having Coffee with the Special One

because she is blessed so much, it all comes from you, and it all can be gone in a nanosecond flat!

Kira really knows now that it's your love, your protection and her faith in you, and relationships, that's what really matters! It's not just the material things that she has Lord. It's the special feelings that she has for you, and the love you have given Kira, and put back into her life.

Lord, you're the light that shines in her, and out of her.

Whew!! What a whirlwind her mind just went through! So many thoughts and pictures and it all boils down to "you in her life".

Jesus is the reason for the season, and always, not just at Christmas.

That takes on such a whole new meaning.

You do know Kira is one that doesn't want fear to control her. Kira lived in fear deep down inside all her childhood when her father was around, yet she never admitted to anyone until after he was gone. It's so funny what you have allowed to let Kira to see now. She could always on the outside make everyone think she was such a happy-g- lucky girl which in all honesty she was because of you. Yet she buried so much of this, and now Lord, you're taking it away from her and cleaning her out. Now Kira can see that it wasn't that important anyway.

Patty Scott

You know Lord, life is sort of a teeter-totter isn't it?? Is it that Kira has just in the past few years realized how it could have been so much worse than it was?

Everything could always be so much worse. When Kira talks to others, in some ways, she finds out that it could have been worse for her and that others have it worse than she ever had it. Lord, when you take away the hurt and the anger, Kira even can see it really wasn't as bad as what she thought it was, and it no longer has power over her.

That's it, isn't it?! It no longer had power over her, and that's the release that you have given her? No one can change the past: God will just help you change the way you look at it.

Kira is realizing now though how her feelings towards men in general— she didn't have a good attitude about them—started. You know it's interesting that Kira even allowed herself to love again after the bad marriage and her dad. She gave another man somewhat of a chance. Kira is very thankful, that you stepped into her life, and brought the man you did into her life. It hasn't been perfect— life on earth won't ever be perfect— but Lord, out of all the guys she dated in the past, Kira realized that you gave her the best one out of the whole bunch, and the best one for her.

Having Coffee with the Special One

She is still learning to love him completely and unconditionally, as you have loved her. Lord, there really is a difference in a person when they add faith, belief and trust isn't there?

Her experience in life has added compassion to other girls and children in general when someone violates them. The sad thing is that it continues through life, and Kira was sort of dumbfounded when she woke up and realized that this crap is continuing. Kira in some ways closed that part out in her life, and for some dumb reason she really thought that since she no longer had to live in that sort of lifestyle that others didn't have to either. Yet that was so, so wrong of her. People still must face situations like Kira's and yet some are even worse than what she had to go through.

Jesus, this is a vicious cycle. It must be stopped, yet it won't be due to the sin in this world. You never wanted us to have to live like this, yet we do. You continue to protect, even though it continues to go on. This free will thing, that's most of it isn't it? Fear is so crippling Lord, and Kira can only speak for what she has experienced. Fear really freezes a person.

Yet we are to fear love and trust in you, Lord, and yet it isn't a crippling fear—it's a freedom fear. If we put our trust in, you!! There is a big difference between this Lord: humans do it to control people, you do it to love us and take care of us, not harm us.

Patty Scott

Trust in the Lord, with all your heart, lean not on your own understanding.

You ever really think about that? Kira didn't really do that until now.

We need (Kira needed) to trust in God with her whole heart, not just part of it. Kira didn't really understand what that meant until now, to truly put her trust in you, Lord, Kira really has had trust issues, hasn't she?

God is our healer and protector even when we don't truly understand. She is understanding it correctly; isn't she? Now that Kira has faced what she was doing wrong and she realized that she wasn't completely free of blame, she has received victory over the demons that haunted her deep down (wow she buried them deep.) Kira can say it a hundred times, and still it all boils down to trusting you, all of this.

Lord, her trusting you with her inner most deep dark secrets, and hurt and pain, she can't go back to her old ways of thinking "Kira didn't do it on her own", you did it for her.

Yes, Lord, if Kira didn't have the trials and tribulations in her life, she wouldn't have learned that she could depend on you. She is fully aware now why she must have them. Also you telling her

Having Coffee with the Special One

that the next few months were going to be rough—well thank you for the heads up and thank you so much for getting her through this far—she knows that you'll help her get the rest of the way through them too.

Each day, Kira thinks she cannot bear anymore, yet you get her through it, and you help her. Kira keeps thinking she is at the end of her rope, yet you give her more to hang on to.

Thank you, Jesus, for getting her through; this too shall pass as others tell her.

She knows you don't give her burdens she can't bare but there are times when Kira says you're pushing the line and thinks there is no way she can deal with the burdens anymore. Kira knows she doesn't have to ask the question because she does already know the answer, and that you're always with her. Lord, you'll get her through this, you did in the past and there is no reason you won't this time.

Lord, you had to get her attention and keep it. Kira is one that gets closer to you when she is facing trials and tribulations. She also will need to learn how to stay close to you even in the good times, and remember it's all you, no matter what! You there that there is probably two times in Kira's life where she really was going to fall off the deep end in her life: once when she faced the possible loss of her child, and the other the possible loss of her husband. As she looks back these two events were two of the most difficult times in her life and were really hitting her heart. Kira found that if someone wanted to hurt her these were the only two areas that someone could. Don't mess with Kira's children, or her husband, as they mean more to her than any material item in her life.

No, God she doesn't care about them more than you. Kira has just found you could mess with her, but don't mess with the people she loves, as she will fight back. If Kira would have lost Bryne and you didn't save him that would have pushed her over the edge!

Even though she made a lot of mistakes raising her kids (their kids) Lord, she loves them with her whole heart. Kira just wishes sometimes that she could understand and see what they were hurt about. She still doesn't understand that part. All of them are a gift to her from you.

You know how much she wanted kids. Just holding them: you know how much that meant to her. There is nothing like having a child in your arms, or your lap. They are so cuddly! Her kids were all miracles: all three of them. It's just that when Bryne was born it was a totally different miracle because you saved his life and Kira's. Kira knows one day he will make you proud because you have a plan for him, and you'll say well done.

Kira knows she can trust you. RaeLee and Kris have already surpassed what Kira ever thought and she knows that Bryne will too. He is like Kira

Having Coffee with the Special One

in some ways. There are some things in life that Kira is a slow learner. It's funny because at her work she is a quick study, but when it comes to other things in life and emotions, she is slow. Kira just must learn to stop fighting the world and choose which battles she needs to fight.

Each one of Kira's kids have a special gift and talent which they may not use to the fullest yet, but she knows if she finally recognized the talent in herself, then they too will recognize it within themselves. RaeLee has such a gift and talent in her drawing and artwork. It's a gift from you Jesus. Kris with his love-filled personality and quick wit...it's just amazing Lord, how smart they are because you have given them such intelligence! They are all so......so blessed. Please watch over and protect them and their families.

Lord, thank you for watching over and protecting Kira's mom who is a walking miracle too. Jesus she is so grateful, for your mercy and forgiveness. Kira is so grateful that she can be with her mom, and you're giving them the time to build the relationship that Kira didn't ever think she could have with her mom. Kira has enjoyed so much of the time she has gotten to spend with her sisters and her mom and be able to really get to know them again, and who they really are. Not what she grew up thinking, but the truth.

Thank you for teaching Kira to respect her again, and respect others.

Patty Scott

Thank you for saving her every time when Kira gets into these pickles. No one can understand Kira laughing at the things that happen, but if they only knew what you have brought her through, they might laugh too. Kira is telling you Olivia cracks her up!

Like her niece says, Kira is like the energy Bunny because she takes a licking and keeps on ticking. Never would Kira have thought it was possible, but you make it possible so she can live through almost everything. When it's their time to go then there is nothing that can stop it, but when it isn't then there is nothing, they can do to make it happen.

Jesus, you really do have a sense of humor, Kira will say that again.

People wonder why she laughs at tragedy; well sometimes, all you can do is laugh.

We can't fail when it's in your plan! We can't ruin what you have planned for us. It's all in your timing not ours.

Kira realized Lord, she would sit and ask you for help, but she wouldn't really let you in. She wouldn't open her heart and mind unto you. She would ask, then she would jump up, and go on with what she was doing. She realizes now she was keeping you out of areas in her life where she didn't

Having Coffee with the Special One

want to go. Kira just kept pushing them down further because she didn't want to face them or deal with them.

Lord, sometimes she can honestly say she doesn't know why she did some of the stuff she did or handled things the way she did. Now she thinks and maybe even knows, that it all has to do with your perfect timing. It wouldn't all come out until Kira was ready to really face the demons and do something about them. Also, Kira is more mature now, and handles them in the way you want her to.

You have really helped Kira to open to you. Jesus Christ, you have taken the fear away from her, and Kira realizes that they can't hurt her anymore but she had to really let you in and be ready to talk to you about it all. You do know you sent Kira visions or dreams, you let her see you in so many ways, and you put the ideas in her head and the way to get them done.

Lord, you show Kira the way, your way. Lead the way. Lord, you have opened my heart and mind and showed that your way is so much more fun and enjoyable. Forgive Kira if she stumbles and falls at times, but she knows you'll pick her up! Kira also has learned that she can't take you for granted because she won't be a success or have victory without you!

God, Kira knows you have great plans for her life because if you didn't .... well things would have been different. You have saved her for something, and she will fulfill what you want her to do. Lord, you have given her again another chance to do it the right way. You're removing the boulders in Kira's life, each day, that some get put in her path.

You know how Kira has been struggling, and you know how she thought she was doing what you wanted her to do. Kira just forgot along the way to keep you first and foremost in her life. As Kira's life, she will serve the Lord, and be glad in it.

Kira had forgotten the important things, the ones that truly mattered.

Lord, help her keep her priorities in line with yours. Help Kira remember and keep in mind what your priorities are. You're her greatest counselor, and you give her wisdom. It's your will Lord, not hers.

Sort of off track, but Lord, you know Kira is still having panic attacks when she goes on flyovers. Kira doesn't know what the hold on there is but please help her and take the panic away. She is going to fight those fears and not let them win. Will you please help her conquer them?

Lord, you have told her too, to open her home up to others, and she has done that hopefully in the way you were meaning. Also, Kira has a desire to start a Bible study, and it just seems like things are getting in the way. Maybe she missed the punch on that, or Kira is not quite knowing what you're trying to tell her? Or, is she blocking that out?

Having Coffee with the Special One

Praise God from whom all blessings flow, praise him above ye Heavenly host, praise him the Father, the Son, and the Holy Ghost.

When Kira's spirit gets crushed, that's when she is really upset! Lord, you have given her a new and Great Spirit which she wants it to shine through her always. Let it shine.... let is shine all the time. These thoughts come to her at times.

Lord, with your cleansing of her heart and soul, Kira has great gospel songs going through her thoughts. A flicker of a thought will come to Kira and she will notice it's not bothering her or hurting anymore. Then a portion of a song will come through and it really comes from her heart. You really are healing Kira as you said you were doing and like you would. You're staying with Kira like you told her you would.

Kira is realizing more and more every day that she can and does trust you, Jesus Christ. You don't falter. You have given life a whole new meaning to her and a fantastic new outlook on life. The darkness in her life has lifted and Kira is able to rise above her circumstances, thanks to you oh, Lord, Kira is now getting to see where you are again, in her life, and you have been all along.

Patty Scott

You continue to work in Kira and help her see your way. You have a wonderful plan. Wait upon the Lord, for he is good.

You told her that your plans are much better for her than the any that she could have had, and you have showed her that too. Each day of her life, you show her where what she thought was not the best for her, but yours are.

Once we are right with you God, it will all fall into place when you're ready. Here is another way how she gets to relish in your peace and Lord, build her trust in you stronger. Kira has not let it pull her away from you, and this time, she is doing it the right way, because she didn't in the past.

Kira wants a more true, solid relationship with you. Kira doesn't want just the surface cleaned up in her, she wants all the clutter to be removed, Lord, She doesn't want it to have power over her, she wants you to be her guide and yes, she knows she will still make mistakes. Kira may stumble, but she knows you won't let her fall.

She is also aware that Satan was trying very hard to ruin what you were doing in her life but he's not the one in control of her life, and he is not welcome in her life, nor her families' lives.

God is good and with love and mercy, love wins!!

Having Coffee with the Special One

Jesus, she said that in the garage in the past and she still believes, it. It was dark where she was headed.

Kira feels like she had two 100-pound cement blocks on her shoulders, and you lifted them off. Kira couldn't understand or see why no one listened to her. She lost the joy and appreciation for all you gave her. Kira had the wrong driver in her driver's seat. She is so thankful that your love and how you care for her. You cared enough to pull Kira in and yes it was a pretty drastic knock in the head but Lord, look at what all you did for her, her family, her business, the magnitude of the healing, the growth, and the other changes she has seen. It not only affected her but Lord, you were and still are working in and through so many of them!! All of them have made and are making changes.

One day they will hear from you "Well done" ….

Lord, you're still performing miracles.

Kira isn't sure if perform is the proper word to use, but Lord, it's miraculous what you're doing in her life!! Let go so they can grow in you, Jesus Christ.

Lord, Kira can't wait (but she will) to see your power and glory working. She knows this is going to be good!! You have been preparing Kira for this, she could feel you working in her life and even more now! Kira knows she has got to talk about the wreck—it's time—but she needs to finish this so she can move on to that, and tell others how you saved her, Tim and others.

Last night Kira was noticing how you were opening her eyes and heart unto you, Jesus Christ. The miracles of the world, a beautiful sunset again, the beautiful bright full moon, and the bright and shiny stars. And she got to see a shooting star the other night! Kira felt like a kid in a candy store! And dancing...Lord, you know how much she always enjoyed to dance.

Lord, it has been so long since she allowed herself the luxury of your joy and peace, in fact she isn't sure if she ever felt your peace in her life as she does now! Or Kira was so far gone or had such thick brick walls up. She knows she only let people and you touch the surface!!

Lord, you came to her or allowed her the space and pace to where it really works this time. Kira is allowing you deep into her soul and heart where she wouldn't before. Kira is so sorry, and you also knew what the problem was with her. You may have nudged her, but you didn't push her!! You allowed her the space she needed at the time. Now Kia knows you must have cried at the way she was tearing herself apart, and yet, you patiently waited until she was ready to let you in.

You're an awesome God! Jesus, she trusts you now!! Kira wants a good relationship with you.

Having Coffee with the Special One

No! she wants a fantastic relationship with you: the intimate one that you intended for her to have with you.

What a friend we have in Jesus, all our sins and griefs to bear. What a privilege we often forfeit because we do not take it to you in prayer.

She has only herself to blame, and Kira needs to think of that again and remember the verse. It has been one of her favorite songs in the past.

You have given a whole new meaning to the words of the song. "What a friend we have in Jesus", let's think about this. "All our sins and grief to bear".

Take it to the Lord, in prayer. Kira must recognize that it's you. You Lord!

Dear Lord, thank you...Raven is back, and she is opening to the knowledge she is capable of! You answered Kira's prayers.

Bless Kira and her company. Help Kira to flourish in her relationships and help this be good for her and our company. Help Kira do a good job for her clients. While business has changed again during the past few years, you keep teaching Kira. Thank you, Jesus.

Patty Scott

You know Lord, Kira used to tell Tim when they were first married that she had a whole lot of love to give if he wanted it and when she was pregnant with their third child, Tim was concerned how a third child would fit into their lives. She remembers telling him the more we love and give, the more we must give and love. Our cup runneth over with love. The blessings you bestow upon them. Just a few tidbits and items that ran through Kira's head, to show your love is always there and you work everywhere in her life.

You have given Kira so many opportunities to be able to be a child again, especially since she has been blessed with all the grandkids that she has. One time, when she got to go to California to be with Kris's kids, she dug ditches with Kristoph so they could act like they were in the army crawling through the ditches, so no one could find them. Shhhhh be quite so they don't hear us.

The day they had pink day, Rain and Raven came over to Kira's house. Rae Lee was there too. Everything they wore and played with was pink. It was so funny how Raven disliked that boa and attacked it. There was so much laughter.... Raven helped make the day fun.

Also, it was so much fun sitting in the closet with Lee, and Rain, when they were over at Kira's house. They pulled stuffed animals in with them and flashlights, so they could pretend that they were in the jungle with all the wild animals. It's

Having Coffee with the Special One

times like these that you can't buy because they are priceless.

Lord, you have made it to where Kira is full of thankfulness, and she feels like dancing again. You know Lord, in life she always tried to live her life to the fullest, be as happy as she could be, and adapt to her environment. But it wasn't the same as it is now because there is so much more appreciation for life in Kira and appreciation for another day. You have made Kira whole again and filled her with true love for her family.

There are times when parts of Bible verses come to Kira's mind and the one now is: "That whosoever believes in you will not parish and will have everlasting life."

Lord, you know what a gift you give to us: not only do we get to enjoy a relationship with you on earth, but the true one is in Heaven where we will get to see you in your full glory.

The changes you have made in Kira.... but it's interesting how she can tell when her will steps in because it isn't as refreshing as when it's your will versus her will. Kira hopes this will make her more aware of when she's trying to take control and that she should open up to you and let you be in control, not her.

Patty Scott

Friday was a particularly good example. They were changing out the internet system and updating the phones at the office, and nothing was going well. Kira had to go to the doctor too because she has another sinus infection. But moreover, they only have eighteen more days for the last major deadline for the year, and of course there are so many returns to complete.

All the claims she tried to finish within the last couple of weeks are missing information and clients need to be called. And.... Kira had already missed one day of work and lost her voice another day! It's like.... seriously God?! Kira knew you would get her through everything so she did what she could do and got it done.... then she would see how the rest went. Obviously, she wasn't in control here.

Lord, you've also been helping Kira remember how much she loves her family and putting her family back in in the right place in life. There are times when Kira gets upset, but then she takes a step back and remembers why she is there in the first place.

Kira has received the feeling of being loved back and giving love back. Her feelings are so different, now—sort of a more mature love, one that truly shines. Kira hopes when she gets upset, she can remember it's important that it's not the act that upset her, but the person that did it....but it wasn't intentional, and stop taking things wrong.

Having Coffee with the Special One

Most of it's the way Kira thinks rather than what it really is. Kira has learned the difference after you invited into her life, versus not really inviting you in. It was you, Lord, who was there during the first years of Kira and Tims' marriage and their lives centered around you. They get along so much better and Kira knows back then she let love show, not so much frustration.

Kira has found that it really is important to let God be the center of her life, and the head of it.

Lord, thank you for the cleansing and healing you have done within Kira and showing her that she is loved, how special you are, and how important it is taking the time you have with her.

This is real, true joy from you Lord. True happiness and peace. You're the light and the way.

Kira is so thankful that you forgave her. Lord, Kira truly is glad to be alive and to have this opportunity to grow and see you in her life. What is it now, the third or fourth chance? Each chance you have given Kira, she has grown in you, but this time, Lord there really is something different about it and she feels like she is getting the whole meaning of trusting in you. Truly trusting in you. You forgave her, and all her sins.

It has been years since Kira really enjoyed looking at the stars in the sky and the moon so bright! It has reminded her of what she had been missing out on in life! Kira was in prison in a way, staying and working so much inside the four walls.

God, Kira doesn't want to do that anymore, because you have showed her there is more to life than work. Please don't get her wrong, Kira loves what she does and the people that God blesses her with to help. But she has learned that the fourteen- or sixteen-hour days were not what he you, Lord, intended Kira do when you blessed her with the ability to do what she does. You taught Kira that you, Lord, family, then work, that's the proper order, and when that's in the right order, then everything else will fall into place.

God gives us beautiful paintings each day of our lives with the sunrises, the awesome sunsets, happiness, and peace.

Thank you for helping Kira to bury the hatchet, as her cousin Zed told her that she needed to do when they were leaving San Diego to go to their grandma's funeral in Bridger! You know that one day you'll have to do that, is what Zed told her.

Having Coffee with the Special One

Lord, thank you again for showing love and compassion to her family and all who she is blessed with that crosses her path. In your name I pray "Jesus Christ".

There are times when Kira feels inadequate with her relationships still, but she also knows one day this all shall pass, and they will build on their love again. It will be deeper and stronger. Lord, you know you have made it to where we give love, we get so much more back. Why is always it so hard to hang on to that and believe it?

Kira knows that she just needs to keep you in the head of the family and first. You know God, you have made so much possible in her life. You have given Kira's family so much more than they could ever dream of or ever even ask for, and you give it so freely.

Kira watched another faith-based movie last night about a young man that had siblings from two different mothers but the same father. One of the half-brothers was having a hard time because the father favored one of the other sons and the half-brother was very jealous of him. So, the half-brother beat him up, dumped him in a semi and asked the driver to drop him off in the middle of nowhere. After that, his life was getting better for a while then—wham—his whole world was taken from him when he was thrown in jail for something he really didn't do. Until he gave his life over to you and really resigned to being in prison, things didn't change much. He had always been a believer, but once he surrendered to you totally it was different. Eventually he got out of jail and went home. His brothers didn't recognize him. In the end, he went through his trials and troubles, so that his brothers could be saved.

Kira thinks that she forgets that maybe some of the trials and tribulations she goes through aren't always for her but maybe it's for someone that's in her life or had crossed her path. Maybe God is giving them the time to do what is right and turn their lives around.

Kira has to remember that too that it isn't always something she needs to learn, and maybe—just maybe—she will have an effect on someone else and they too will turn their lives over to the Lord,. Isn't this in a way what it's all about? Aren't we hoping that someone else can be blessed, through you? You're the only one that can fill that empty hole in their hearts instead of with food, or something else.

It took Kira a while to realize that it was how she pushed God out of her life. So how can she expect anyone else to see how important you are if she doesn't act like you're important?

Our happiness comes within us, it isn't anyone else that can make us happy. The Spirit in us is how we get to have the joy and shine as we are supposed

Having Coffee with the Special One

to shine. Everyone has their own journey that they will go on and everyone has their own cross to bear. Now, Kira understands what people were saying when they said that. And sometimes, you have to move us out of the way so that others can learn: like the guy in the movie, God had to move him out of the way to be able to get to the other boys. The change in them was amazing, and what came out of it was a lot of love for each other and forgiveness. Forgiveness played a big role in it.

You lighten the heavy loads Lord, you carry the heavy burdens, so we don't have to. You promise us so much and it's there for us always, if we will just listen and trust you!

Right now, Kira needs to listen to what you're saying to her, because it will make a big difference in her life how she handles what is going on. Kira thought about her car wreck. You know insurance companies do not want to stand by their policies, and they don't want to honor what they are taking your money for. It's sad that they do this to people. It's been a long, hard battle with the insurance company and Kira is tired of it. She must find that one person that gives a crap and does something to help.

You know God, you're the only one that can help, and you're going to need a strong angle to help. This is a difficult situation. It has been going on for way too long.

Patty Scott

The star that Kira watches at night and has picked out is bright, shining and dances a lot! The right one for her. The clouds in the sky are beautiful again and she loves the clearing in her mind that you have done, because you've taken out the trash!

You're giving Kira a new way to look at things and you have lightened her load.

Thank you for answering her prayers where her family and loved ones are concerned.

God you don't lie, and you don't break your promises.

Love like you haven't ever been hurt. That too takes on a whole new meaning, and Kira understands what that means is when you open your heart and mind to Jesus, the hurt and pain goes away. You see that some of it was, well, blown out of proportion, it wasn't the big giant it seemed to be, and it squashes the power you had over you.

Love like you haven't ever been hurt.

Forgive so that you can be forgiven.

But most importantly, enjoy your stay on earth until the day you get to see him in full glory.

Having Coffee with the Special One

Even though to Kira it seemed as if she always had to do things the hard way, now she understands how the phrase, "if it's easy, it's wrong", came from. God's way is the hard way, but that's how we know, Lord, it's your will for us.

Kira understands that now, and just because you're a child of God doesn't mean that your life will be easy or problem free. That's something that she thinks is a misconception of others just as it was of her.

Why do we think that if we follow the Lord, we won't have problems?

Kira has heard this out of others, too. It's interesting that she isn't the only one that thought that if it comes from the Lord, then it's not going to be hard. Even when we suffer, God will get us through it. That's what he tries to tell you: he's not going to take away all our problems, but he will get us through them. And he'll help in his own timing, not ours. So, don't think that it's going to be tomorrow, because that may not happen. Who knows though, it's God we are talking about here, and he will do as he pleases. Maybe he would get it done quickly; it just depends on what he is wanting from the experience you're going through.

Patty Scott

It's interesting Kira thinks, how he plans everything so well, and how there are miracles that happen in each person's own life. Recognize it for what it is and be incredibly grateful. That also is something that Kira had to learn to be thankful and grateful even for the hard times. There is always a happy ending to them. Always..............................

Kira remembers to her it seemed that it was hard for her to have a baby. However, it wasn't hard for her at all.... she just had to wait for the right person to be the dad and the man in her life for her children. That's when you brought Tim into her life.... then wham! It seemed like all she had to do was look at him, and wham! There she was having another baby. Again, it's all in your timing, and with whom you chose.

Lord, by the way you chose properly, because we have three beautiful children, that turned into fine adults.

Another time is when Kira tried and wanted to have her own business and work for herself. It just didn't quite work out in the beginning but on your plan and road for her it eventually happened. Kira got to go out on her own and start her own business. You have been training her all along for where she is today. The jobs she started out with were always in a position in the accounting

Having Coffee with the Special One

department or as a full charge bookkeeper. Kira didn't have official education and training other than the record keeping classes in high school. You gave her the gift and intuition to be good at it and she enjoyed it.

Then Lord, the tax world changed her direction. Kira remembers the day in Daniel's office where she was responsible for updating the changes in the tax law. Kira would sit and read the tax law changes and soak it all in. It was all so interesting! See Lord, it's all in your plan from the very beginning. I hope you're chuckling, because it wasn't you that had to be convinced was it? It was Kira that had to be. Yet she didn't know until now that all along you had a plan for her.

You sparked an interest in Kira that led her to where she is. That's why you can't give up on your dreams, you don't know when they may come to pass. Maybe they won't come when or how you think they should, but they will come. One thing too Kira found out, it isn't all glory and fun owning your own business. You must continue to work hard and—one thing that Kira lacks—make the right choices at times. Kira goes on gut feelings, but sometimes she must not be listening to what it's really saying because she doesn't make the right choice. Sometimes it turns out for the good, then sometimes, it doesn't. Kira hangs on too long and needs to learn when is it time to cut ties.

It's funny when Kira purchased the third leg of her practice, she and Tim decided to purchase an office building rather than rent one. Kira had to get a life insurance policy to cover the debt on the building in case something happened to her before it was paid off. The insurance rep was a friend that Kira had met in a networking group she belonged to so when they were discussing the policy and other insurance, he told her that one day she'd stop being the mom and taking care of her kids. Kira had employed some of her kids, so he told her that she couldn't do both at the same time, be a boss and a mother.

Kira finally figured out what he meant and realized that sometimes she didn't make the wisest choices and business decisions because she was thinking about them as her children and that she needed to take care of them. Finally one day it clicked with Kira what it meant: she had to do what was best for the company and her clients, and her kids who were grownups needed to do for themselves (honestly it was the best for them too.) Sort of let them go and let them grow. None of this was perceived as negative. Kira loves her kids more than anything, but she also wants what is best for them, and for her.

Kira has a deeper and more respectful view of them now. Kira can see she wants a more meaningful relationship with her kids and understands why you kept telling her to not act on feelings, because feelings can change. It's true, there are so many factors that come into place regarding the way she was feeling. Kira yearned for a lengthy relationship deep down in her soul with you. Now

Having Coffee with the Special One

you're helping Kira see how her thoughts and feelings could have been misguided or misplaced. It all has to do with trust and belief, doesn't it, but more on the trust side right? Because Kira had always believed in you, it will always fall back on the fact that she didn't truly trust you, won't it?

Kira knows at times in her life she was mad at you and blamed you when and where things went wrong and for the actions of other people. She really got mad at you and pulled away from you. She thought you had let her down when it wasn't you at all. It wasn't your fault.

You give Kira free will to do what she wants. You give choices and sometimes, she just makes bad ones. Kira lets what she wants to get in the way, and she loses sight of you. Oh! That's where stress comes from (a light bulb just clicked on in her head.) Kira thinks things should happen right away and she wants an overnight success. She forgets that sometimes you have a reason for taking longer than Kira thinks it should take.

You're preparing Kira and putting things in her path, so she knows she is on the right track. But Kira gets in a hurry and wants it done before it's time. Before you want us to have it or do it.

You say slow down and take each day one day at a time. Stay present in the presence of the day.

Enjoy the journey that she is on. You really know how to let her understand that, where she didn't before.

In all honesty, your path and journey is so much more peaceful and fun, where yes, Lord, she was under so much stress that when she stepped back and let go and let you be in control, all things happened for the good and your _way_!

It's such a freedom to be able to turn it all over to you. It's so much more fun in your way. Kira hopes she doesn't forget this again. She hopes it's not one of the mistakes she will make again. She doesn't know how many times you told her this or someone else told her. She hopes it sticks with her this time!

Kira has learned to listen, and she is even taking the steps—realizing that's part of the problem—with communication with her family, co-workers, and Tim. She wouldn't stop and take the time to listen, so Kira shut them all out because she didn't want to hear what they had to say, which wasn't fair to them or to her.

Kira causes a lot of the problems herself, just because of communication. Still a work in progress there, but hopefully Kira will remember to take the time—just fifteen minutes a day—to let them know she does care. The problem too is having a medium-sized practice like she does, there are times when the workload is sort of an overload. Kira isn't in a position where she can add staff, and

Having Coffee with the Special One

so everyone gets overloaded at times. What do you do in situations like this Lord?

At times they need more people to help, while at other times they need less help. Kira can see why some people hire a bunch of part-time people and let them go when times are slow. The problem is there are times when Kira can't judge how the workflow will come in and no one works a lot of overtime. So, Kira doesn't know how to judge the workflow all the time. It just seems to be a never-ending battle at times.

Then Kira remembers who it's all for, and she can calm down because she knows it's all for your glory. It's to show you through her heart, and it's to enjoy you and keep your peace. As they say, God is on the move so when someone wants to be of service rather than being served, you know God is helping you get it done.

Kira realized that God couldn't care about her or for her if she wouldn't let him in or talk to him. Even though he knows your innermost thoughts and feelings, you still must open to him, bring it to him and tell him about it. You can't let your pride get in the way, and that was what Kira was doing. Kira thought she had to be strong for everyone else because they depended on her.

Wait a minute! It isn't her they should depend on, it's you they need to depend on! Kira needs to stay out of the way there, allow you to do your job and she does her job.

Patty Scott

Lord, you're helping Kira see what she was doing wrong, and by helping her you're opening new doors, and showing her there may be different things down the road.

You have awakened Kira's creative side, and you're letting it shine. She really loves sewing—for her sewing helps relieve stress—and she loves writing and talking to you. You're bringing Kira back to what really is important in life which includes love, laughter and the precious moments she gets to share with her family and friends.

You know that she has spent more time with her mom, Olivia, and she really enjoys being with her because Kira is getting to know Olivia on a whole new level. Lord, Kira does the best that she can. It's so nice to go home again, and to be there around her birthday.

Last time Kira went home she landed in Denver, so her sister Dawn took some time and went home with Kira. Her other sister, Jag, couldn't go this time because she had just bought and was moving into a new house. That's always fun isn't it?

Moving? That's a whole different story for Kira, because she moved so much, she felt like she should put it all on roller skates and just drag all her junk behind her car.

Having Coffee with the Special One

While home, Kira got to see almost all her family, she even got to see her younger brother, Lee, who she hadn't seen since her youngest brother Donnie passed away. Geez, that was almost three years ago now, and then that was the first time she had seen Lee in about twenty years.

Kira has found that even if you don't like the way a person lives, or you don't agree with them, you don't stop loving them and caring about them. She just learned she couldn't care for them. But to Kira, now, what matters to her, is that she gets to see them and is around them, to share the exciting things like trips, or just dumb stuff together. That's what she is thankful for, the time that she has with them now.

If Kira does ever retire or cut back, she is going to spend more time with her family especially since she found out she could get less expensive tickets to Denver. She got lucky a couple of times and purchased tickets for less than $400.... but that was a fluke for her. Her family comes to Texas to share in celebrations, so it's sort of like old times when we are all together for baby showers, birthdays and holidays. Kira doesn't want it to get to where it's just for funerals—that stinks—she wants the good times too.

This is the Glory you show us, and the good things in life.

Kira thinks when we let your light, Lord, shine in us, how could she be so dumb to let little things keep her away from the ones she loved? Some of it though was just because they lived so far away, and Kira and Tim weren't in a financial position where she could go flying around. Plus, the kids were in school, so really, she couldn't be flying everywhere. Kira could have tried to see them a little more often, but the money got spent in other areas. It had to do a lot with where Kira's frame of mind was at the time, and to be honest, she really didn't think she could do it. Jesus, thank you for opening Kira up and having her let people back into her life. There is nothing in this world that can top love, and family, because good or bad, they're your family.

Kira remembers when her kids were old enough where she couldn't spank them anymore, she was glad that she had read an article that helped prepare her for when this happened. The funny thing one of them was thousands of miles away, so Kira realized they couldn't be ganging up on her. Then Kira thought well it's probably because they were so close in age. But that's when they all decided to open up and let Kira know what they didn't like about their upbringing. It wasn't bad that they decided to open up about their feelings, but it was the fact that it happened, in unison, and almost all at the same time. At first it sort of shocked Kira, but then the words in the book she read came to her mind, so she was able to handle that better.

But it didn't change what did come out of their mouths. Kira realized that she didn't have to act

Having Coffee with the Special One

on all of them, she just had to listen to them so they could get their feelings out. Kira knew what they were really saying was everyone wants to be heard and their feelings validated. Even Kira needed that at times. Thank you, Lord, for the knowledge you gave her ahead of time to help soften the blow.

Thank you for helping her understand that they weren't mad at her, and they didn't hate her. Her kids just needed to talk about it and get it out. Kira should have understood it too, because that was exactly how she felt at times: she just wanted someone to validate her feelings and know that she had them. It used to be that Kira didn't want to talk about things because then that made them true. That was dumb too, because Kira had always been so vocal in the past, but the problem was she didn't have filters. Sometimes Kira made people feel like she was attacking them.

Kira knows full well, that when that happens people retreat and they don't want to talk to anyone that makes them feel that way, so nothing goes resolved. You have taught me how to stand differently and watch my tone of voice because that had a lot to do with it.

Thank you, Lord, you give Kira the strength and courage to face her mistakes and to help her find another way—a better way—to handle them. It isn't easy to face what mistakes you've made. It's funny when it all boils down to it, what everyone really wants is love and to know that someone cares. That seems simple, yet why at times is it so hard?

When Kira opens to you Lord, she can feel a river of love flowing through her. It's so warm and comforting. And, it's so much better than what she let in before. You have taught her that Kira doesn't have to fight the battles of the world...she doesn't even want to anymore. Kira surrendered to you—she waved the white flag—but not in defeat and the feeling of hopelessness, but in knowledge of faith and hope. She knows you're there, and you'll be for always.

All she had to do was to let go and let you....

Time. Lord, you have given Kira more time. And, once you lose time, you can't get it back!!

Kira is no longer going through her days like a horse with blinders on. Well, Kira hopes she isn't now that she thinks about it.

Maybe it was good for her to get sick, even though it's not the best timing. Maybe Kira just needs to readjust again, and maybe not shut everyone out. She has been so busy again, but maybe it's time for her to slow down and take a breath, regroup, and reassess.

Having Coffee with the Special One

At times Kira feels like a little kid in a candy store, seeing all the surprises that are there. The clear crisp mornings.

Lord, you're clearing Kira's mind finally from all the muck and lifting the mental fog, so she is getting clarity. There was so much clutter in her mind. She still was hanging onto problems rather than giving them to you to take care of. Somehow, Kira has got to convince her mind that there is no room for negative thoughts because she had way too much joyful thoughts and memories to hang on to. Kira found out that it isn't just temporary, it's always.

You know it's funny how Kira thought that when she was younger how she thought about things. She was finding out that she wasn't as smart as she thought she was, and there was no way that she knew everything. She guesses this is an awaking, for all young adults. With you, Lord, all things are possible. Kira can reach for the moon and the stars, or she can just sit and relax and let it all go on, on its own course. She doesn't need to try to take control because no matter what you, Lord, are in control of, whether she gives you credit for it or not, you still are. Kira learned that the weight of the world on her shoulders is just too darn heavy! It wears her down, and that's not fun or what she wants anymore.

Kira is glad that you opened her up and showed her that what she was doing, many times others tried to tell her? Maybe Kira is still too young to completely retire, but as she said earlier, it's something she wants to think about, or just maybe change what she is doing, or the way she is doing it. Something must change; she just doesn't know what.

Kira had taken on the responsibility of what others did wrong, and she realized, or you showed her that was wrong. They are responsible for their actions; she can't control what they do any more than they can control what she does. We all must be held accountable for our actions and what we do. (We can't hide from you, Lord, can we?)

Kira felt inadequate at times and in many areas of her life, Lord, you're the only one that truly knows what is in her heart. Sometimes Kira's mind takes over and she struggles with what her heart says, versus what her mind says. Then this comes to her "Listen to your heart and what it's saying!"

You're her heart. As you, Lord, said or the minister said we can dress up the outside and look great to the world but it's the inside that needs to be fixed, to be <u>healed</u>! So many times, this comes to her mind because it's so true.

Kira is a clothes freak. She loves new clothes and <u>shoes</u>! But she also wants to feel fresh and clean on the inside. Kira wants to open her heart and mind unto you, Jesus Christ. Kira wants the inner beauty you have given her to shine on the outside. She wants it to be real. You have put the bounce back in her steps. She wants to wear the ponytails

Having Coffee with the Special One

and dance around!! By the way, she did enjoy putting her hair up into the ponytail. It made her feel young and spry!

"Lord, there is something about a ponytail!" When she fixes her eyes on you Lord, it does make the days brighter. You keep telling her, Lord, to fix her eyes on you if she heads to the area where sadness starts taking over. She is weak and you're strong.

What a friend we have in Jesus, all our sins and grief to bear.

You really wanted Kira to open to you didn't you, Lord?

Here is another issue Kira has: she always goes over and over issues in her head. She always thought it was so could figure it out, resolve the issue, and yes, Lord, it would hurt over and over.

Lord, that's where she was having a problem and issues with getting close to people. Kira is one of those feelers—she hurts when other people hurt—and can truly feel their pain. Sometimes it's just so overwhelming, that Kira can only imagine the magnitude of your pain, Lord, and what you felt dying on the cross for all our sins.

Yes, Lord, Kira has had to stay focused on you, but it's just overwhelming at times. You're right: Kira isn't strong enough to carry these burdens because they aren't her problems. She just needs to learn what is it empathy, and where she can care but not take it on as her own.

Sometimes it's as simple as just a cloudy day that makes Kira so emotional. She needs the sunshine. Oh, it can rain all it wants but it must be sunny too.

Is that too much to ask for?

Kira needs to hold onto you, Lord. Let your presence shine upon her and give her peace. As you say, she needs to relax and now that she has learned to relax, Kira has changed a lot in the past few years.

You know it's funny: Kira has been asking you, Lord, to remove the yokes from her because she thought they were holding her back. But the fact was, Lord, you were protecting her. Slowing her down so she could breath. relax and take time to reevaluate her life and learn from you. It wasn't to hurt her and stop her from growth even though Lord, you didn't really care for where she was headed. The yokes were placed on Kira to watch over her and let her see your way.

Lord, you know you keep bringing up some very valid points—and some of them are redundant—

Having Coffee with the Special One

but you have helped Kira with each one. Some of the issues just went away and stopped bothering her, while others you just resolved them. Kira kept praying for you to remove the yokes, but she realized they were there for your reason. Lord, I am sorry!!

Kira didn't see them as protection, she was seeing them as brick walls or hurdles that she couldn't climb over or was having difficult in doing it. At the time she didn't realize you were working in her life, but Kira knew something was steering and you were preparing her for something she just didn't know what it was.

For several years this was happening, and Kira now sees you, Lord, were preparing her for many changes, and you were protecting her and getting her through it. You put others in Kira's path and life to help watch over her and protect her, while you worked on healing her. You kept Sheila, Jim, and Nancy in her life to help protect her and watch over her. All them really have been a blessing in her life.

Thank you, Lord, for the many blessings you have given her. In so many different ways you have showed Kira just how important that she is to you, and why you did what you did or allowed what happened to happen because all of it was for the greater good.

Patty Scott

Kira mistakenly thought she was uncaring if she didn't try to resolve negative issues.

She didn't realize she didn't have to give it another thought. Kira didn't need to dwell on them.

The Lord said Kira is to apologize and move on. She shouldn't get lost in the thought because maybe it's not always her that hurts someone, maybe it's something else and she just talked into the middle of the situation.

You showed Kira that it's you, Lord, not people that she has to please, even at work because in reality you really are working for the Lord.

You're not doing his job, that's not what he means, it's that whatever you do, do it with gladness in your heart and do the best that you can do, give it your all.

Sometimes there is no pleasing others, that's just the way it is. Remember you can do all things through Christ who strengthens us.

Having Coffee with the Special One

Kira is glad that you told her not to allow any one person to define her or who she really was.

It's interesting how that starts to happen. In some cases, it's when someone has done something wrong, and they want to either sweep it under the carpet or just hope it goes away. They try to put the blame on you, so you feel bad, and you start feeling like it's all your fault. That's what everyone needs to guard against, and that was what Kira was facing.

It's a good thing that Kira was doing her Bible studies. It's amazing how each Bible story fit into what was happening in her life, and it was through these studies that you, Lord, were talking to Kira and keeping her informed. No one will probably believe it unless they are true believers or have gone through it themselves.

God really does talk to you through the Bible. You can find anything you want in some of the verses of the Old Testament—even stuff you probably don't want to learn—because there really were some bad people and bad times. Kira can see why Jesus had to die on the cross to save us. We needed saving.

Kira knows that the Lord, promises not to hurt her. He promises to heal her, and he tells her how much she means to him and how much he loves her. That's all in the Bible. Each day Kira reads the

Bible, she is just amazed what is in there. It's really true that God will talk to you, and he promises to take care of you, so you don't have to worry about anything.

Lord, you also are teaching Kira that with you on her side then who can be against her? Just because you may lose the battle that doesn't mean that you lost the war.

You have always told Kira to be strong and courageous, and don't let them intimidate her. Well, there have been several times in Kira's life almost daily where people have made her feel like they want to overpower her or knock her down.

Take it to the Lord, in prayer, he will give you peace.

Kira gathers that you're telling her to quit rehashing the past and to let it go. She can't change any of it, and it already hurt her once, so why would she want to hang on to it so it can continue to tear her down. Kira wanted to learn from her mistakes so that she didn't continue to do the same ones, and if she did then she would know which way didn't work. What she does see Lord, is that when she pulled away from you or didn't keep you close in heart and mind, then her life became a mess.

When Kira keeps you close to her, she still makes mistakes and there are still problems, but for some reason, they just don't bother her as much. As you

Having Coffee with the Special One

tell Kira, she doesn't focus on the problem, or dwell on it, she focuses on you, and you give her your peace, the peace that surpasses all understanding. You show Kira a better way. It makes the problem seem so small. It doesn't always go away; she just doesn't let it destroy her.

Thank you for taking your time to teach Kira and let her see the difference so she understands what you're telling her. Lord, why did she doubt you? You have been in Kira's life since before she was born, and you tell her that too.

Kira understands that she was in the hospital a lot with pneumonia when she was a baby. Olivia, her mom, said Kira almost died, but you saved her, and she is still here. There are many times in Kira's life that you have showed her that you're there, so how could she have ever doubted you? You saved several members of her family from disaster.

Kira apologizes for the doubt and she is sorry because she now knows you have always been with her family and in her family's life. You have always been there watching over and protecting them. Remember when her Dad would load them up in the car and drive them to the Children's Home and tell them they would be there one day? (Chuckle) Yes now Kira can laugh because they never ended up there, because you kept all of them together and safe from harm.

Who would have wanted to take on so many kids anyway? You kept them all under the same roof, and you kept them safe. Kira is so thankful for that, and you removed the problem which was her dad. It just hit Kira, that's why he was always working jobs in other areas, so that you could keep them safe and him away from them. That really was a blessing to her family.

Kira's mom Olivia would constantly tell them how much you loved them. Kira remembers her mom sitting Kira and her siblings down on the floor while Olivia sat on the couch so she could read the daily devotions and passages from the Bible. Kira doesn't remember all the words, but she remembers her mom doing that. Even with all Oliva faced daily, she always hung on to her love for you, Lord, Kira's family was in your presence, or should she say they were under your care all along.

Kira wanted a loving father, and she found that in you, Lord, because you're the father that she needed. Kira wishes she could talk more about her mother. As Kira gets older, she realizes there was so much wasted time because it was Kira who got mad at times, not her mom. Kira is the one who missed out on love she could have been enjoying. Lord, you gave Kira the right mom. She is grateful for her as Olivia is so strong and beautiful thanks to you, Lord!

Olivia never gave up or gave into the trials and tribulations that she was put through. Now Kira really sees it for what it is: so many miracles in her life, they really do still happen. Lord, again Kira is sorry for pushing you away.

Having Coffee with the Special One

You tell Kira to go to you with all her needs.

Kira thinks sometimes she gets sort of arrogant. She thinks well you know what her needs are already, and some of her needs, Kira gets embarrassed about.

Kira thinks you gave her an intelligent mind, so she should be smart enough to get through this. "Yes" Kira gets the attitude she can do it herself. It's funny that was before, not how she is now. Today, Kira realizes it's all you and "She can do all things through Christ who strengthens her." Kira can't forget it's you, Lord, that gives her the strength.

Kira must remember you may be using her to have someone that's close to her learn something: you may be using her as a tool. She can't take it as a personal attack against her.

Lord, let your light and your spirit shine through her. Keep the dancing flame in her smile and her eyes!! She knows it's the Holy Spirit in her. Kira has your presence in her and she doesn't want to let go of it, or the light to go out.

Patty Scott

Kira has been asking you, Lord, to change the world and the people who are close to her. But maybe it's Kira that needs to change and change the way she looks at them and at things.

Where does she get off thinking she is so great? You told her you weren't going to change all the problems, but you would show her how to look at them.

Maybe it was that Kira needed to change her attitude to gratitude and gain a thankful heart that really needs to open unto you Oh Lord, There have been circumstances where you did show her that if she would just take it differently or look at it differently than the problem would be resolved. But sometimes the wrong button gets pushed, and Kira reacts how she shouldn't. You know that the ones that are close to Kira know how to push her buttons, and she has learned to just walk away, and not let it get to her.

Lord, help her to look at things the way you do and with a thankful heart. You know maybe Tim is trying to reach out to her and he just isn't sure how to do it. Kira never thought of that. Maybe their Friday night taco nights with the kids are a start for them to get closer again. Besides, they all really like tacos and those family meals. Maybe Kira should work on leaving early on Fridays, help him get the meal started, and stay focused on one thing.

Having Coffee with the Special One

Oh, yes, another thing Kira gets into trouble for is jumping ahead: trying to see the future, and what is in store for her. Sometimes, Kira just won't sit and enjoy what is happening now. Learn to take one day at a time, and be in the present moment, that's why you call it a present. Besides, she has enough to do, just taking care of what is happening right now.

Kira knows she has a bumpy road ahead, but you're going to be there. In fact, Lord, you're already there to get her through things. There is a light at the end of the tunnel and once she gets through this, she will be so thankful and will see the blessings you have for her and the people in her life. Kira didn't realize that the bumpy road was going to last for so long, and there were going to be several of them along the way.

Thank you, Lord, for always giving her a head up so at least Kira knows that you're going to be there right by her side. Lord, Kira has learned to trust you, but she must learn more because she is allowing things to get to her, while she knows this isn't done yet, there is more to come.

It's really getting crazy what all is going on, and trying to get in between you, Lord, and Kira. Kira knows she must stay focused on you and your love because for her some of it's overwhelming and she thinks she is at the end of her rope. But you'll be there to replenish her and give her strength to go another day. Kira is grasping your hand so you'll carry her through, so she can let it go!!

In the past you have always fulfilled your promise, so Kira isn't going to doubt you now. You're already there to answer her prayers. There are times when Kira has wondered how long are these bad times are going to last, but what she should be doing is asking where are the blessings in this situation and what does she get to learn from this?

The blessings are there. Kira just needs to look for them and see them for what they are.

I can do all things through Christ who strengthens me.

What Kira sees is that everyone will always have trials and tribulations, but you show them the way to endure and give them strength so they can get through the rough, rocky times.

In all we do, Kira needs to trust that you won't leave her side. She just must hold on tight to your hand. "Don't let go of her Lord," God's way is the hard way, but don't give up!! Letting go is not giving up.

That's one of the things Kira had to learn. She got them confused and thought they were the same thing. Letting go is putting your trust in "God", letting him lead the way. She may not fully comprehend this at the time, but He will enlighten her and give her the answer when he is ready to.

Having Coffee with the Special One

Once she figured that out, the rest of the journey was fun and exciting. Especially, when she isn't afraid! With God in the lead her journey is fun even during troubled waters. And it's funny sometimes, Kira doesn't see it until she does step back.

Do not feel guilty for the blessings that I have bestowed upon you says the <u>Lord</u>!! The Lord says to glorify him by receiving blessings <u>gratefully</u>! You can really enjoy his presence and what he wants you to have!! It's God's choice and will, not ours what you do or don't have or someone else may or may not have.

This is something, that Kira was not aware of, she never even thought of it this way. She used to feel guilty for having nice things, or a nice home when someone didn't have that. Thank you for telling her and informing her it wasn't up to her. Geez Kira used to take on a lot of stuff, that really didn't have anything to do with her, didn't she?

These times with you Lord, are really showing Kira just how naive she had been in the past, and how she allowed too much of what others thought of her get in the way. Funny saying that too, because Kira never thought she really cared about what others thought of her, yet she turned into a slave and forgot who her boss was exactly.

The other day you told Kira that she was surrounded by a sea of problems. Yes Lord, she was. Some of the problems that she was facing were ones she faced almost every year. You got them through in the past, so why wouldn't you do it again? You also told her not to give up. She needs to come to terms with the fact that this is a never-ending cycle. She is aware of it and knows it's just hard because some don't understand this is the way it is for now.

Lord, it wore Kira out when she tried to do it without you, so now she is going to include you in all of it. Even though you know it and see it before she does, you still want Kira to bring it to you. There are times when Kira thinks she just doesn't want to do it anymore, it's wearing her down too much. It's always at the time of year when finances need to be ok so she can enjoy Christmas, her favorite time of the year because you were born, and she gets to enjoy your birth. There are times, though when Kira would rather not have to deal with the stress and what happens at the office, but she has learned at least not to let it ruin everything. OOPS! (Chuckle) Okay Kira needs to follow and understand what you're telling her.

Okay you're telling Kira not to try to figure it all out. She must accept it with blind faith and true trust in you; you have a plan that's better than hers! Look for you to work it out!

Lord, she knows your plan is better for her, it just doesn't happen at times when others expect it. Kira wants your peace because it's hard for her to function properly if she allows herself to get overwhelmed! She strongly needs you in her life, to

Having Coffee with the Special One

help her through and everyone around her. Kira hopes and prays, Lord, that she won't give in and she stays steadfast in your love. She doesn't have any idea how this will all turn out, but just think of the fun while waiting to see what you do. Your way is always better than hers. Kira doesn't want to misunderstand you either Lord.

Lord, Kira thanks you for all the good that will come out of this. Everything Kira is going through, she knows there is an ending to it, and you'll turn it into something beautiful. You haven't ever steered her wrong in the past. Lord, Kira will put her trust in you because she has seen how she messes things up when she tries to control them.

"Do not be afraid for I am with you says the Lord," When she gets in the way, it just takes you longer to resolve it which has been proven to Kira. Lord, Kira can't read your mind, but she can listen to you. Trust in the Lord, with <u>all my heart</u>. (Not just half of it or a part.) Do not be afraid for I am with you, says the Lord.

This can go for every circumstance that Kira is and was going through at the time. Lord, when you say you want her living on the edge with you, Kira really thinks she has because she's been told that she goes through life by the seat of her pants. She sort of lives each moment as it comes. Is this what you mean when you say that?

What a good way to look at it, walking on a tightrope. It's a balancing act and it's <u>trust</u>! Kira

Patty Scott

for sure is walking on the rope, the edge. Lord, you're really making Kira think and see in all the areas of where she didn't completely lean on you. In the past, Kira never really thought about some of this, but now she's looking at life and circumstances in a whole new way. Is that where changing her attitude and Kira is really turning her life over to you?

Kira has always been a risk taker...the dare devil type. Yet Kira would allow someone else make her question her judgment or, what should she say, influence her, or make her give in. Lord, every year you get Kira through things and now she's aware of it and thinking of it. How can Kira explain to others that even though she has always believed in you, her life was not the same as it is now. It's so different. Kira had other growth periods in her faith, but she doesn't think it has ever been what she is experiencing with you right now. Kira means she really is hanging on to you and feeling you in her life, because she is more aware of your presence.

Kira feels the peace that she knows is you. When she feels the joy and she gets to laugh, it's from deep down within with that deep throaty laugh! This is not just on the surface.

Jesus, Kira thanks you for this, as she guesses this is the difference of having a relationship with you and then having an intimate relationship with you. There really is a difference in how she feels, and

Having Coffee with the Special One

how she pays attention to what you say to her. You're revealing so much to Kira.

You're showing Kira so many areas where she really was a control freak, and really did try to control the world. Geez, no wonder she got burnt out!!

Lord, she really did get burned out. Kira can see that now. At times she allowed life... to suck the life out of her!! Do others go through what she has at times? Kira was headed for disaster, or she was the disaster.

No matter how hard she tried, Kira felt like she couldn't make anyone happy which was true because she was doing things the wrong way. Kira guesses this is where you get to tell her again that she was a people pleaser. Kira never looked at it that way, and she still doesn't like it because she doesn't want to see it that way. She thought she was a caretaker, is that the correct word? You know there are givers and takers; Kira considered herself a giver. She read somewhere two different things: it's the givers that have to set the boundaries because the takers will keep on taking, and it takes the takers to make the givers happy. They both make perfect sense.

Lord, now Kira is enjoying accepting and taking your blessings that you're bestowing upon her and seeing how you think she is worth it, and worth your time, your love, and your forgiveness. Why does she always wait until things are just so bad to really call upon you?

She really gets to magnify your glory, doesn't she? People can see how you have worked in her life and through her. They will know it was all you. Lord, she hopes they all believe it too, that it's all you, not her; because she doesn't have the strength, unless she has you.

You have weaned Kira from depending on her work to bury herself in it. That was a false sense of security that she held onto. Kira should have gone to you and talked it out with you, but she was mad at you. She was hurt and she could not understand, she should have opened to you and poured her heart out to you. You know exactly what happened and that it would happen before it did.

Lord, Kira did figure out that it was hard to have a good relationship with her spouse if she wasn't ever around. You know it takes two to have a good relationship, not just one person. And some people aren't strong enough to be alone as often as others. It doesn't make it right if something goes awry but it's the way it is.

Kira found out too that she was a lot nicer when she wasn't so rushed all the time, and she quit blaming the world for her short comings. It's ok that Kira wanted her own business, but it just

Having Coffee with the Special One

wasn't ok to put it first in her life, and ahead of you or her spouse. Kira was really walking on the edge there for a while. Thank you for being there at that time in Kira's life. She knows you were there because at first, she did talk to you and you did help her.

Kira can picture you standing in front of her like a father with a child when they are first trying to walk, "come on you can make it, your almost there!" She is not afraid of falling Lord, she was scared that she wouldn't get back up. Each day that fear lessens in Kira because she knows you have a reason for what all is happening in her life and you have a much, much better plan than the one she had for her.

You have been working in her life, or Kira should say, she has been more in tuned to you working in her life ever since the forgiveness process with her ex and—as she looks back—really for a long time when you really opened her heart and mind unto you, Jesus Christ.

When Kira truly let go and let You—as she said before brick by brick—the walls that she built in her and in her heart have been torn down because she just really started opening up to you and letting you in! Kira could feel the walls just falling away in her. They are crumbling...the negative power no longer has power over her.

Small baby steps...holding her hands in the process...leading her on.

Patty Scott

Why is it Lord, that when Kira gets glimpses of you, it's you holding her hand and she is a child? Is it because of your special place in her heart, and how you say blessed are the little children? Kira just thinks it's interesting (and by the way, she has her hair in pigtails.)

You know Lord, Kira is starting to see where our society is waking up more and more, or it's that she is looking for you in everything. It's probably that she is waking up. Her pastor said there has always been spiritual warfare, it just wasn't that apparent to Kira as it is now. Kira sees you're everywhere, in the clouds the angels that she sees, in movies, in books she reads, people she relates to. Kira thought for a while that society needed to wake up but maybe it was her, that needed to not others! Watching and seeing what is happening and bringing you back into her work: Kira doesn't remember working for a company where they let you pray at your job, or with clients. Kira not only needs you Lord, —others do too—to watch over us and protect us. What do we have if we don't have you in our lives?

Kira notices more and more that she is calmer and peaceful. She noticed it yesterday but also the storm (at least one of them) is around, but she's calm. She knows it's only because she has let you in, and you're now a part of her everyday life. Kira knows you were knocking on her heart before, and

Having Coffee with the Special One

she wasn't listening to you. She says she is sorry and thank you for forgiving her. Kira knows that there are more storms in her life coming, and she knows you'll help her through them. Kira doesn't ever remember sitting down and writing to you everything that was on her mind and she doesn't ever remember, being that close to you or even wanting to do something like it.

You have shown Kira that's what you really want from her, just for her to sit and talk to you and bring you in. Thank you for this time, thank you for being able to sit with her and thank you for getting her to talk, she needed it more than ever!! Until now Kira really didn't want to face this or to deal with the hurts and disappointments over the years. Kira knows, she thought she was in control.

Kira does regret at times thinking she should have made other decisions. She understands what you're saying Lord; it wasn't working out that well when she did that was it?

Lord, Kira is searching for your way as she was so tired of this never-ending cycle. Even Rae Lee said, well if this continues like it has been, then maybe it's you, or in you, not everyone else. Kira felt Rae Lee had a valid point there. It was partially because Kira had such high expectations of others. And who is she to put that kind of responsibility on others? She thought it was okay because she expected so much out of herself, and she thought well she didn't expect any more out of them than what she did of herself.

Patty Scott

It's also funny, Lord, how you shine through during trials and tribulations, and Kira wants to thank you for the truth coming out. It's funny how people will do something that may not be the best way, and yet you always prevail and always bring out the truth eventually. You let it shine; no one can hurt Kira if she has you by her side.

Help Kira to remember that and hang on to that as it's going to be a long ride. She wishes it's something she could talk about but right now she can't. Kira knows this is something she must wait on until you want to do something about it. It doesn't mean Kira enjoys this struggle, but she knows she has to wait on you. You're giving them the chance to stand up to the plate and act responsibly. It doesn't mean that they will, but you have a plan, and Kira has done all that she can do. Now it's your turn to do the rest!!

Lord, Kira can honestly say she thought there were people out there that needed you more than she did, and she didn't want to bother you with her problems. "<u>Yes,</u> she thought she could take care of it herself." Now she understands you didn't ever want her to do it alone. Lord, you never intended for any of us to do things on our own or alone. Kira can depend on you to help her.

You promise to be by her side every step of the way and no matter the result, it's in your hands, and what happens is up to you. Kira just must trust that you'll fulfill your promise to her. You don't let your sheep get caught up in the wrong gate, and

Having Coffee with the Special One

you protect them. Lord, Kira is one of your sheep. Lord, you save her in so many ways!!

What a friend we have in Jesus, all our sins and griefs to bear, of which we often forfeit, take it to the Lord, in prayer.

What a privilege to carry all our sins to God in prayer. We are never alone when we have Jesus.

Kira can see you opening her path, moving the stumbling blocks, changing the way she looks at things, and showing her how she can help others. You're showing her the way—where before she wasn't listening—you, Lord, are the light and the w

Lord, you told Kira she would have stormy waters ahead of her and you would reduce the waves so she could get through them.

Kira was thinking I sort of weakened yesterday, but once I calmed down and relaxed, I started listening and remembering what You told me. You told me to hold on tight, and you'll get me through this. Lord, I am searching for your way to get through them, and I do see your blessings in them. What is your way that you want me to handle this? I am not liking owing so much to others. I don't want them to think they control me. Lord, I want to do it your way, and I don't want them to push me. It's what it is, take small baby steps and get through this.

Lord, you told Kira that she just seemed to know exactly what to say and when! Thank you for telling her that she doesn't have to be a "goody". Thank you for telling her know it's ok to be human. It's okay for her mind to wander, because that's what happens. Kira goes through examples of situations so it can make sense to her, can understand what you're saying and what you want her to learn. You're giving Kira examples so that she can truly let go and trust you, trust you more.

You're all knowing; she can't keep anything from you. You know Lord, even though Kira fell for a bit yesterday, she didn't panic as bad as she would have in the past. Kira knows they are going to get through this rough time. You brought her to where she is today, so she knows you'll get her through this.

You're allowing Kira to see so many miracles. Each day there's a tiny miracle—sometimes more than one, and sometimes a major miracle!

Look at how you, Lord, helped Mathew, the little boy who had something in his ears and the doctors had to cut off his ears to get it out and sew them back on. Man, "Lord," you're amazing in what you do and what you help doctors know how to do!! You helped that little boy. Thank you, God!!

Having Coffee with the Special One

Look at how you changed the mind of the mother that didn't want her daughter learning about you. "Lord," there are so many miracles!! It's just so awesome to hear about these stories!! They are the truth!!

Kira watched others trust you and depend on you as you walked with them the whole way. You got them through the rough patches; you can get Kira through them too!!

She needs to watch for and count the blessings along the way, Lord!! There are so many!! You're taking care of Kira, her family and others at the same time.

How do you?

You're the I am, the Almighty. You can handle it all!! Kira can't ….

You're the way, the truth, and the light.

Oh Lord, thank you for shining through Kira so others can be blessed!! The two people who came in yesterday, Lord, that was fun!!

Kira can be a good example for others when she handles things the proper way. Others can see you carry her and get her through hard times and other situations, so why wouldn't you do it for them? Right!!

If Kira panics and falters, why would they want to believe in you? Kira can't magnify your glory when she stumbles and falters. She must hang on tight and let you guide the way. There are so many people watching her!!

She must let you shine through her because Kira can't glorify you, Lord, if she is a raving lunatic. If she lets anger control her that's not allowing you in.

Kira knows you understand her. You see her deep down inside.

She can't hide anything from you.

You know, Lord, the best things in life are free. Your love, your grace, your forgiveness, your strength, your care; everything, everything from you is freely given to us.

All we must do is let you in our lives. Love, honor, and cherish you. <u>Trust</u>!!

Why do we work so hard in life? When it all comes from you, Lord, you give us what you want us to have, and you help and guide us. It's all planned out.

Having Coffee with the Special One

As Kira looks back over her life, she can see each step of the way and how you had it all planned. Even when she sidestepped it, you brought her back on track according to your plan. Kira can see all the blessings in her life that you bestowed upon her and her family.

God, she gives you praise and thanks you for the blessings in her life. The people who love her, the people who help her, the people who care about her: Kira's life truly is blessed by you. Kira is so glad the seed was planted long ago when she was a child and growing even better now that she is an adult. Even though she forgets at times, Lord, to tell you but you're her knight in shining amour, you're her protector, her teacher, and her friend! It's so different than the love that she has for her family and her husband. But it's a deep love, that no other can share. Kira wants to make the most of each day! It's funny some people think you must do things like that to be a Christian, and Kira thinks, no you don't have to do anything, you just need to want to do it.

There is a difference there: Kira wants to show people you're the one leading her and guiding her. Whatever happens, Kira trusts You, Jesus. She knows that you want the best for her in life, and Kira owes it all to you.

God, you gave your life for us to have all that we have.

Patty Scott

God, Kira thanks you even when she didn't get her own way which happens often. Kira sees what you mean now: when everything goes our way, we tend to put you on the back burner and forget that it's you that's with us and it's all for you. We are not supposed to put our trust and faith in ourselves, but to continually praise and give you thanks for all that you do for us and help us with.

Kira is realizing more and more where she sort of pulled away and didn't depend on you. She was giving credit to the wrong person, and Kira must stop and remind herself that it's all yours and for you. When we seek you, we find you and you're in all that we do. Lord, you fill us with your peace. It's forever if we hang onto it. It's not temporary, as worldly things are. Money comes and goes, new clothes turn old, and the shiny dulls. But, Lord, our life and breath shines always, and gets brighter the closer we get to you. There is nothing in this world that can take your place, or even touch what you do.

You're constant and never changing. Kira can see that now. You're always the same—yesterday, today and tomorrow—and can always depend on you because you're there for her.

It's not like human relationships, it's so much more........

Having Coffee with the Special One

Kira is coming to the belief and realization that there is always going to be trials and tribulations, and there is nothing she can do to stop them. She just needs to learn how to handle them.

There is no excuse why Kira just flies off the handle. Some days she can take it smoothly, but others not so much.

Like the other day when the darn programs stopped working and some of the work that they did the day before had to be redone. Geez, things were just rough. She did not handle it well. Sometimes, she can take it, but other times she just gets so overwhelmed.

Kira was reminded that she had to take a step back, and breath. She was reminded of some important opportunities that she missed the mark on. You don't know what is going on with a person, until you ask. Try not to fly off the handle, and think you know what is going on.

Kira realized the other day that she had a chance to get to know one of her uncles better, and she totally missed the mark. He went to Kira and said that he might be looking for a new accountant because he thought his was retiring. At that time, Kira had it in her head she wouldn't be doing this much longer, so she wasn't too interested. Let someone else step in.

Why does Kira keep doing things like that? Now she knows she should have grabbed his arm, and said, let's take a walk and talk. She really would have loved doing that with him, but noooooo she had to miss the whole opportunity. Even if he didn't change to her, that would have been an awesome moment, one that she could have hung on to for a long time, since especially now she won't ever get another chance. This just breaks her heart.

Kira has got to stop and listen sometimes to what might not be being said. Kira just gets so wrapped up in her thoughts that she can't see trees through the forest. She knows now that even if she had cut back, Kira still could have taken care of him.

Another part of her problem is—besides missing the mark—she has tried to do EVERYTHING. Kira was trying to be super woman, because she thought she had to do it all on her own!! And she didn't trust anyone to do it right!! Kira kept talking to you, but she wouldn't really listen to you! Thank you for forgiving her and she really is sorry.

Kira hopes that she is wiser now that she's older and now that she knows to ask you for wisdom, and discernment. She knows when it's a good decision to do something, or not. There are times, Lord, Kira has taken baby steps to let go of the crap!! She doesn't want the burdens of the world on her shoulders because she doesn't have the strength and power you have.

Having Coffee with the Special One

Kira is nothing compared to you!! You really do give her relief and when she turns it all over to you, her load is not heavy!!

Let it go, let it go, let it go. Let go and "Let God."

Clean out my heart and renew my spirit!!

Lord, thank you for getting her attention back to you.

Take each day, one day at a time. Do you know how many times that runs through Kira's mind?

Kira knows that she just needs to try to accomplish one thing at a time and quit trying to take on the whole load and do it all. Kira really is trying to learn more how to delegate and get done what she needs to get done.

Baby steps. Just one day at a time. One step at a time. One case at a time.

Kira wasn't built to multi-task, and it doesn't work out for anyone really. Even when Kira was younger, she could only do one thing at a time.

Lord, you keep her informed and you smooth the path, so each storm is easier to handle and a little less devastating. That's what you're trying to teach her: that each problem isn't the end of the world.

Patty Scott

It's not that we won't have problems; it's that you make them seem smaller. You take the power of the problem away and help Kira see different ways to get through them. (Light bulb goes off in her head.)

Help her look for your way Lord, to get through it all. Help her to follow your lead. Be very bold, so that she knows it's you, and she isn't hesitant to take the steps you want her to take. When Kira didn't look for your guidance, she just pushed everyone away, so they weren't a bother any longer!! There is a difference when she let go, rather than pushed away. Kira had to make room for you in her life, the important thing!! (As a person walking through a crowded room, pushing his way and people out of the way to get closer to you.)

Kira knows she asks for a lot from you, Lord, she is full of neediness, in all aspects of her life. She can't remember when she did face it and say that's what it was. Kira never allowed herself the privilege to even feel a need for you in the past. She always thought that she had to do it on her own. How could she be so unintelligent? Not give you credit where credit's due. You know Lord, Kira doesn't think the lesson would have meant so much to her if she hadn't gone through what she is having to go through. She doesn't think it would really have even gotten as much attention from her.

Thank you for staying with her and not giving up on her.

Having Coffee with the Special One

Lord don't let her go. Kira realizes she really wants you, and she does need you. But the most important thing is that Kira has learned that she wants you to be in in all aspects of her life, not just what she picks and choses. Lord, you need to be in it all..............................

When Kira does have trials and struggles, it's so that she can have quiet moments with you and take time out of her busy life to remember what is important.

This is something she had forgotten. Lord, how could she not know the peace that you give her, would be so warm and healing? Kira knows she never really put her trust in you.

Thank you for the day she had time to relax, time to cook, time to play, and time to enjoy the warmth of the sun during one of the days that you made. Kira was glad and rejoiced in it. It was a wonderful, peaceful day.

Hey, were you surprised when she did take the time to cook something? It even turned out "great" thanks to you.

Lord, she had fun, thank you! You know she isn't much on cooking, but when she isn't in a hurry and takes the time to do it, it's kind of fun to do. Thanks....

Patty Scott

You know Lord, Kira thinks it has finally soaked into her thick skull that she used to complain when her mom, sisters, family, husband, or kids wouldn't spend time with her. They wouldn't visit or they wouldn't call. Yet Kira fell into the same trap and did the same thing to them.

When it all comes to a head and relationships are ruined, it comes down to this: people just want to know they are loved, important to you and in your life. Kira wanted that from everyone and yet, she pushed them away! Kira remembers thinking the kids had their thing, Tim had his, and she needed to find hers and do it. Where Kira went wrong was that she didn't know how to have a career and a family because she just couldn't work it all out and didn't know how to turn it off.

In the meantime, everything was going wrong, Kira was being pulled in all directions, and she wasn't even taking true time to be with You. You're showing Kira the way and how she can have both her family and career. She just must keep things in the proper order: you, Lord, are first in her life. Kira must keep you at the head, then her family, and then work. Work should not beat the top of the list, that's the difference.

Kira kept trying to compare how she did it when she worked for someone else versus having her own company. She let the company own her and run

Having Coffee with the Special One

her, rather than her running it. Kira is sorry she wasn't putting you first in her life. Kira didn't make room for you in her heart and mind as much as she should have because when she got so overwhelmed, she cut out the wrong things in her life.

Kira sure was looking at things the wrong way, wasn't she, God? Here she thought you were supposed to come to her, and it was the other way around. She had to go to you, hold on to your hand and let you guide her. You, Lord, were not running along with her in the muck of things, as she was thinking it was supposed to be.

Kira will take time for you, especially in this busy time. Lord, she will need you always. In fact, she's always needed you, she just didn't know it, or wouldn't admit it. Kira doesn't want to put you on the back burner anymore. She must stay with you and keep you in the forefront of her life and her thoughts.

She's not supposed to fight what you're doing for her and in her life, yet at times Kira continues to fight it. You know, Kira fought everything and everyone who crossed her path during her younger years as she was growing up.

She even fought what You were trying to do for her, until Lord, she finally (after all those years) realized what a burden it was becoming. Kira realized she does want love, she wants intimacy, and she wants a close relationship with you, her husband, kids, and friends.

She doesn't want to be a martyr. But Lord, she wants to do it for you first.

Kira can see where you're working in her and her husband; you saved them both, not just Kira. The hearts are softening………

Lord, you know how Kira loves the creative side of things. You blessed her with the use of both the creative side and the analytical side of her brain.

Kira feels the creative side in her waking up again. It's so exciting as it provides a new release and a new adventure in her life. Kira always enjoyed that part of her; it was the fun side, while the analytical side is the more serious side of her. Kira just got out of practice and glad her creative side didn't die. It's just dusty, and she will blow off the cobwebs.

Kira is reminded often that it's your time schedule, not hers. Sometimes, she feels the old her popping its ugly head out and wants to hurry up and get things done. Lord, she doesn't want to let you down. She's not the one in control, you are. Kira is holding on to your hand Lord!! You guide and lead the way. You and Kira are not done yet, are they?

Having Coffee with the Special One

Lord, Kira wants you to lead her through the rest of her life.

She can't enjoy your peace if she is rushing around everywhere, and she doesn't remember to say "Jesus". It's easy: just say "Jesus". As Kira has heard several times you can do everything to dress up the outside and make everything look great, but it was the inside that was broken and needed to be healed.

Just a thought Lord: Kira's brother needs to be healed too. What we don't let have power over us in our lives, can no longer hurt us. Don't give them or it the power to hurt.

When two or more pray the same prayer, you'll listen. Jim and Nancy are praying for Kira, for the business, and she'll bet, for all.

You do know, Lord, they are a blessing in Kira's life. You gave her something nice in that relationship. Thank you, Jesus.

What! Because Kira feels and thinks she has paid her dues she is thinking that she deserves a problem-free life?

Okay, Lord, you say part of her is still hungering for the resolution of all difficulties. Kira guesses that for some reason she thought you would deal

Patty Scott

with all her difficulties and resolve them all. It didn't click with her until now that it won't ever happen. Kira will learn through your guidance, Lord, to handle them so the difficulties she faces won't destroy her or weigh her down—even though there are a few that do weigh her down.

Yes, Lord, Kira must learn your way of facing difficulties and depend on her faith and trust in you to get her through it all.

You're not only the perfect one, Lord, but you're constant and true in this ever-changing world. You'll show her the way?

She thinks you already told her to pray, love and trust. You'll lighten the waves of the stormy waters. Something good always comes out of the bad when we have you in our life. Praise and thank you Lord, even for the bad times, because without them we can't see where the difference is, and we can't magnify Your Glory if it was always good times.

Besides, we would think we didn't need you, Lord, and it was all us, as sometimes we mistakenly still think. Kira must get it into her head that she isn't being punished as she had thought at times. It's about bringing her closer to you, Lord, as she puts her faith and trust in you.

Kira knows she can only speak for herself, because others may not believe as she does, or they just may not be walking the walk as she is. Everyone is

Having Coffee with the Special One

different and they are all on their own journey. One thing that Kira has learned is that she really couldn't speak for others. Who knows what their thoughts are and to begin with, they're not any of her business, as you, Lord, have told her many times?

You allow the trials and tribulations for a reason, and it's not to be mean. Kira must learn to trust you more and deeper.

Kira is finding out, Lord, it's possible to enjoy you and your peace during all that's happening in her life.

God, Kira knows you're there because she isn't the raging idiot, she used to be in times like this. Yes, in her head she tries to solve the problems, but she has got to stop trying to solve others' problems....you keep telling her that...and hopefully one day it will click, and she will stop.

God, Kira hopes that it's soon, as she is tired of all the problems running through her mind and keeping her awake at times. Kira knows that's so wrong, yet she can't always stop it. She doesn't have control over her thoughts and mind when she is trying to sleep, and she was waiting for you to clean out the muck.

Kira needs to ask you, Lord, for the answers, then sit back and wait for you to show her the answer and know that your way is the best way. Kira needs to learn what problems will take care of themselves and which ones she needs to take care of. She sure can't handle all of them, so Kira needs to leave it up to you, so you can decide what you're going to do or not do. Kira will do what she can, then Lord, you do the rest as you always promise to do.

When Kira looks back and sees what was going on, Lord, she now can see how you were there and working in her and through her life. Kira felt everything was going wrong, she was being hit from all sides. You took Kira out of the picture so that you could conquer the issues and she wouldn't get in your way. You removed her, so you could clear the way, and make the path for her to handle things, your way Lord.

But that's where Kira went wrong, wasn't _it_! Kira would try to deal with it on her own rather than turning to you. Kira let her pride get in the way even though she knew better than that. She buried herself in her work, rather than bringing herself to you, Lord. That makes sense, because now she can see what you're saying.

Lord, Kira hid from everything when she didn't know how she was going to deal with it, or she didn't want to deal with it. Kira would say "_I work_," so I stay out of trouble. Just yesterday she said it to herself rather than trusting you to help

Having Coffee with the Special One

her and to take care of it. Kira is like a bird in the sand, burying her head in the sand. Kira shut off all contact and she pushed people away, even you. So many times, Lord, so many times Kira did that.

Lord, help her stop this bad habit. Life is too short to keep doing this. What time you have given Kira, she wants to enjoy it and make the most of it while she is here. She'll try to remember that doesn't mean a problem-free life.

Kira must respond in the proper way, but, Lord, you do know too already that sometimes she will fall. If you help her up, she will be okay. Here she pictured you leaning down, holding her hand, and helping her up!

You'll be there for Kira when she falls. Lord, you always are and were there for her.

If two or more pray the same prayer, you'll listen.

Do we do it at the same time together, each time?

Just because Kira lost the battle doesn't mean she lost the war. Kira must remember she can't win them all, but it doesn't mean she is a failure.

God always comes out strong in the end. <u>God</u>! Love, hope, and peace conquers all!

Patty Scott

Kira watches so many faith-based movies. The nice thing is they are all based on true stories about amazing trials and tribulations people had to go through. Yet in the end, Lord, you always win, you stand out and shine, you get them through it, and they win with you. It's so much encouragement in not giving in or giving up. It gets so close at times. Sometimes, Kira just doesn't want to keep fighting the fight, then a song or a phrase pops into her head, and you're there telling her not to give up.

That who so ever believeth in you, shall not perish. You have better plans for us than we have for ourselves!! Sometimes it's just hard, to wait upon you.

You saved Kira's marriage more than once!!

God, you saved her children as young adults, her friends, and associates.

God is great!!

All the Time.

Why is it that when something is bugging the heck out of Kira, she cannot let it go?

In church yesterday the minister was preaching on being set free because the truth will set you free. Well, one day the truth will come out, and Kira will

Having Coffee with the Special One

be free. She just doesn't know how it will happen because the end results are up to you Jesus, not her. She must accept that and whatever the ending is, Kira just knows it will be good.

Kira has just got to learn how to lighten up and laugh at her mistakes and situations more often. She takes things and circumstances too seriously. Kira's mind went to her friend Maria. There was so much fun laughing with Maria.

Lord, Maria is healing, and it was fun for both. When Kira stops worrying about everything, and keeps her focus on you, everything will fall into place. Is she understanding it properly? Instead of focusing on the problems at hand, she can or needs to focus on you. Teach her how and show her the way.

Kira thinks she understands rather than allow a negative circumstance to direct her, Kira can look up to you and ask you to guide her and make the proper decision. She's not to act or do things with the wrong intent or for the wrong reason. When Kira stops fighting the changes, you're making in her, her life will be much better.

In your eyes, the world is so small, and Kira's problems and issues are so small. Kira must remember to look at them in the same way! Is this correct? It doesn't mean to go hog wild, but it means to trust you, Lord, look at things in a different light and not make it so big in her life.

Patty Scott

Does this mean that the fact that Kira lets you in her life, depends on you for guidance and listens to you that she won't let you down? If she lets herself be human and makes the mistakes and laughs at them, it's okay, and you still love her? Geez, why does Kira let those moments get to her?

The fact that you're with Kira and taking the mornings to sit down with her, means she isn't disappointing you and that she means something to you, Lord. Kira hopes that soaks into her heart, Lord, and you don't have to tell her one hundred times.

Lord, Kira said that she saw the angel in the sky the night before last night. It was awesome!

The way the eagle and the angel came together, they let Kira know that you're there, and she is protected. The angel was so majestic and beautiful. Kira felt the change in her heart.

How many times in the past did Kira miss out on these kinds of things? She has always seen characters in clouds at times, but nothing like you have been showing her lately. It's just amazing seeing the trumpets and the angels because Kira knows you're watching over her and you care about her.

Having Coffee with the Special One

Lord, you know everything about her. You can see in her heart and in her mind. You know how she thinks and what she thinks. Lord, she got so off-track. Kira is sorry how negative she got. She is so glad that you're a forgiving God and with your grace she is forgiven. To Kira, those are still some powerful words.

You know, Lord, what Kira has to say about the world and government that they are pushing you out of our lives and our schools. She did the same thing! She stopped doing what was giving her the peace and making her happy. Every single time in Kira's life when there was hurt, suffering, and pain, she didn't keep you close in her heart and mind, or in her life. Kira sat there, looked at her marriage and blamed someone else for the errors or the separation. Now Kira can see it was because she didn't keep you close and didn't put you the head of the family.

Kira can see the difference in her life. If you're willing to take the time with her and heal her, she knows you'll do so with her loved ones too. Kira can see her faith and trust in you is becoming stronger as we draw you, Lord, closer to her.

Not only does Kira know you're there, she trusts that you'll be there forever. Trusting you makes fears go away and talking to you and listening to you, Lord, you're setting her free. Kira couldn't ever be a prisoner because she likes her freedom too much. Yet, Kira let fear and anger keep her prisoner.

Patty Scott

She just pictured a cowboy sitting on his horse with his lasso gathering the cows. When you told her to lasso her thoughts and take them to you, it's a process. Lord, it will all be the way it should be in your time. Kira can't let her life sink into the darkness of worries. That's not a fun place to be. She was allowing them to control her.

Lord, with you in her mind, you push out what you don't want there. As some say, you're pulling the weeds, and taking out the spider webs. Lord, Kira is at peace, and the problems become so little. The problems don't go away, but they just aren't so scary when Kira puts her faith in you. Kira knows at times that she repeats some of what you tell her, and for some reason, you must repeat it. Maybe it just doesn't soak into her thick head, or maybe Kira is struggling to understand what you're meaning at the time.

"May the light shine upon you and give you peace."

That's what you tell her, now that she is listening to you. Brings on a whole new meaning.

When you're the center of relationships, you fill them with love. When they can give love, it was a cycle. Give more get more. You put harmony in the family dynamics, so much joy and laughter.

Having Coffee with the Special One

The kids were there at her home, and she enjoyed them, in fact, she loved having them. Kira knows she wasn't the best, but she tried. Kira let things in life come between you, Lord, as one of the old adages is, the family that prays together stays together. Well that's so true, and there is so much proof in Kira's life that all you have to do at times, is pray, speak your name and you'll be there, as you're always close.

Why would Kira want to give that up?

Kira loved having her kids, what caused her to.... oh, never mind. Look how they are getting back together.

Lord, forgive her for the days and times of resentment. Thank you for giving her the chance to see her faults and change things before it may have been too late. Kira is extremely fortunate that her kids do want to be around her, and they all enjoy being together because it really is important to her. Kira loves those hugs, and those smiles, or the wave hi. The sparkles in their eyes, the laughter in their voices, coming through the garage, she likes to surprise them as they are coming in, and to hear them laugh.

Kira just must remember to stop, take time to rest and relax so she can enjoy life, and the love that's there for her.

Kira never looked at it as worshiping, the junk, but she guesses, that's what she was doing, because she didn't let it go or even sit and talk with you about it, not until now, now that she knows what you were meaning. As much as she can't stand anything having a hold on her, she was surprised she let that happen.

Lord, Kira's trying not to stand in your way of what you're trying to do for her life.

God, Kira is living proof you're real and you love them. She made so many mistakes in life, and you keep forgiving her. Lord, you saved Kira even though she has sinned against you. You're in control of her life; she can't forget that no matter how many times it may come up.

Kira hopes when you're reading her mind and thoughts, you do see that she truly loves you and trusts you, Lord.

After all these years of muck Kira allowed to get in the way, she finally realizes she was hurting your relationship, but she was the one missing out. Kira didn't fully trust you, Lord, as it should have been.

How many times have you shown yourself to her and she knew you were there; but Kira just didn't have a lot of trust?

How many times did someone tell Kira she had to trust someone, yet she wouldn't do it?

Having Coffee with the Special One

Lord, Kira hopes she doesn't forget the angel! It was just awesome! And heartwarming.

She still needs to be able to define the feeling of warmth deep into her heart and soul.

It was like her heart wasn't broken anymore because you put it back together. You squeezed it to let Kira know she still has a heart. You have given her a strong one, that's for sure.

She is realizing where she went wrong finally. Kira hopes she doesn't keep making the same mistakes, (chuckle.) Yes, so she can make new ones!!!

Lord, Kira loves you ......

Kira doesn't know if she will ever be able to describe the difference in herself since she has taken the time to spend with you: what you have done for her, the openness, the warmth and the love. It's just so much Kira didn't have before, or realize it was there before. Thank you for opening her up to it.

Even in her work, Kira has had to work on some challenging things, and you gave her the answers. You were guiding her, everything balanced, and it made sense to her. Kira had a better understanding of what she did! She had been struggling with some of the entries she worked with and you gave her the answers even when Kira didn't even question you!! She got to learn something new. Kira had a difficult client to deal with, but you helped her deal with him with humor. Her client defused and even got a chuckle despite having a difficult day. Kira forgot that was one of the gifts you gave her was the ability to make people laugh.

God, Kira was taking everything in life so seriously. You have helped her lighten up.

You're teaching Kira how to delegate too and learn that it's okay to have someone else handle challenging situations. Sometimes, it's best to keep Kira out of it because she still has flaws and weaknesses. You know what all they are, and she knows you'll help her with them. Why is it that some things are easy for her to let go of and others...... well not so much? Kira knows that most of the time, or even really all of the time, when the flaws come to surface, she just has to trust you to take care of the issue, or it will just go away. Kira knows that just as sure as she is sitting there.

When Kira struggles with something she realizes that maybe she didn't turn it over and leave it with you, Lord, Jesus, Kira will give it all to you. She just gets in the way of your plan and delays what you intend to do. She is sorry, and she needs to be more aware it her errors.

Kira knows you're keeping the enemy away and protecting her right now. There have been so many things happen, but you have cleared the way for

Having Coffee with the Special One

new work and for us to be able to think and to enjoy your peace.

Kira says: "Lord, I am not afraid, I know you have a plan".

Kira has known it or realized it for several years. She could feel you working in her life, and while Kira knew there were going to be changes, she just didn't know what the changes would be, but she had to make room for positive growth.

Thank you, Lord, for giving Kira the strength and the peace to get through each day. Sometimes Kira really didn't want to face what she thought the day would be like, you know that!

That's not how Kira feels now, and she doesn't dread going to the office anymore.

She even enjoys and looks forward to going to the office again. You know it seems as though when one problem is resolved, there is another one in its place. (Chuckle)

Guess that's the meaning of job security in your life, the never-ending cycle of always having problems, just some are not as serious as others. The atmosphere is so much better in this day and time with you in Kira's life. Everywhere home, work........

Patty Scott

You know what to tell Kira every single day!! You know she has dinner guests coming tonight and she has a lot to do today. Kira had a concern if she was up to it, you already told her You have it all planned and worked out.

Like the weekend she had Lilia over, her energetic three-year-old granddaughter. She is a ball of energy, Lord; Kira enjoyed the time with her so much!! She is a gift from you and a blessing. Anyway, you got Kira through the day. They baked sugar cookies, frosted them, and painted them. Something Kira didn't do much when her kids were young, and she sure didn't take the time to do something like this. It was so much fun!!

Kira can see the areas in her life where she had been praying and you're answering her prayers. Thank you, Jesus.

It means a lot to her—she can't say what—but she is thankful.

Kira thinks, Lord, you know sometimes I must step back and pay attention to where and how you're showing me the way. I must let it soak in and feel your presence.

Lord, I want others to feel and see your presence in my life. I want it to be true and real, not fake, and showy. I want people to know you're there for them

Having Coffee with the Special One

too!! All we must do is ask in your name, and our joys will be complete.

Lord, speaking of watching over and protecting me, we left one of the office doors unlocked when we went home, and no one walked in or messed with the office. You watched over and protected it ... and it could have been bad!!

Kira says, I also know you're watching over me and protecting me on the roads. You're shielding me from harm.

Lord, I truly thank you for being in each area of my life daily. I know you're the Almighty. I'm telling you Lord; I don't want your job because I could not handle all the neediness of people. You know how I feel and hurt when people hurt. There is no way I could do it, and you do it all to save us from sin!! You take on the burdens of the world. You don't give them power.

Take each day one step at a time and stay in the moment that way nothing will seem so overwhelming and you won't let it get in the way of God's peace. The problems won't seem so big!! God will help you tackle and conquer them. Tackle is a gentler approach, than to conquer.

Let God be the one to conquer the world. You may lose a battle, but it doesn't mean you lose the war. Your life will never be trouble free, but God is always there with you and he will get you through. It's such a freedom and a feeling of peace to focus on the Lord. The chains that were binding are dropping, one by one as God is taking the burdens off Kira's shoulders.

It's not fake or fictitious; it's real! The peace is there. He does what He promises you, and all we must do is trust Him, thank Him, praise Him, and believe He will get us through the mess we are in. It doesn't mean one day you wake up and all your problems are gone, but you'll just feel like they are, and you won't let them control your life!!

You get up, you smile, and you push through each thing that you're faced with. It's so refreshing!! It's so nice to have joy and peace from you, Lord, Kira feels like a whole new person!!

She feels alive again!!

God has removed what was damaging her. He is healing her, her bones, her nerves, her neck, her head, and her heart!! It's a process and it takes time.

As they all kept telling Kira, it's coming on two years, and what a journey. God has been with her every single step of the way. He hasn't left her side for one second!! He even carried her on the days she didn't think she would get through!!

Having Coffee with the Special One

God, Kira thanks you for loving her and caring for her, and for her healing inside and out.

All the bruising, all the pain, all the muscles, all the swelling...God thank you for loving her enough and telling her she was worthy of your care. Kira thanks you Lord, for what you have gone through together with her!

God, you have showed her a better way!! A better plan, and you did not leave her. "Oh Lord," thank you for <u>this</u>!!!! You have cleaned her heart!! Also healed the ligaments and tendons. Kira knows you're still working in her and healing her but she knows one day none of the hurt will be there, unless it's to give her a nudge and help remind her you're there and what you have done for her in her life. Lord, can she even thank you enough??

Bless me Father for I have sinned. You do bless her every second of her life, you love her even when she does stupid stuff ...... (will always bring a smile)

Lord, are you telling Kira to just take one problem at a time when you talk about climbing the mountain rather than try to resolve everything at once as she does at times?

Thank you for telling Kira you don't want an overnight change and you're telling her not to expect one either. She has allowed many things to get to her for so long that they are all piled up. Kira guesses this is where she sometimes gets lost and can't see the trees for the forest.

Sort of like when she was driving back home to Wyoming from Denver and was pulled over for speeding. In all honesty, Kira didn't realize she was speeding. For Heaven's sake she was driving a Vega which didn't have any power to be speeding, so how the heck could she get a ticket for that! HA Oh yeah, Kira didn't have any shoes on either so driving without shoes, and only $5.00 in her purse. And her youngest brother Donnie and her youngest sister Gay in the back seat... hmmmmm what did the officer think? Well Kira was a runaway surely? No, she wasn't, but he made Kira drive all the way into Greely where she was hauled to the police station to get a mug shot taken (and had to help them work the camera!.)

She got her one phone call, so Kira had to call her mom. Her mom then called a friend who got a bails bondsman to get her out. In the meantime, there was a parade going on outside, and Donnie was screaming and yelling because he wanted to go watch the parade and was cooped up in the police station waiting room while Kira was otherwise detained. (HA HA)

It wasn't funny then, but now it is. You got Kira to court and it ended up not costing anything but the filing fee. Thank you for having an honest officer who cited Kira that her odometer was broken. That's why Kira didn't know she was speeding!

Having Coffee with the Special One

Thank you, Lord, as it could have been so much worse. But you saved Kira and kept her out of trouble.

You showed Kira that she doesn't have to get through it all on her own because you're going to have Your angels always watch over her and if she stumbles, they will pick her up! If Kira messes up and she does something wrong, they will be there to get her on the right path, and you'll still love her and forgive her.

Lord, Kira is sorry when she doesn't take that step back and flies off the handle. She needs to understand what you're telling her today. There are several things running through her head all at once: maybe that's the deal, she needs to talk about just one thing at a time!! Right now, the only thing that keeps coming to mind is the financial situation at work which you, Lord, have so kindly helped with and corrected.

There are times when Kira wants to tackle the whole mountain at once, but Lord, you're going to lead her to an easier path??

Kira is at a loss here this morning. Lord, is it because maybe she isn't listening properly to what you're saying??

Okay Lord, Kira gets that putting her faith and trust in you to get her through situations doesn't mean she can see how we're going to do it. She just must trust that they will do it, and your protective angel will be there to get help her get through whatever it is she needs to face.

Lord, you, and Kira are on a journey that's going to take a while (for the rest of her life) to accomplish your goal. Kira is building her faith and trust in you more and more each day. She may not be able to see the how or when, but she just needs to know it will be completed.

Does she understand correctly?? Even when she sins, you'll forgive her if we take it one step at a time? Lord, you're showing Kira that you'll fulfill your promise to her—and some have been completed? How could she have ever doubted you?

Funny thing is even today, she said you know if it's easy, it's wrong. Kira thinks that you're telling her there is an easier path. If you're there with her, then she will know it's your way, not hers.

Now people tell Kira that she does things the hard way. She knows you're not only going to help her, but also the people around her. You know where they are right this second, so she doesn't need to keep telling you. Kira knows that she needs to keep practicing her focus on you and not the problem, because it's a waste of energy and time. As you say she has no idea how or what will happen in her day.

Having Coffee with the Special One

All Kira must do is remember to ask you, Lord, to be with her. She needs to hold on tight to your hand and not let go. Lord, you'll be right there by her side. You have been every single day too; not once did you leave Kira.

Lord, Kira needs her mind renewed, as you have cleared the fog.

There were so many unkind, negative thoughts going through her mind that it was awful!! She was allowing the problems to take hold of her, and it was so overwhelming. Kira was so lost in her head and problems that she had and was going through, that she forgot about you. Kira knows that you're fully aware of that too. You're only informing Kira of it, so she knows now what to do and guard against that and try to stop doing it.

Now Kira understands to work like you don't need the money. Lord, that's so much more fun. Chasing money really stinks, because it's a never-ending circle, and it just wears a person out! It doesn't do any good either. Kira doesn't even want to think of it anymore, because it made a mess of her, and "Kira was an unhappy camper." (Figure of speech.)

Kira is beginning to let what you, Lord, told her yesterday to soak in and she is opening and understanding what You were saying to her. Help her to get up and walk around.

Lord, Kira can't have her body stiffen up to where it hurts to move. Like the stupid meniscus that she tore six times in her right knee. Man, that hurts like heck, she can't let that stiffen up!!!

It's kind of like pinning the tail on the donkey right now, going through the days by faith and trust in you. Not knowing what is going to happen but enjoying the journey. All Kira knows is it will be good. Negativity is getting behind her, and you're showing her a better way to get through it all.

You're opening Kira up to options and your choices because her choices weren't the correct ones. Kira finally faced that and made some changes. Now she is opening to you, Lord. In return, you have given her signs to watch for when she is making the wrong choice.

Lord, Kira knows you brought Sheila to her for a reason. Kira needs to dig down deep to get the junk out of her and see that you're there. Lord, you're climbing your way to the top, so she can know your presence, and see you have always been there. Kira just piled so much junk on top!! It didn't end the way that Kira had hoped with Sheila but, she knows that she was there for a purpose and the purpose was served. Thank you, Jesus. Kira prays for her healing too.

Having Coffee with the Special One

Lord, you're not only around Kira, but you're also within her.

Kira knows, Lord, that when she focuses on the negative or the problems, she loses sight of you. She must keep working on that and can't continue that road of out of sight, out of mind. That's what her kids get so mad about too.

Kris was really upset about that. She needs to work harder and keep them close in her mind too, not only her heart. She needs to stop hurting you, Lord, and her kids. Looks like Kira must apologize for a lot of things these days, because you bring so much to the forefront. At first it really shook her up. Now she knows she must face it with you, repent of the error and hold on to you. She needs to figure out how to positively handle a problem.

It just clicked with Kira: she must remember that you're always there even when she doesn't see you. Yet even when you always show her that you're there, Kira just wasn't opening to you in the past. Great example you're showing her!! Kira needs to learn another way. She doesn't want to forget you, as Kira doesn't want to forget her children, or the work that she must complete. She must find the way that works for all: keep you in the foremost of her thoughts and her loved ones, all in the proper <u>order.</u>

Who is the most important one?? (She knows so that was a rhetorical question.) Get her priorities straight!!

When you say you're renewing Kira's mind, Lord, she hopes (which she really does know it does) that she gets the proper values in place.

Kira sure has gotten way off track, hasn't she? Kira fell into the trap and allowed people to define her, or something rather than you. Kira is so glad that you're there, and she doesn't have to face "<u>anything</u> alone!!" She is having to face a lot of things right now in all aspects of her life; some of it's hard and some of it's so joyful and pleasant! As she draws closer to her kids, Kira sees where they have matured and grown into adults.

"Let go and let them grow."

Yes, Lord, when Kira stays in today—the present— she gets to see the joys and gifts you give her, and she gets to see where You have been with her the whole time. Kira sees the light and she's almost there! There still are times, when Kira feels like three steps forward and two steps back, but she is gaining some ground. You give her examples so she can understand and see you're telling her, so it makes sense to her Lord. Kira sure is glad that you're on her side, you watch over her, and you protect her. Kira wouldn't not know what she

Having Coffee with the Special One

would do if she had to face this alone and without you in her life.

Lord, you watch over her even when Kira isn't watching, which is sad on her part, because she misses out on so much joy and freedom when she doesn't look to you or for you.

As you tell her: "Don't worry about tomorrow, for today has enough problems of its own." Kira kept looking down the road. What the heck did that matter?? Today is what is important. She can let go of that now. Now she sees all her planning and hoping that "one-day."

Geez, Kira's life—or anyone's life—can change on a dime (and their pretty small.) Whew!! Did she ever look at things differently! You know even with her seeing a new path and a better one in her life and seeing where she was on a different one, you, Lord, are showing her the way while being gentle about it. Kira had to lean on you more, and as she does lean on you, Lord, you're opening the world up and getting the negative things out of the way!! She is not weighed down so much, so you two can fly.

"One day at a time."

Patty Scott

Kira has got to stop viewing being busy as a problem. She needs to be thankful for what you're bringing to them, because if it wasn't for this work, they wouldn't have a job. They wouldn't be where they are.

Lord, why does she feel like she's on an emotional roller coaster? Kira knows the answer before it even gets out of her mouth: but it's a flaw or weakness in her, because she is forgetting to focus on you.

Lord, you're also listening and answering prayers. You're bringing work to them, and Kira is ever so thankful. You're listening about other people and care enough to pray for them also. There is so much that Kira wants to talk to you about, because so much is happening, and she sees You working everywhere. Kira sees you're surrounding her, her loved ones, and the people she cares about.

Kira sees you're working in their lives too. Please help Bryne: at least see that he needs to trust in you, and show him that you're there for him, when he trusts you. Lord, you saved him, now please take the hurt and anger from him. Kira guesses age doesn't really have to be the defining point when people mature. It's when they ask you into their lives and asking to see, and for you to open their hearts and minds unto You, Jesus Christ.

Having Coffee with the Special One

As Kira saw in devotions today, she doesn't want to conform to the way of the world. She wants to follow you and <u>trust you</u>! Trust is such a big part in the whole relationship with you and any other person. But with you it's the important one. You're what matters in all things. All who Kira prays for will one day see the light and they will feel the way she does if not better about it.

It just dawned on Kira that when she was younger, she was appreciative of the opportunity to be able to work and to get a job. Kira was so eager to learn, to soak it up like a sponge.

Lord, that was a time Kira was close to You. There sure is a difference how our lives go when we do trust you and depend on you. We let you in, then when we push you out.

Lord, something is messing with Kira's mind, she thinks it's allergies, she's not sure, is it a of joke of yours? There are weird noises going on outside. Sorry, it distracted her for a moment there. Didn't mean to get off track.

All we must do is trust God. Ask God in His name and our joy will be complete. God does answer prayers.

Kira has had the pleasure lately to be around her youngest son. She turned him over to you, and you have done wonders there. Kira was getting so frustrated, and she got in a hurry because she wanted it done today, as usual. Finally, Kira let go and let God.

Kira has had the pleasure to watch him mature and take on responsibilities, but still it isn't as quickly as she would like to see, but there is a wonderful change in him. Even Kira has learned to look at him in a different way and really see him. She sees him for the young man that he is and how he really loves his family. It's the simple things in life that mean something to him.

Kira can see you working all around her and answering her prayers. You're showing Kira in so many ways that you, Lord, are there. You're always present in her daily life and by her side.

Lord, you have opened her eyes to so many things. Kira is understanding so many things that have been heavy on her heart and mind for so long. Now it's funny because all she had to do was ask.........

Kira has been reborn.

Lord, you're showing her what it has been like with you—and without you—during her life. Now Kira knows the difference and that it's you, Lord, who made the change in Kira and her life.

She prefers the life with you in it; with you in every nook and cranny of her life. Kira can't say it enough: she thinks that you have made such a

Having Coffee with the Special One

difference in her life. She is calmer, she takes things better most of the time, and she knows now how important it is to truly forgive because it's such a Heavenly relief. Everyday Kira sees that it really made a difference in her life, and she is ever so grateful for it. Thank you, Jesus.

Lord, Kira is sorry to say that she was allowing fear to control her. In some ways, Kira thinks it was to punish the people who hurt her but during the process it was Kira that was being hurt, not them. She was just closing her heart off to you and everyone around her.

Kira was having a hard time with trusting people in her life; not only you but others around her. She was holding on so tight to the things that you were trying to get her to let go of. You're right (as always.) She had to let go of her controlling grasp around their necks, let them grow and stand back so you could do your work through them. Kira does believe that once you grasp on to them, there is nothing that you'll let get in the way of them becoming one of your sheep again. We all must go through this, and you even tell Kira that everyone must be born again to really know why we need you.

It was scary for Kira to open herself up to people and to you because in the past she felt vulnerable and people could hurt her. When she holds on to your hand, it's always as Kira being a child. We are always smiling and laughing. Kira has long blonde pigtails, and a dress on. She is so young, and joyfully skips along the way. You hold her hand ever so gently, yet tight enough to where she doesn't slip away. All she can see is your arm, your hand and your long robe, and the glow from your smile but never your face.

It might really be your angel for Kira, but he is hanging on to her anyway. Kira's mom always says, we can't ever see your face. Well, Kira hasn't seen your face, but she knows your smiling. Kira wants the spirit that you have given her to dance and laugh, to come alive!! She remembers when they lived in Fort Collins and their daughter was between four and five. One day she had a tutu on and danced around the table singing "don't mess with my tutu". It was so fun to watch her because she was so free and so happy.

That's what Kira wants to feel everyday of her life, even in times of trouble. Trust in the Lord, with all your heart. Not just half of it.

Thank you for telling Kira she can have as much of you as she wants. Lord, she wants to trust you totally and especially she doesn't want her time to be wasted on worry. Kira wants to be free from worry, not let it control her life!!

Dear God, help Kira make the correct choices all day, every day. Please give her your wisdom and discernment, so she can make the right decisions.

Having Coffee with the Special One

Kira knows life won't be perfect, but she wants your peace while she goes through it.

Trust in the Lord, with all your heart. Lean not on my own understanding. Acknowledge you, Lord, in all my ways, as you'll lead my path straight.

There were times when Kira was feeling selfish for needing you so much. She thought of others who needed you more, so she didn't want to bother you all the time. Lord, you have showed Kira it's no bother at all. You even like listening to her, and what is bugging her now.

Kira is glad you said she could have as much of you and your peace as she wanted or needed. She wants it, she wants it all Lord. You showed Kira where she is getting off your path in her life, and she can see the difference you make in her life. Kira doesn't have to be mean to herself anymore and punish herself for her mistakes that she made.

Lord, Kira has learned from them and she is going to use the lessons in making her a better person. Maybe she will be able to use what she has learned and share it with others. Maybe it will help just one person, if that all it's for.

Kira will be more loving, more kind, more trusting in you, Jesus. Every time we get to the word trust, Kira can just see where she was so ignorant and didn't realize she had put you equal to or in the same category as the men in her life who she didn't trust. Now Kira can see that and stop it.

Patty Scott

Thank you for showing Kira where she was going wrong even when she doesn't want to hear at times what she did wrong. Kira didn't think that's what it was about, and it was for her to take her problems to you and you were going to fix them for her. Lord, wasn't that what was in her head in the beginning?

Every day Kira can see her growth in her faith and belief in you. She never thought about this closeness before, but now she knows it's the most important thing in her life. You have never steered Kira wrong or hurt her. Even when she may not have always gotten her way, you never hurt her. Your decisions and choices in her life have **always** been for the good. You make Kira whole; you complete her.

Let your face, Lord, shine upon her and give her peace.

She will hold onto your hand and you'll walk with her. She notices Lord, that you never go ahead of her or behind her; you always walk by her side. When you look down at her, there is always a smile on your face and a twinkle in your eyes. It's like you truly enjoy the time with Kira. You never rush her along the way and tell her to hurry up.

A lot of people want and need the time and special moments alone with God, where it's only them. No matter what they must face each day: trust you!!

Having Coffee with the Special One

Kira needs to let you in and keep you with her.

Get away from the negative and stay in <u>God's</u> peace.

You always give us choices Lord, you never force us ......The free will thing, well that doesn't always work so well. (Chuckle)

Kira's not sure what you're trying to tell her today. You're teaching her a difficult lesson that only she can learn through hardship.

Lord, Kira grew up poor. When they lived in Casper, they struggled. When they lived in Denver, they struggled and basically, they were poor. When they lived in California, they weren't any better off. Maybe you're not talking about financial? Why does she automatically think it's financial? Kira knows she can live without money if she must, so that's not what she thinks you're trying to show her.

Kira does know that when she turns away or let's go of your hand, her life is in shambles. Lord, even in bad times she wants to stay close to you. Kira wants to hang on to your love for her and your hand to walk along that sandy beach with you, Lord. She wants to throw those pebbles in the water, watch them skip along the top and the water ripple a little. It's so calm and so peaceful.

Patty Scott

Water is very peaceful to Kira. That's why she can sit by the pool for hours and just relax when she takes time to do it. Kira knows that whatever she must face she doesn't have to do it alone. Lord, you're going to get her through whatever it is. Kira will keep her trust in you, and you Lord, have and will do right by her, even when it's a hard lesson she has to learn. Kira also must remember that it isn't always her that needs to learn the lesson, maybe it's someone around her or is involved with the situation that needs to learn something. Lord, you trust her to get through what you're trying to teach someone else.

Lord, Kira knows she had turned away from you before, but now she is getting to the point where she really knows that she needs you in her life, and she really wants you there. Kira understands more now that she won't always win in life. God, she just doesn't want to lose the closeness with you.

Kira will hang on and hold your hand no matter what happens. She knows now that the result is your choice not hers, and you're not going to tell her how it's going to end, no matter how much she pushes you. It isn't going to happen!

Lord, you're the peace, the joy, and the light! "I am the way, says the Lord!"

Having Coffee with the Special One

Lord, thank you for giving examples so Kira can utterly understand what you're showing her. Drawing her a picture really helps her understand what you're trying to tell her, so she can see the difference how she was and how she should be.

Kira loves to see and hear people laugh. Yesterday she was reminded why people like to be around her because they laugh together.

Lord, thank you for yesterday. She was hurting. Please help her heal.

That's what makes Kira happy too, "Lord, how long has it been?" What was it about the move and the change? Kira lost touch with you. She let go of your time together, but now you're giving back to her and bringing her back. (The good parts, right?) (Chuckle) She forgot what was important! Planning and planning and not paying attention. Losing herself each day, it was just slipping away.

At times, Lord, Kira felt like she had nothing to give you, but then she'd remember, it's her you want. You want her love, her trust, and her faith in you. That she can give to you so freely. Kira is sorry she forgot this important fact. When we are right with God all things just fall into place.

Kira didn't give herself time to mourn the loss of her friends. Earl and Herb meant a lot to her Lord.

She looked at them as mentors. Kira respected them, (even though at times, she thought they were wrong.) Kira should have really asked Herb questions. Lord, he did things differently, but she wasn't sure if it was wrong, it was just different. He was well loved and respected. Earl was (oh man, Kira really respected him) probably one of the best attorneys she ever met (until Rob) and he was one of the most compassionate men she ever met.

Kira is sure they weren't that way when they were younger, so she is glad she met them when she did. Earl and Herb were both honest men. They were both so down to earth, it just hit Kira they didn't have anything that they had to prove to anyone because God mattered most to them. Kira knows Earl was struggling the last year and a half of his life. She just didn't know how bad it was for Earl. Kira knew it was a rare form of cancer related to exposure to agent orange. Kira didn't understand until it was too late.

Lord, Kira respected these two men because of how much they loved their families and they trusted you. They helped Kira. How could she have questioned their integrity, even for a split second. She shouldn't have done that. Everything always proved out so why does this industry make you so untrusting? Hope this stays in the rolodex of her mind, so she doesn't ever do that again. These relationships were too important, and she misses them.

Having Coffee with the Special One

Kira is going back to being like a child: she listens and learns, stops thinking that she knows it all, and doesn't believe her way is the only way. Kira can still learn and has opened herself up to you.

Kira can't shut everyone out; she just wants to shut out evil and wrong. The truth always must come out and shine right or wrong, but it must come out.

Some of the struggles Kira was having she discussed with the Lord.

She feels like her nerves are raw. Kira is emotionally exhausted.

Kira knows everything she has buried has to come out, and she knows it's hard to face a lot of it. Yes, Lord, some of it she was ashamed of; thank you for forgiving her. Kira knows that the truth always comes out and it's what sets you free. You know someone told her that they liked how she was such a strong person. In fact, it was three different people who told her that, and it was you, Lord, who gave her the courage and strength, and the attitude that she can do all things through you, who strengthens her.

Where did she go wrong, to where people were getting upset? Why does Kira always take on the mistakes of others and think she is the one that has control over what others do?

This is something else that Kira needs to ask your help on. These things in her life that are just haunting her, they need to be resolved. Kira knows she can't tell you when to act on them, or when to finalize them. She just hopes that she wasn't lied to in the beginning and she is really doing as you want her to do. Kira will be so glad when it's all over and she can really talk about it and tell others, so it doesn't happen to them. Hopefully one day Kira can laugh about it, that would be nice wouldn't it?

Lord, when Kira gets drained like this, she is fearful in some ways that she is going to go back to the old her and lose what you have worked so hard to fix in her. When she feels like this, she reads more of the Bible and know you keep telling her not to give up or give in.

Your spirit dances in Kira's eyes, Lord, Kira gets to see it every single day, and she doesn't want to lose that either. She loves seeing that in her eyes!! Lean on me when you're not strong.... sometimes that song comes in Kira's head and she thinks of you.

Kira has got to get emotionally strong again and build on what you have done for her.

Lord, you're showing Kira that her weakness is where she draws on you and your strength. Where

Having Coffee with the Special One

you hold her up and keep her moving on. All she must do is ask in your name, seek ye shall find, knock and the door will open. You really do that for us. Kira is finding out it really is true, and it does happen.

By the way, Kira changed her mind on the office rental deal. She realized you had other plans for that and is glad that she didn't lease it out. It was another blessing in disguise, and Kira realized maybe that wasn't your intent for the extra spaces but thank you for finding at least someone that would rent just an office space from them. That helps with the cost of utilities.

Another thing that has been bothering Kira is, that Lord, society is pushing you out of schools, our children are being harmed by people that want to hurt them, they are trying to remove You from our money. Our world was created by you and while we can't stop what is happening, we don't have to go along with it.

Kira has found for sure that she is in your presence daily. Lord, you saved <u>her</u>!! You have been with Kira every single step of the way. She knows that because there is so much proof of you being there. Lord, Kira can feel you inside and around her, through that soft breath of air, the clouds that form, or the peace when it's a storm in her life. There are just so many times that Kira can't understand how others just don't believe it's you and give you credit. In some ways she can understand it because she was there one time. But it didn't affect Kira as it does now to be so close to you and open to you and your love.

Lord, Kira knows that evil was messing with her, her life, and people around her. She was almost going to tell them they may not want to be around her, but then Kira realized that was a little dumb, so she didn't say anything.

You have been drawing her closer to you for several years. You sent Sheila to work for her, and to help make her a better person and make her whole. Lord, sorry to get off-path, but she just had a glimpse why does she think or want to have sort of a publishing company? Is that her will or yours??

Oh Lord, Kira wants to be on your path not the wrong one. Ideas like this go through her mind at different times, and Kira just isn't sure what you're trying to tell her. You delivered when Kira wanted her own tax practice, you'll deliver when and if there is something else you want her to do. It has been a few more years and Sheila did quit and moved on to something else. It didn't quite happen how Kira thought it would, but it happened, so Sheila had served her time there and did what you intended her to do. It just sort of shocked Kira how Sheila left and say what she said, but that's what it is. The tax industry is an incredibly stressful industry, so many deadlines and due dates. There is no forgiveness for mistakes, and if you cost a

Having Coffee with the Special One

client money, well they are not happy about that, so it makes it even harder to do your work. Thank you for the years you kept Sheila there and for staying when she was needed the most. Thank you, Lord, Kira is ever so grateful.

You know when we stop and take each day one moment at a time, we don't miss out on the little things, like a bird chirping, a child's smile, a cloud formation, or a shooting star. Life in general is so much more enjoyable when you take it one moment at a time.

Lord, Kira knows she is going to continue to have problems; she just doesn't want to allow them to mess with the newfound peace in her life. She doesn't want fear to set in and control her. Kira doesn't want to turn back into a bull and grab everything by the horns because she did that so often. In some ways Kira still does it and it just keeps biting her in the butt. When will the light bulb go off in her head on this one?

Lord, she wants to get through life with peace and laughter. Kira just pictured the spirit in her dancing and flittering here and there. Kira just doesn't want her problems to get her down or to overcome her. The peace that surpasses all understanding, keeps her heart and mind unto you, Jesus Christ.

Patty Scott

You know the song: what a friend we have in Jesus all our sins and griefs to bare, what a privilege to carry all our griefs to god in prayer. Aren't we so lucky to have a friend like him, one that never talks to others about us, or walks away from us? Instead he sits there, and he listens to us? What a privilege that's.

All these issues seem so small when you're with Kira. Lord, let's dance and laugh more. It's always so nice to be with friends and get to visit with them: the laughs, a nice dinner and nice fellowship that we get to share. When Kira doesn't get this time as often as she would like she misses it, and it makes her miss her family being around more.

Kira has had problems in the past with relationships. Sometimes she is sort of stand offish and acts like she doesn't have time for friendships. Kira thinks at times therefore people that aren't so strong in faith think Christians are arrogant.

Lord, we know we can rise above the problem with you helping us, so maybe at times we make people feel or think that we think we are better than them. But that's not what is going through our minds at all. ("Sorry, that may have been out of context here, but it just hit her")

It's like Kira at times when she is hurting so bad on the inside that she hangs on to you, Lord, for the strength to move, go on. At times she feels like she's walking on clouds and you, Lord, have lifted her up. She takes charge!! She won't let her

Having Coffee with the Special One

weakness show and allows your strength to shine through. Lord, Kira doesn't want to stifle you shining in her life, but people must know it's you shining, not her.

Now Kira sees how, where, and why it's so important to take small baby steps, so she doesn't rush through it. It has true meaning when Kira realizes you got her through it and there has been a change within her how she treats others and thinks of others.

One moment at a time and you, Lord, can't be rushed. (Chuckle) There is no way that you, Lord, will allow anyone to rush you because it's all in your time so that the lessons can really soak in and maybe Kira won't keep making the same mistakes. Kira knows that she's going to keep making them, she just doesn't want so many at once, and to let you help her with them. Maybe the lesson will stick with Kira so she can share with others or at least not make the same mistakes again.

"When there is doubt you cannot succeed." Kira has read that and said it over and over in her head. Yet there are times when she doubts herself and if there will be a resolution. The knowledge that you gave Kira, Lord, she sometimes can't process properly. When it comes from the heart, it's from you, Lord. She must keep that in mind. When it comes from the heart, it's from God.

You know in financial struggles; you learn so much about yourself. God, you really have so much more.

Kira's mom used to tell them when they were young that they may have been poor financially, but they were so rich in God's love.

That sticks with her and she thinks of it often. You really have so much more because they may have been poor financially, but they were so rich in "God's Love" and they were so blessed with God's love and protection.

She can't even begin to tell you how many ways they knew that God was there and protecting them. Kira now sees that they had so much more than some people ever have or have had!!

All things are blessings from the Lord, even the rough times in your life. We just must "Trust the Lord." We can do all things through "Christ" because he strengthens us. A person needs to slow down and put things in proper perspective and take time to be alone with God and enjoy the peace that "God" gives us. You can't feel the peace when you're rushing everywhere. This also bangs around in Kira's mind; how can he help her if she won't slow down to listen to him speak to her?

At church, the people have gotten her attention one way or another. Lord, they have helped Kira heal. They have made Kira realize how rough her compassion for people was. In fact, she isn't even sure if she ever had compassion in the first place. Looking back on how she raised her kids, Kira doesn't think that was a facet in her life. Not

Having Coffee with the Special One

something she is proud of; how does it even get there?

Facing all of this and going through this has been hard on Kira. Yet it has also been a blessing that she won't ever forget. Kira really does hope that she will be able to share her story, in a movie or somehow, because there are others that have been in the same place, if not worse, and they too need to know God, that you're there for them. It's not just Kira that you're there for all. It's all thanks to you, that you have given Kira your mercy and you have forgiven her too as she has been able to forgive others.

Forgive us our trespasses as we forgive those who have trespassed against us.

A whole new meaning. Kira truly does feel blessed, Lord, and even the trials and tribulations have been a blessing. It shows her that love truly is stronger than any other emotion. "Love wins." The love you have for us is like no other...............

You know, Lord, if Kira hadn't gone through these experiences, she doesn't think she would have been able to experience or have known what true love is.

Again: "What a friend we have in "Jesus," all our sins and griefs to bear, what a privilege we often forfeit, when we don't take them to you, Lord, in prayer.

You turn the pain and sorrow into great blessings!!

Look at the friends Kira has, the love she has, the people that care about her.... never would she have thought she could be in a place as to where she is right now!!

You opened her heart and soul up to you, and that opened the doors to others.

Lord, you're opening the skies for Kira as she has been watching and learning.

You're showing her the way and you're holding her hand.

Whatever happens, Kira will get through it; she knows that now.

Whatever the result is, Kira knows you're there for her and with her.

Lord, is this where you're telling Kira that she needs to make the proper choices. She cannot get so busy and forget about you, Lord, or try to make the resolution happen faster. Kira is enjoying spending this time with you, and she hopes that

Having Coffee with the Special One

she continues to do it. She really doesn't want to give it up this close intimate relationship with you.

Kira doesn't think that a person can really understand it until they themselves go through it with you and that this time with you is so important. Another interesting thing that was pointed out to Kira was she and her younger sister Dawn were driving home to visit their mom for her birthday, Dawn told Kira that 'Lead us not into temptation but deliver us from evil" in the Lord's prayer, well that was for "us" not for "you": we are asking you to keep us from evil temptations and from doing wrong.

Kira never really thought about it before, and now that Dawn has pointed that out to her, she thinks of that often. We are asking you to basically keep us out of trouble. It's just another way that you help us in our lives. It's interesting too, Kira noticed that a person can't really say the Lord's prayer unless their heart is clean, and they realize what they are saying it. That was another thing that she is noticing in herself, too, that when she says it, it really has true meaning to her, it just isn't the words, it's the meaning behind it, and who she is talking to when she says it.

It's a good thing that Kira found the Christian Rock station to listen to, or she was going to have to get some more gospel CDs because she was wearing out the ones she had. Kira loved listening to "Souled Out". She must admit, now though that she has found the radio station and gone to some other concerts, Kira has sort of changed who she listens to most of the time. Sorry to say that, but Kira just realized that it's been a while since she listened to them. Wow, she will have to get their CD out again.

You know, Lord, Kira prays for them to continue spreading the gospel through their music. She also prays for the new ones that she listens to on the station along with "Souled Out". You gave all of them their great voices, and they surely know it. They praise you, Lord, so much in their music. Kira is just in awe at it, especially the male vocalists because they put so much heart and soul into their music. You blessed them in that way.

Kira knows she has got to get her priorities straight and in line with what you want of her. Honestly, Lord, will she know that it's your will and not hers? Kira has a hard time deciphering this at times, so will you help her to know which is the right way, and to know it really is what you want of her to do?

Lord, on one trip Kira could have witnessed to someone, yet she messed it up!! She has got to learn to be more prepared to witness to others. You know you do hold the doors open when it's something that you want Kira to do. Maybe Kira did what she was supposed to and that's all you wanted from her. Maybe it was someone else that was going to witness to that person, at the time.

Let your light shine upon me and through me and give me strength. We will get through this with the

Having Coffee with the Special One

help of God. All the trials and tribulations that are going on in Kira's life, it just seems at times it won't ever end, yet she knows it will, she just doesn't know when. It's all in your timing not hers, it's out of her control. Kira just must keep that in her mind and rise above them.

Kira may be cheating some on the lesson plan that she is going through right now with you, Lord, because she is a person that needs to know why. It helps Kira understand better what she is going through, and it helps her hang on to You and Your peace.

You know that she has emotionally dark days. Kira thinks maybe that's one of the reasons she got so hardened in the past. Kira didn't know how to weather the storm, so she would clam up. You know Kira didn't want to break down and cry, but now she knows it isn't a bad weakness in her, it makes her human, it makes her alive and it cleans her soul.

Yet it's hard for Kira to let go and let it flow. She just may have done so much damage to herself, it may not come. Waiting for the right time and the right place, maybe there won't be one. She kept herself so busy in the past that she couldn't feel; she didn't want to think about it or what she was doing to herself. Kira doesn't want to be one of those "oh poor me" people.

Thank you, Lord, for pointing things out to her, so Kira gets a better understanding. You explain it to where she can understand it and it means something to her.

Lord, Kira has become more peaceful, and calm. Somedays Kira just wants you to know that she is noticing it, and that you're doing that for her. Kira thanks you for that, Lord.

You know Kira's way of handling things, was just wearing her out, draining her. She is so glad that she wants to get things done your way because that's the right way. Your way is so much better, and carries no guilt, no regrets, and no ill feelings. You're helping her so much!!

Lord, Kira is catching the small stuff and learning to understand. You're opening doors up to her in the good areas you're bringing her back, oh, and man!! The bubbling joy inside her. Lord, Kira loves the feel of your peace and your working in her. It's funny when she wakes up sometimes in the morning, Kira can just picture little men running from one side to the next with their hammers and chisels, breaking through all the negative and getting it out. You work so hard for others.

Their youngest son talks to Kira differently and now she will listen to him. He is so mature now; it makes sense to her. Lord, though she missed some

Having Coffee with the Special One

of what he was saying to her, he shared his plans. With Your guidance, Lord, you'll lead his way; help him follow through what you want for him. He must finish what he starts. Unless it's you changing his ways. Keep your peace to weather the storm. It's all in your time, not theirs. Kira needs to hold on to your hand tight.

"Lord, you're still by her side." Thank you for not leaving. Just another way you're showing Kira you're there.

Lord, you're what is best for Kira.

Sometimes Kira still messes up with having a conversation with someone. She understands there is a time and a place for a conversation, but Kira must pick the right time and the right place.

What happens is what she says just comes out—with no filter—and in the process she ends up hurting the person who is with her. Lord, please help Kira with her filters so she doesn't embarrass others.

You have blessed Kira with the opportunities to sit and visit about you with others. Again, all she needs to say is "help me Jesus", so that she doesn't open her mouth and insert her foot. It's been a long time since she just sat and listened to someone talk; but she's getting to do that these days, and she's showing an interest in them. Kira has had to slow down to stop and listen to others.

Man...all Kira was doing was pushing everyone away and digging her hole deeper. Wow...all people want is to know they mean something to you, and they want someone to listen.

Kira used to be a good listener. She used to love to just listen to what people had to say and have them share their stories. No wonder Kira felt so alone: she was shutting everyone out including even You, Lord, in a way.

Kira was talking to you—telling you all about it—but as she said several times, she wasn't listening.

Lord, forgive me for the stupid things I have done wrong, Kira prays.

Pray.

Prayer is the way to help Kira and change her destructive thoughts to good ones, Lord. You use the minister at her church and others to tell her to get away from and release the negative thoughts.

Kira couldn't quite understand all the negativity and why she was surrounded by it. She kept running things through her head. Kira was buried in negative thoughts and so miserable. She allowed

Having Coffee with the Special One

people to take her joy and bubbliness away. Kira was turning into someone she didn't even like.

It's so nice to be able to think of the true way that Kira feels about you, Lord, and she still is in awe how you care about her. It was you that she was missing all along: she was missing her relationship with you, Lord. Kira wasn't letting you in yet you're the love, the warmth and the peace she was missing. "The Peace."

Kira can't fight all the battles: there are too many. They wear her down. She wants to know what's important to you, Lord, not the rest of the world. "Love, Honor, Cherish." Forgive and forgiveness.

Kira should have turned to you rather than worked so much. She thought she was doing the right thing by working all the time because it kept her out of bars, but not out of trouble. Kira buried her head in the sand. It sure was far too long that she did it wasn't it Lord? Where did it get her?

Kira couldn't understand why she was involved in so many arguments. There were just too many arguments partly because she and the other person just didn't know how to communicate with each other. Toss in stubbornness and the person not being around.... then how can anything get resolved? It's hard.

Lord, a thought just occurred to Kira. Everything in her life and the lives of others is accomplished on your time and you do give them choices. You're very patient with everyone and slow to anger. You don't force them or try to control them.

Lord, you have been in Kira's life and heart all along. You've allowed Kira to do what she did so she could really learn and see the difference her life is when she tries to control it versus when she gives it to you. Kira has learned there is a big difference. Kira is incredibly lucky and very blessed by you to be able to see the signs, hear your words, and see you.

Some of the lessons have been extremely hard ones that Kira has had to learn from. Kira hopes and prays that she doesn't let go of you again. Each time Kira did let you go, you safely took her back. And each time Kira has gone through a life-threatening experience, you've watched over and protected her. Kira hopes she doesn't run off her guardian angel.

Wear your peace with regal dignity. What an awesome way to show it to us and in a way, let us feel like royalty. Let us shine; let it shine.

The peace that surpasses all understanding, keep our hearts and minds unto you, Jesus Christ. Kira is truly beginning to understand in more depth, "the Father, the Son, and the Holy Spirit."

Three in one. It all makes sense to her.

She doesn't want to let go of or give up her time with you, Lord, Kira looks forward to spending this

Having Coffee with the Special One

time with you each day. Yes... as you say, she "enjoys the treasure hunts." It's <u>fun</u>!!

Kira used to be ashamed of her life and the mistakes she made, but now she really knows they all happened for a reason. All along, Lord, you have been with Kira, and carried her through her trials and tribulations. Man, she did some dumb stuff. You forgave her and you still loved her. "Unconditional Love." "True Unconditional Love."

You know how much you as a mother loves her child..."no matter <u>what</u>!!" Well, that's not even one tenth of how God loves us. He forgives us for the things we do wrong or dumb things. It only makes sense that we should not hang onto the hurt and pain caused by our errors. That's not what Jesus wants of us.

We need to love and forgive those who have hurt us as God has forgiven us for us hurting Him. He died to save us from sin, not because we are perfect or will be (because we aren't yet.) Sometimes we don't behave in the way God wants us to or listen to him. Kira can't blame God for what she does wrong or what someone she knows does wrong, it's not God's fault. But He does allow the experience to happen, to see how she will handle it, and, for her to ask for His guidance and help.

We all have free will. God doesn't push us, but he will nudge us and talk to us. He lets us know he's there, and he will lead us and guide us when we ask and when we let him. Kira also has realized and accepts God's guidance.

God the Father, the Son, and the Holy Ghost, who so ever believeth in Him shall not perish, but have everlasting life ....

Stand tall and stand proud, for God is your shield of armor.

He is your Savior and your Protector. No one can destroy you.

Kira was the one that was forgetting about God's love for her.

Lord, Kira wants to listen to You, as you're her guide. Who can be against you when I am with you says the "Lord?" No one really.........

"For nothing is impossible with God."

Lord, Kira isn't wanting your time together to end or be over. She loves every second she gets to be with you and when her day doesn't get in the way. There is nothing comparable to the peace that you give her. When Kira has your peace, she wonders how she ever lived without it. Not very well, that's for sure. You know her so well, Jesus. She is just so excited about what you're teaching her and letting her see. In a way that's wisdom, isn't it?

Having Coffee with the Special One

Kira wants to share it with the world. She really wants to shout it out at the top of her lungs!

Jesus, you have saved Kira more times than she had thought about until now.

Kira turned sixty-four last fall. Yet it's taken her this long to truly trust you and thank you for all that you have done for her and are still doing for her. She's a late bloomer, God?

Kira knows so many people who are fighting cancer in one way, shape, or form. Lord, they are your special people too. Kira loves them and thanks you for bringing them into her life. At first, she was having a really hard time with facing it. Kira cares about them and it hurt so bad to see someone she cared about or heard about having to go through this. Then you changed Kira's attitude and the way she was looking at it. They are a blessing to her because she gets the chance to get to know them and she gets to tell them about your love and your peace. They get to share you, Jesus Christ. They get to share your love and to see the miracles of your love.

Do not be afraid for I am with you, says the Lord. It's all about your love and your divine power, to heal, to keep them safe, to let them know you're with them every step of the way. Hang on to your hand tight; you're with us.

I am sorry, Lord, when I was complaining. Maybe it was that Kira was just so excited because she wanted to get things done. She doesn't want to let you down or forget to share your word. There are times when Kira feels she's letting you down and she doesn't want to. It's ok for her not to be perfect and let go of her pride.

Kira can't mention the names of other people that she can see you're working in their lives too.

Lord, Kira hopes they will share, and she hopes they recognize it as all from you. They may not see it either until later in their life. It took Kira a while to see it, and she doesn't think she has seen it all yet either. Kira knows there is more to come, and eventually you'll show her all of it.

This is about you and how you're working in her life.

This is about your time together.

This is about the miracles and wonders you're giving to her and helping her through.

This is about you, Lord, all your glory and peace, and rebuilding relationships.

Trust in the Lord, with all your heart. Lean not on your own understanding and acknowledge him in all your ways. He will lead your path straight.

Having Coffee with the Special One

Lord, in so many aspects of Kira's life this all means the same. Yet, when "a light bulb goes off in her head" and she sees it differently, it gives her new meaning.

Here is another area in her life Kira needs to trust you fully and completely. Deadlines and due dates have been controlling her life so much in the past, that Kira has forgotten that you were the one in control, not the deadlines and due dates. Kira put way, way too much importance on tax season and deadlines and due dates, just too much.

God, Kira let the deadlines and due dates have power and control over her, but you set her free once she said she was sorry, and you forgave her.

Kira really did push you, Lord, out of her life or she just got her priorities in the wrong place. Lord, when Kira did that, nothing was going right. There were so many negative forces attacking her. All Kira had to do was stop and listen to you and get back to the basics of life: Love, honor, and cherish you, Lord, and put you first in her life. Geez, Kira was out of control—her life was out of control—until the day you saved her, and you got her back on track!

Lord, you saved Kira more than once during her life. You love Kira enough to give her a second chance. You could have taken her that day when she had her wreck — really any of them—and you didn't.

Patty Scott

Kira can tell it's time to start talking about that day. Kira's known all along that she can't keep it balled up inside her. She needs to talk about it—get it out—so it doesn't haunt her anymore.

Kira said, I promise to tell others, so they know you don't ever let us go. You stay by our sides always. Six vehicles and at least twelve people. Lord, you saved us all that day.

Kira says as she's sharing time with you, Lord, "Give me a little more time and I will talk about that day and share it with others."

Lord, it was so close. One more hit and Kira would have been gone.

Lord, you knew that. You had it all planned to the very last second. But you saved her!!

Help Kira glorify your name.

Kira wants to share what you have done for her in her life and helped her to live. You continue to help her in addition to healing all the scars that have been forming and tearing down the walls that have been building up.

Jesus, Kira loves you and she thanks you even for the bad times. If Kira didn't have the bad times,

Having Coffee with the Special One

then she wouldn't appreciate the love and the care you give her and do to heal her.

Lord, it's your miracles. It's by your hand that Kira is saved. You could have taken her away that day, but you saved her.

Kira wants to share the news with the world so they know you're there and we all need to hold on tight to your promise, "For who so ever believe in you shall be saved," and have everlasting eternal life with you, Lord, in Heaven. We are on the road to you. You'll lead us and give us the right path. All we must do is ask...and we shall receive. Our joy will be complete.

Kira thought, Lord, you don't lie.

What is it about us that the moments that inspire us and give us good feelings, we doubt you, Lord, or back away from you?

In the past Kira acted like she didn't need you because she had the attitude that she could do it herself. She was the one that put herself in that box....and she apologizes Lord, because now she's aware she did that to you.

Kira closed herself off from everyone and everything. How many times was she told by Lynn or David or someone else that she had this wall around her, and a person could only get so close to her?

Patty Scott

Lord, thank you for cleansing Kira and giving her a clean heart. Each day she stops and thinks about what you have done for her. Kira can see just how much you have opened her up. It's also opened her eyes where Kira can see in others around her that they too need to let you in too. Just by the change in Kira is she able to see what others were saying to her. Now she understands what she didn't see before.

You have renewed Kira's spirit and refreshed her soul. Opening to others and letting them in has allowed Kira to see just how much love she really does get from others. For example: the beautiful job that Raelee did when she painted the walls and the artwork that was hung in the office. She did it all out of love and caring. Raelee is so talented Lord, thank you for that gift too.

Kira can see all around her that you're working in her family members' lives and bringing them all back together as a better family. They're more respectful, more caring, and more loving of each other.

Lord, you have given Kira back the loving feelings as you're teaching her compassion. Compassion is something either she lost a long time ago—or she is just now learning it? Kira still needs to hang on to it and learn more, but at least she knows now what you mean when you say to be compassionate.

Kira thanks you, Lord, for the time they have together. Even in the way you so gracefully,

Having Coffee with the Special One

carefully planned it all so Kira could slow down and spend this time with you.

Lord, Kira is fully aware that you pick every second out, and you carefully plan just how you want things to turn out. You have a way to make everything right even when there is some damage that needs to be repaired. Lord, you know how to keep everyone safe and alive.

Kira thinks about sayings she's seen on peoples' t-shirts. It's a way for you, Lord, to let her know you're there. Even in these small ways.... Glory to God in The Highest!

Lord, you know that sometimes the only way to get our attention is to knock us on the head and say hey!!! wake up, it's time to come back to what is right.

Kira has realized that sometimes she doesn't—or didn't—realize she was so bad off, until she wasn't anymore. Thank you for the blessings you gave Kira the day she opened to you again and let you in.

Lord, Kira knows in her heart and soul you were there, and you saved her each time in her life. Everything she has belongs to you and Kira is just a caretaker of your glorious gifts.

Even in her darkest days you were and are with her. You carried Kira every step of the way. You gave her peace, and Lord, you got her over each steppingstone she needed to cross. With the people you have put in Kira's path and the love and care that they have given her and showed her, it's amazing—and kind of sad—that she shut that out too. When Kira was all closed off, she had to let love in to be able to give it back again and to accept it.

Yes, Kira can see the old going away, and in some ways, it's a smooth transition. She has noticed that when she let go and stopped fighting the change was more peaceful. Kira guesses in a way now she can see the old person in her had to die, so that she would learn that she could live. It makes sense now that she can see it and has been a part in it. Kira doesn't know if she can explain it well enough but there truly is a difference in her how she feels on the inside, and how she reacts to somethings. It's so different than it was a few years ago.

Lord, the inspiration and the hope you give Kira are such refreshing feelings inside her!!

You're helping Kira come to life again. You give her hope. You give her <u>life</u>!

And yes, Lord, it's challenging because Kira is living on the edge with you. Walking on a tight rope. Kira does get those fleeting moments of hesitation and, yes <u>doubt</u>! But when Kira listens to you and brings her focus back to you, your love for

Having Coffee with the Special One

her then shines through her and gives Kira the peace that she needs to hang on to.

"Do not be afraid, for I am with you says the Lord,"

Doesn't that tell you a lot? Doesn't that let you know that he will fulfill his promise to us? Do not be afraid to open and let love in.

Now Kira knows why in the Bible it says to love one another, it really is what is important and what makes a difference in everyone's life. When you lose love, you don't even know what happened to take it away, yet you can pinpoint every moment if you think about it. When you let go then you realize that it really doesn't matter what was done in the first place. Why did you allow love to be taken away from you in the first place?

Kira can see how much of a change you have made in her. She also sees where she went wrong. Kira hopes that she remembers that you're the hope and the salvation within her.

She is beginning to understand the meaning of "open my eyes unto you, Jesus Christ, help me to see what you have placed in my day!" Help Kira to look for your presence and treasures in each day of her life, and know it comes from you.

As Kira finds your presence the treasures each day, she can talk more freely about you to others and share the joy that you have given her. It isn't that Kira thinks she has to, but she feels that she wants to. She wants to share the love you have given to her, and in that way, Kira is trying to watch and see how she gets to talk with the ones who are around her. Just yesterday Kira had a conversation with Nancy, and was able to share you with her, and being at peace while doing so.

Lord, it's our attitude towards our circumstances that makes the difference. If we let it tear us up, then it will. If we don't and we look to you as you ask us or instruct us to do, then.... well they can't tear us up.

When Kira opens and shares things with people, she gets so animated, and passionate about how she feels. Kira needs to know the difference between bemoaning and being honest and passionate. Kira doesn't sound like a whiner or negative about what happens, when it isn't the way she thinks it should go.

There are times like yesterday when Kira got all emotional. Yes, Lord, Kira feels as though she is on an emotional roller coaster at times. Kira was sort of surprised to hear that the judge in a case where two people were badly injured in their car when a piece of metal flew into their windshield ruled that the insurance company wasn't or didn't have to pay some sort of settlement to them. It's her understanding; the female was seriously hurt.

Having Coffee with the Special One

Then it hit Kira and she remembered that you're in total control of our lives. It's not up to us to be the judge, and we are not to question the outcome. As you told Kira before, it's not up to her who you bless, how you choose to bless them or when you choose to bless them.

It's your will not ours.

Kira wants so badly to share her stories with people, but she doesn't want it to sound like she is preaching.

Lord, let your words come into my heart and soul, so that I may say what you want me to say. It's your will not mine, so I may get off track at times. When I get off track, pull me back to what you think is important to share with others, and what you want them to hear.

Lord, Kira wants to tell the story of Jesus and his love, and how each day she learns just how deep that love is for all, and how deep it is for her.

Even when Kira sleeps it's better, and she wakes up with you on her mind. She knows that you're running around working so hard to make her the person you want her to become.

Lord, in your mercy hear my prayer, help Kira to stay on track, and stay in your love. There are so many areas in her life and in the lives around her where she can see you working; you're answering her prayers...she can see that you are.

Lord, you're healing so many that are so close to her. Kira doesn't think they realize how nice it was to have someone take care of them when they couldn't do it for themselves.

There are very few times in Kira's life that someone else took care of her, but as she looks back, she really wouldn't ever let anyone take care of her. Each time Tim tried to take care of her when she was sick, she just didn't appreciate it as she should have. Now Kira sees where she shut people out. Not that others wouldn't try to help her, she wouldn't let them, just as she wouldn't let you in. On top of that, Kira wasn't someone who would stay down.

Remember when Kira was young, and she had the measles and the mumps? She just wouldn't stay in bed and rest because Kira didn't want to miss out on anything in life. Now Kira knows how important it is to allow your body to heal and resting allows us the privilege time with you.

Kira used to blame others for not wanting to help, but how could she do that when it was her that she wouldn't let them? Is this where you're not to judge others until you pull the log out of your own eyes? Kira blamed others where she was the one at fault. Lord, it started at such a young age in her, why wouldn't she let others help her?

Having Coffee with the Special One

Lord, Kira doesn't think she ever had this close or intimate of a relationship with you.

"Wow!" she has really missed out on something special. Kira is thankful to be able to enjoy this opportunity now!!

Thank you for spending this time with her. Lord, we all need this with you. Even today you still make the time for her, after all this time. <u>You're the "I am the Almighty."</u> You're in Kira's heart and soul. Kira is happy to be surrounded by God fearing people who love, believe in, and trust you, Lord.

<u>No matter what Lord, I trust you Jesus.</u>

As Kira reflects on how she is now she sees how, Lord, you're making her life better.

You've given her so much more than anyone has ever taken from her physically, emotionally, and intellectually (even though everyone around her thinks she is losing it.) You became her friend; someone Kira can talk to Lord, about anything, no matter what. You're on her side. With you by her side, then who can be against her? You're her strength and her courage to continue on and move forward in this life.

Patty Scott

It came to Kira last night, that it doesn't matter what others say about her. You're with her and those that love her and care about her; well, it just won't matter. If someone wants to hurt you or a person, they will find a way to do so.

Lord, Kira can't wait until she can get this debt she has paid off, because sometimes it just overwhelms her, and she gets concerned. She doesn't want to cheat anyone, even as you say in the Bible that sticks with her. Kira doesn't want cheat her workers. She wants to make sure that she can keep them employed and keep paying them. Kira remembers too, what it was like when she worked for someone, and she couldn't cash her pay checks. Kira doesn't ever want that to happen with someone that works for her company.

Kira knows that you'll help her, guide her and pave the way. You always did in the past, and you always will in the future. She doesn't have to worry, Lord, because she knows you're protecting them and keeping them from harm. You're keeping the negative away, and out of Kira's thoughts. Your shield is all around Kira. She prays to be the good steward of what you have given her.

Heaven is her home, here on earth is just temporary. Life is a journey not a destination. For however many years you allow Kira to be here on earth, she must remember that life here on earth is short. It goes by quickly so she must do the most she can and do what she can about sharing your word and your love while she is here.

Having Coffee with the Special One

"For God so loved us all that he gave his only begotten son to die for us, that who so ever believeth in him shall not perish and have everlasting life."

So, when Kira gets down or feels herself sagging or having dark thoughts, all she must do is remember you're there, Lord, holding her hand. "Kira has to hang on tight and not let go."

You'll get her through it. You're leading the way. You're the way, the truth, and the light. Every cloud does have that silver lining. Lord, you shine through in all your glory.

Listen to the Lord, and what he is saying. He will not let you go or lead you astray. He gives you a better life than you can give yourself.

"Lead the way Lord."

"Do not be afraid for I am with you says the Lord."

Kira doesn't know how many times she has said it, or will say it, but when it comes from the heart, it's the Lord. That's how you know God is with you, one of the ways. You or I get these warm, funny feelings; that's when God is in us. We have his peace.

When I trust Jesus as my life works. He is cleaning out all the garbage I hung on to. I am getting to change my perspective and see things through God's eyes. I am looking at things differently.

Jesus was my first true love. He reminded Kira of that. It's nice to remember it too; he is our first love. Kira is learning that what God does in her life and with her life, <u>it works</u>? She just must let him do his work and stop trying to block him or take it from him.

"God has given her a better life than she could have asked for; that she sees daily and knows it comes from him."

Good morning, Lord. How are you today?

As Kira wakes up and says: I thank you for the visions and the spark you give me. Lord, you're talking to me in so many ways and showing me that you're there. The angel and the eagle were awesome; I received so much peace and warmth from that.

You knew how Kira felt about men but you found or made a way to get into her days and talk to her so she would fully trust you. You're the Almighty; you don't let her down.

You know she never really gave much thought to what you had to go through for her. Kira is finding that she has to say she is sorry for a lot. She just

Having Coffee with the Special One

never really thought about how she was acting or what she was doing was so wrong all .... not all of it. Lord, you have enlightened Kira and have changed her.

Ever since Kira saw the Passion of Christ, Kira realized what you had to go through for her and others in her life. She is sorry that she didn't let that sink in a little more. Even at that time it impressed her greatly, but now Kira sees more of what you went through to show us your compassion and love for us.

Lord, Kira isn't comparing you to a human being because there's no way that she can. But she does see what you went through for her. You endured so much for us all. You really do love us and stay with us; you hold on to us.

You know there are—and were—times in Kira's life that no matter what she tried to do the first thing out of someone's mouth was "you can't do that" or "you're not good enough" or something like that. It was almost always on a negative note. Yet look at what you have done in Kira's life; you kept her alive when she was stupid and did things she shouldn't have, you gave her the ability to start up and work in her practice, and people told her she couldn't write, yet here she is writing.

It's a good thing you have been there for Kira because sometimes life isn't kind.

No one should doubt. Don't give up on your dreams, you have no idea when they may turn out or what life will hand you when you do push forward in them. Who or what is success anyway?

To Kira it's just being able to start something and finish it—whether someone else thinks it's a success or not—she tried it and completed it! To Kira that may have to be good enough at times. How else would someone know if they could do something or not unless they tried themselves.

Which is kind of funny that everyone who tells her she can't do it, well most of them haven't even tried themselves. So, what does it matter anyway?

Just a thought.

Lord, Kira's hopes of sharing what you're going through with her will continue. Kira hopes by opening to you that she will be able to tell others what you have done for her in her life, without being repetitious on what she has learned.

Kira loves this quality time that she is getting to have with you, Lord.

Lord, help Kira with her memory.

Help Kira to stop allowing stress to take over.

Having Coffee with the Special One

Help Kira to slow down so that she isn't so forgetful.

Lord, please help her with her ADD.

Jesus, Kira knows it's hard to stay focused, but it does help for her to stop and think of you, and say: "Help me Lord, Jesus,". This is particularly important to her.

She needs to remember to say especially in her line of work, "Jesus help me......"

Kira can see where in the past she didn't properly take the time needed to build this relationship with you, and honestly until now, she didn't know that she could even be this close to you. Kira is just amazed how much of a friend you really are to her, and how much she depends on you to help her and be there for her. Even when Kira may miss a few days, when she comes back you there, and you just pick up where they left off without asking questions or criticisms. You're kind and loving, and you just know.

There are days when what you say Lord, makes sense and there are days where Kira really doesn't understand. There it goes. She lost the connection to you for a second there.

You're the Alpha and the Omega.

Lord, you're showing Kira where being humble is not a weakness or a shortage, and where it really is important that she can see that in others and how it has helped her to deal with people.

Being humble is a softer and better way to approach people. They will be a little more open to you and talk more freely. They will be so........ friendly. Kira sees that other people's needs are just as important as hers, or even more so.

Lord, you got Kira through the hard time when she and her husband, Tim, were separated. When they were fighting like cats and dogs you didn't give up on them, nor did they. Instead they just had to get through it together but Lord, you helped Kira.... you helped them.

There was a time when Kira lost trust and respect for Tim. She also thinks he felt the same. They just lost what was important to them. Lord, you fixed the brokenness, and the separation was the best thing for them both. They had to decide if—and see—they really did love each other, and if they wanted each other.

Now Kira knows what it means to love as you have never been hurt. Once you forgive the other person and you forgive yourself, it really doesn't matter what was done in the first place. Not when you truly forgive. You don't forget but you do forgive, and the anger dissipates and goes away.

Lord, Kira does know she let Tim down too. Marriage is a two-way street because there are two in the marriage. In some ways both spouses are at

Having Coffee with the Special One

fault when things don't go right. No one needs to understand that maybe a couple—or individual—is having a hard time because there are things that they need to deal with within themselves.

Sometimes what a person is dealing with can't be seen because it's in the inside, and it's hard for them to let it out or talk about it. Don't condone the wrong that was done, but it does help to try to understand it. Kira just needed to know and understand how to be with him, and how to be the respectful wife without feeling like he was trying to control her. Or was it still the trusting him that she was missing?

This is something that Kira learned: you can't really have a relationship with anyone if there isn't trust there. Even with you, Lord, Kira had to learn that she could trust you and she did put her trust in you. What a big difference that made in her relationship with you. Why would she think it would be any different?

Kira trusts you, Jesus ....

Yes, Lord, Kira knows that she can't compare you to others, but it sure helps to understand what you're trying to tell her, and it makes things clearer for her. Which leads her to another matter or subject....

Patty Scott

You are what you are, and you are who you are. You're the Almighty powerful Lord. You're the great I am.

It's what it is Lord.

Kira realized that it really doesn't matter in some way that when she went astray and you want her back, you make a way for her to get back to you. There is really nothing that can get in your way or stop you from doing what you want. Yet you do this in the gentlest way.

Lord, even in the car wreck, Kira felt your presence and your peace. You could have taken her away that day, yet you didn't. Instead, you saved her. Even with all the pain Kira was going through, you were with her every step of the way.

Lord, you never left her, and you never let go of her hand. It was a miracle that she was walking around.

Lord, you got Kira to the best doctor and the proper care she needed. Kira is still amazed what she went through. Lord, you carried her, so she wasn't really, really scared. Kira could feel the peace once she truly let go and trusted you. You knew exactly where to stop the vehicles how the impact would happen.

Lord, people say Kira must talk to someone about this; well you're the only one that can really get her through it. When she talks about what happened

Having Coffee with the Special One

with you, it makes it real. When she doesn't think about it, then she can pretend it didn't happen. Besides you're the best counselor there is around, and yet, you don't cost one penny. You won't lie just to get paid, and you give her the best advice. Who else can heal the body? Only you. Doctors can repair, but you heal because you listen, and you help.

It just dawned on Kira that when she doesn't talk about it and holds it in, then she is cheating you. This is a way that Kira can share your miracles with others. She is living proof to the ones who didn't believe in, trust or have faith in you, they can see where you always were be Kira's side. Oh man! Kira didn't look at it that way before.

Lord, how many times will Kira have to tell you she is sorry for missing the point of what happened? She didn't want to break down and cry!

But Lord, Kira knows that she will have to shed tears of joy once it's all over. That's when she will probably break down and shed the tears.

Lord, help Kira tell what you want to be heard, and help her say it in a way that will move people, help people, and get your promise out there. Your words are the truth, the light, and the way.

Patty Scott

Help Kira tell the story of the day you saved her. It's been several years since the accident, yet she is still healing. Then Kira and Tim had another accident, and you saved them again.

God, Kira will share her stories of you, and you'll lead her or show her the way. Last night Kira could see why you told her it's not her concern or up to her how, when, or why you bless others.

Lord, it has a lot to do with attitudes, doesn't it? When we truly learn to be appreciative and thankful, then we truly see how we are blessed.

Lord, Kira genuinely believes you saved her. And she truly trusts you, Jesus.

Kira has learned to change her attitude to gratitude. You know no one owes us anything and you don't have to save us or help us, but you choose to do so. No one owes us a free ride in life, and it could always be worse than what we're facing—not that we want to ever do something bad again—but it could always be worse.

Kiss. Keep it simple stupid.

That's a very good phrase and really a good way to structure things. It's the simple things in life that mean so much.

All we need is fifteen minutes of someone's undivided attention. A smile, a hug, or touch to Kira that's a simple act. It's so easy for Kira to give

Having Coffee with the Special One

someone a hug, or to smile at them. Touch, oh how she is a touchy, feely person. Kira has had to learn to back away or keep her hands to herself that's hard for her. Not everyone in life likes to be touched or wants to be, so she has learned to give them their space or to ask them if they would mind a hug or to be touched.

Kira is thankful for you putting the dance back in her step. You have made her feel that it's ok, to build friendships with people that she works with. You're stirring up the pot. Even with the pile of work on her plate Kira has enjoyed being over at their client's office talking and sharing with her. Nancy has been an exceptionally good friend and shown Kira that it's ok to mix friendships and business with some people. Kira has also learned from Nancy, while she could feel your presence and peace.

Something hit Kira while she was there with Nancy. You have helped Kira live with a condition that could have been serious, yet you have kept her safe. Even when she had the flare up, it wasn't as bad as it could have been. Lord, there is no way Kira would have wanted to have a colonoscopy. Funny how some conversations can trigger something that hadn't been thought about for years.

Thank you for helping Kira and teaching her how to care about herself and to make sure to eat correctly: just another way that she should have realized it was you all along that kept her from harm. Kira saw what could have happened to her, she is grateful that you helped her.

When we sit like we do each day, I get to learn what it really means to have you as a friend. What a friend we have in Jesus. All our sins and griefs to bear. What a privilege we often forfeit when we don't take it to you in prayer.

You gave Kira such a strong spirit. You have always shined in her smile. Kira was humming the song, and her spirit and your friendship came to mind.

As she was reading, Kira thought of something else: the world around her doesn't offer peace because Lord, you're the only one that can give peace to her. The world around her is total chaos, and there is so much destruction and so much mistrust.

Lord, thank you for making Kira a person that people can <u>trust</u>.

Trust is an especially important factor in relationships and thank you for putting Herb and Earl in her life.

Lord, Kira still thinks about them often, but she was still mad at them for leaving her. Kira is so sorry for some of the doubt that she had. Those two

Having Coffee with the Special One

were strong, so kind and so giving. Your spirit was in them too, Lord.

Herb and Earl gave Kira so much encouragement and guidance. She hadn't met many people like them in the past. Kira used them as mentors and they were happy to help her, and her family as if they were their own. Memories that she will get to hang on to and sort of cherish.

Kira knows that you, Lord, are really the only one that can give her what she needs. She also knows that you put others in her life, and path to show her there is kindness and to help you send helpers even though it may only be temporary.

You're the Almighty, the: "I am."

Each day Kira gets to think about how you're helping in her life and what you do for her. Kira used to think if her life was at peace that meant she had to die. But that's not so. Kira is born again.

If Kira didn't believe in you so much now Lord, she wouldn't have believed her own eyes how you're working in her life. You have brought her a long way. You have had a lot of clean out and clean up to do in her. Kira had so much deeply buried inside of her. What freedom you have brought to her. Kira's hopes are that her family can find the freedom that you have given her. She hopes that her siblings and loved ones can see what you're doing for her, and that they will know it all comes from you. Thank you, Lord, for giving Kira the determination that you have given her and the strength that she needs to carry on.

Your peace is the bucket of gold at the end of the rainbow, Lord, now that Kira really knows what it feels like to be at true peace, she hopes this stays with her and she enjoys every second of it.

Lord, Kira can't remember feeling like this in the past, and she doesn't want to go back there. Life is too short and goes by too quickly. She really wants to bask in the peace and tranquility you give her. It really is fun and <u>man</u>!!

She enjoys the daily treasures you leave for her—the little things in life that mean so much—like a whisper, a smile, some laughter… just pure joy. Kira hopes everyone is soaking in your love and peace while they are on the cruise. Lord, are you trying to show her that she could have gone on it, or that she was meant to miss it this year?

Kira feels there was a reason why she didn't go this year. All the gospel music, and musicians they just glow with your spirit within them. When Kira got to go on the last one, she knows how you worked through her and it was so great how you changed her, and the way she looked at things. It wasn't about Kira, yet you're working in her to heal her. Lord, you gave Kira so much more than people took

Having Coffee with the Special One

from her. Being humble is a peaceful way to be. Again, this is where you showed her it's true.

You have showed Kira so many times too, that she can trust that you'll help her with what is important and guide her on want you her to do.

Lord, God, Kira has learned to trust you and know you're taking care of things. Kira can see where she missed out on so much joy when she was so lost in thought. She has seen too that you can work, and you can play, and when you play you play hard. You taught Kira all she must do is depend on you and thank you for helping her when she needs you and to acknowledge that it comes from you. You have taught Kira to stay in the present moment, so she doesn't miss out on what is happening at the time and what is important. Stay out of her head, stay in the presence. Watch and see what you do for Kira; you have taught her to live and to love.

It's always so nice for Kira and Tim to have their daughter and her family over for dinner. One of their youngest grandchildren is really growing up, and they're ever so grateful that he is here with them so they can see his bright smile shine. His beautiful, bright, and happy face; and crystal blue eyes.... Kira just loves to look in his eyes and kiss his face.

Lord, she is so glad that you saved him, and her daughter is so happy. Kira can see your spirit in them, and she knows it's you that shines through them. Kira loves getting to hold, kiss and hug them.

Kira has learned how to work with the small disruptions in her life, without getting so upset like she did in the past. She still has a hard time at times, but she is working on it. Kira's time and days won't always go as planned and she has to understand that. Kira must accept that there are going to be interruptions and her plans will change, moment by moment, but in the end it will all be good. Her grandchildren just bring so much joy to her, it's worth every second that she is around them whether at the office or at home, they bring life to her life.

Kira kids that if she had known how great it was to have grandkids, she would have skipped the kids and moved to grandkids right away! Maybe this is what others meant when others told Kira (while she was raising her kids) to treat them as they are your friend's kids and you won't have any problem with them. Kira treats her grandkids as someone special...maybe that would have helped when she was raising hers.

There are so many areas in Kira's life that she needed your help. She needed help with her family and with people at work—the two groups of people she spends most of her time with. Learning how to appreciate others and what they do for her is important to Kira.

Having Coffee with the Special One

Gosh! Why couldn't she just take people at face value and appreciate what they have to offer by way of knowledge or guidance.

One problem Kira has with people is when they make the same mistake over and over. She doesn't have an issue if they make a mistake, but Kira wants them to fix or resolve the mistake, so they don't make the mistake again. Is that too much for her to ask? Does this stem from how she looked at herself, or the fact that you have given her an ability that if she makes a mistake, she normally only does it once?

Kira's ability to understand and learn from her mistakes is a gift from you, God. Even as she says this, Kira has realized there were sometimes she just didn't get it and missed the whole point of what something meant or what it was. Maybe this is the same thing in Kira's work, or other abilities: there are just some things that are hard for her to understand. Maybe Kira needs a little more compassion in this Lord, is this why mistakes happen and why she needs to deliver more compassion in her?

Maybe that's the point you're trying to make with Kira. Teach her patience and understanding, so that she isn't so frustrated when things go wrong. Besides that, how in the world can she expect someone to learn if they don't make mistakes along the way? That's how Kira learned she made a lot of mistakes and then learned from them.

It's funny because Kira was just thinking that she should be thankful for what they do get done and all they get done. How they work together and how the clients trust them. That should be more important to her.

Now Kira can understand why they get so upset with her and she understands how it felt when she was growing up. Kira isn't a perfectionist in everything. She's only a perfectionist when it comes to her work....and she does let her pride get in the way a lot. Maybe Kira is too prideful, even though in the Bible it says she isn't supposed to be that way.

Kira thinks she is beginning to understand why when she was growing up and tried to help around the house, she'd get frustrated because it was perceived as not good enough. One time she was ironing some shirts for her dad, he laughed at her because Kira didn't do a very good job and couldn't get all the wrinkles out of the shirts to make them look nice. Kira guessed she never would iron again. No way! She wasn't even going to try it.

Maybe Kira is making them feel the same way. Maybe she should stop, stand back, and figure out what the problem is, and why the problem is happening. Maybe the person making the mistake needed to be shown or told a different way. You know everyone's reason for making mistakes is different, and the way they learn is different. Maybe Kira should have more patience with them

Having Coffee with the Special One

because it does seem to work better for all who are involved.

Afterall Kira really isn't a mean person; she just comes across that way at times. Hopefully, this too shall pass, and you'll help her in this area. Let the peace that surpasses all understanding come into play here.

Kira is learning some hard lessons and should be thankful that her employees even want to work there. The tax service industry is a stressful industry at times, and really there are a lot of deadlines that must be met. You're almost always under the gun to meet some deadline—the industry is deadline driven. What's sad is many clients wait until the last moment to get their information to them for tax filings. That makes it hard on others.

She's going to have to change the way she looks at things and be grateful.... really feel it in her heart. Kira needs to see the important things: learn from you and learn what really matters. A lot of times, there is peace in the office, and Kira would love to keep it there, Lord. Knowing that you're there with us it makes all the difference in the world says Kira.

Kira keeps feeling at times she is being so selfish hogging up your time, but to her it's so important to have that time with you. Kira thanks you for allowing her this time to explain things to her. She doesn't want to turn her need into greed though.

You're too important, Lord, and Kira doesn't want to take you for granted. She knows it's you, Lord, that's helping her be the person that you want her to be.

Each day, Lord, God, you're healing Kira in one way or another. You're peeling away the hurt, fear, frustration and the loneliness (it's gone you took it and filled her heart with your spirit), and bringing back the love, joy and peace.

Kira still thinks that she can't thank you enough for all that you're doing for her, because you really are protecting her – she sees the twinkle in your eyes and feels your warmth.

Lord, you're getting Kira back to the basics in life: to look at and for the good in people. Stop criticizing them. There are times when Kira is bad about that Lord. That's a sin she needs to stop with the help of you, Lord.

No wonder! Kira needs to look at the good in people and stop picking out and harping on their faults. We all have faults, and no one likes them to be pointed out constantly, not even Kira. So why does she do it to others?

Kira tries to praise them for their good works too, but sometimes, that's not enough. Sometimes people need kind words, or a thank you. Just stop

Having Coffee with the Special One

and think how you feel when you see your own faults—you don't feel well about them—but you don't beat yourself up because you don't need to.

"Mental note to self."

Lord, Kira says I really need you in this area, because I am bad here.

Kira looks around and you're everywhere. Yesterday at work (thank you very much for the new business), Kira really enjoyed talking to the person that works as an administrator that sets up meetings.

Lord, help Kira get her story out. Help her to write it down, as it will be so healing for her. Kira isn't sure if maybe she asked the wrong thing here. Thank you.

Yesterday when Kira went to the Christian bookstore, Lord, she could feel the warmth of your presence. She really enjoyed being there and getting to talk with the salesclerk at the register. The salesclerk was so nice and friendly. Kira likes being able to—I guess you call it witnessing? — well, talk to others and share what you have done for her. That's one of the reasons why Kira keeps going back to the Christian bookstore: it seems almost every time there has been someone that she could visit and talk with and share you with them.

By teaching Kira to be in your presence, Lord, you have helped her realize something more meaningful.

Kira thought back about her childhood and how there were eight kids in her family. Lord, Kira knew how she felt just raising three kids; her mother did the best that she could raising eight kids with your help and presence, Lord, in their lives while growing up.

Kira can still remember her mother sitting all eight kids down in the living room and reading the devotions. Lord, she had to be their mother and dad. She kept you, Lord, in their home as much as she could. Lord, you made her an extraordinarily strong woman. How is that for you to be in a household where both evil and good lived? When their dad was around, it wasn't full of fun and laughter always, as when he was gone. They are so thankful that you stayed in their home with them and watched over them as you did, Lord.

You're teaching Kira that this world is so big, and it isn't all about her and her woes. Life, it's about love, laughter and faith, and about friendships and healing. There is more in life than just us. There is something much bigger than life and bigger than us, and that's you, Lord. It's all about you and how we can glorify your name. Kira gets it now that there is a greater purpose for all of it.

With each lesson you're teaching Kira she is learning that you have been with her all her life.

Having Coffee with the Special One

There isn't one thing about Kira that has escaped you.

She can see you everywhere and you have trained her to look for you everywhere. It's sort of embarrassing when she messes up and then realizes you were next to her and you saw her do it. Kira needs to be more careful. Kira knows there isn't anything she can hide from you, and there isn't anything you don't already know about her and what she says or does.

Kira is finally realizing that most of the bad things that happened to her was because she made bad decisions in life. She was given choices and she chose the wrong route. Even when things were out of her hands and out of her control, Kira still should have taken them to you and talked to you about them, rather than act as she did. She could have made better choices. Kira had such a bad opinion of herself, and she was sub-consciously hanging on to stuff that really wasn't that important in the first place. Now she sees that.

This is an example how Kira must remember to keep you in the forefront of her thoughts, and keep her heart and mind open unto you, Jesus Christ.

That's what you're telling Kira, isn't it? Don't let go of you and don't forget that it's you. Kira wants you in all areas of her life not just part of them. When you're with her, she seems to do what is right and she is a nicer person.

Kira has realized that she can't do it without you and she never did.

Lord, why is it that Kira can't notice an issue sooner and draw into you before she really gets into despair or trouble?

Yes, you give Kira a choice, and she sure hopes she remembers that she has a choice. Kira needs to drill that into her memory bank.

Dear Lord, Jesus, let thy will be <u>done</u>! That who so ever believeth in you shall not perish but have everlasting life. <u>Amen</u>!

Your peace and love surround Kira. Kira feels like she's in your protective bubble as you surround her.

The peace that surpasses all understanding, keep her heart and mind open unto you, Jesus Christ.

You're welcome in her home, her office, in her car.... anywhere and everywhere Kira goes.

Now is the time for her to listen to you, Lord.

Having Coffee with the Special One

Dear Lord, you have given Kira such a good life with who she is married to and has been for many years.

You blessed her with so much love and joy.

Kira can see where you have been present in her life but when she and Tim struggled, it was because she set out on her own independent way. It wasn't because you left her. You dropped Tim in Kira's lap when she wasn't looking for someone. She sure didn't know how to make good choices on her own. Just look at the ones Kira picked before him. She always ran the decent ones off.

But it's okay, because you gave her the one you wanted her to have. Kira didn't always appreciate what you did for her or what you do for her. Lord, you have shown Kira so much love and she doesn't deserve it. As you told Kira, it was almost like she worshipped the pain and anger, rather than trusting you.

Now Kira understands the wonderful feeling deep inside her heart: it's you! No wonder she loves the feeling because Kira loves the feeling of being in love and being loved. Kira understands it now that no person can give her that feeling or fill that empty hole in her heart, only you can, Lord. You're the only one that can fill that need and want!! Kira gets it! Maybe now that she freely comprehends it, maybe Kira won't let go of it again, and she won't let go of you, Lord! Kira let the worst in her take the place of the best in her. You, Lord, are the best in <u>her</u>!! It's you; it's you; it's you!!! (Another light bulb goes off in her head)

Every time Kira felt like this was when she was close to you and let you in. Lord, Jesus, thank you for giving her again another chance. Each time you do too, it seems to get better. Hopefully, Kira won't forget again, and she will keep building on this.

You have blessed Kira's life with a good man. Forgive her Father for she has sinned against you in thought, word, and deed. Kira let her selfish ways get in the way of what you have given her.

Jesus, you have given her so much more than anyone could ever have taken from her. They can't take your love from Kira, if she doesn't let them. Kira will hang on tight to your hand!!

"You, Lord, are what matters!!

We never know who is watching us. However, Kira does know the Lord, is he is looking over her shoulder. Resting his chin on her shoulder. Lord, you're there with her. Kira needs to listen to you so they can have that love back; you'll be their love.

Having Coffee with the Special One

Dear God, it was you all along!! Kira had to realize it.

She was giving credit where it didn't necessarily belong. It was you that led Kira and gave her the peace!! Kira had to ask for forgiveness from you, and she had to forgive before she could have your forgiveness!!

Forgive us our trespasses as we forgive those who trespassed against us.

Kira had to forgive him, for the lies and deceit so she could profoundly move on in life of love and laughter. Kira didn't know the full impact of those three words, I forgive you.... Wow! All Kira had to do was forgive her ex-husband for the walls to tumble down. That's when the joy that Kira and Tim now share, began. Kira laughs more and enjoys the good memories. She knows there are more memories that she hadn't thought about for a long time.

Kira is glad that she didn't have to die to receive your eternal life. Lead the way, Oh Lord, Let's skip and dance the rest of the way. Hey, Kira can enjoy the rest of her second childhood. It's funny how she could open her heart up to her grandkids and let them in so easily.

Patty Scott

Dear God, they are such a blessing Kira. She thanks you for them.

One of Kira's memories that came to mind is sort of off track in a way, yet it shows how your mercy is involved. Remember when Tim and Kira had recently moved to Texas and their teenage son was still living with them? He liked to mess with electronic items and code the phone for emergency numbers. One time he was supposed to be sleeping but when he was coding in 911 it went straight to dispatch. Kira can't remember if he fell asleep with the phone in his hands or if he didn't know what to do once he hit the numbers, but he either hung up right after dialing or something. The police showed up at the house and woke Tim and Kira from a dead sleep. Luckily, the officers could tell that they had been sleeping, and checked and verified that Bryne was ok, and all was well.

Kira can laugh now, but that wasn't really funny at the time. You know the local police department can charge a large fine for a false emergency call. Well, Lord, this is where you stepped in. No one was hurt, and no one was fined. Ahhhh the things that kids do to their parents out of boredom, or oneness.

You know, Lord, that was an interesting sermon today because something hit Kira. It was where we asked for forgiveness for the things, we have done wrong and the things that we have left undone.

Having Coffee with the Special One

Kira hadn't given that much thought about that because she thought she had pretty much done what she said or told others that she would do. But then Kira realized it's not always promising others that you would do something, it's how it would be kind to someone if you did it for them. It could also be if someone asked you to do something, and you say you'll do it, but then you watch TV, read a book or do something else. Kira is sure that there is more to this, but she found it rather interesting.

Kira saw another area of her life, that she needs to watch and ask for your guidance. Kira can't seem to get the "oomph" to finish tasks or other things that she has started months ago.

Kira honestly didn't realize that was a sin against you. Now she can see what you mean there, and it makes sense to her. There are so many things that Kira is in the middle of but she's like a squirrel and can't stay focused on a task. It seems like other things come along, Kira gives in to being tired or she just wants to sit. That's not bad either, but finish what you have started and get it done. Especially if someone else's feelings are involved in it. Someone may be counting on you to do what you said you would do.

It's interesting that you tell Kira that everyone has their limits, so was she using this as an excuse to put things off? (Chuckle.) Kira has been told that a few times before and that she expects a lot out of people. She has the fault or problem of comparing things and all that does is cause frustration for her and everyone involved. Kira needed to realize that some of that just wasn't what was important. This in some ways is where she needs forgiveness. What the heck got into her??

She can do all things through Christ who strengthens her.

Lord, you reminded Kira again today that there isn't one thing in her life that you didn't have control over, and she can't succeed without you. Kira doesn't want to succeed without you because you make it so much more fun and the end results are up to you.

Thank you for humbling Kira. She really is grateful that you cared enough to do so.

Kira is sorry!! She knows she is the human and you're the divine one. You choose who you want to do what and when you want them to do it!! You have put so many beautiful people in Kira's life, and in her path. She is now fully recognizing them as a gift to her, even though they may have some traits that absolutely drive her crazy. Kira is still learning to love them and to love being around them. She doesn't fully understand them, nor will she, but she will be kind, instead of ungrateful.

Having Coffee with the Special One

Love and compassion are something Kira was lacking. But Lord, you're showing her love and compassion through the people you put in her path.

Lord, it's all about your glory, your love, and your forgiveness.

Even when we sin, you still love us. Now Kira sees why you're her Father: a father loves his child no matter what and you show that unconditional love for her. She now sees what you have done for her during her life, and yet, you forgive Kira and sent your son to die on the cross for her.

<u>Lord, Love Wins</u>. You love us so much.

Kira has felt the power of forgiveness and that was <u>awesome</u>!! And powerful!!

If the power of you is more than that, you're correct...as you always are. Lord, Kira is so glad that you allow her to talk to you as she would to any friend. She knows you're the Almighty, the most powerful.

<u>She knows that</u>!!

You're just so easy to talk to. Before Kira wouldn't open up to you and let you in, but now she does. Who was she hiding from anyway?? This is where you have really been in Kira's life and helped her.

It's funny she can't get away from you now even if she wanted to (but Kira doesn't want to!.) Kira knows now how important it is to have this time with you, and how you do answer her prayers in due time.

"I love to tell the story of Jesus and his glory, to tell the old, old story of Jesus and his love."

You put the song in her heart.

Kira can picture you sitting with children and laughing with them. You paint a great picture for her. You glow with love!!!!

Lord, Kira knows your peace and love shines upon her!

Kira has to say that was totally unexpected. Yet, she knows you prepared her for that day.

Kira will miss her baby brother, she thinks of him often, even though he was an ornery one. Kira has a lot of memories of joy and laughter shared with him and several other fun moments. It never failed he would text her at the most inopportune time—it seemed as if it was always when Kira was the busiest—and at that time she wasn't smart enough to just put down what she was working on and talk to him. That's all he wanted; he just wanted to talk to Kira.

Having Coffee with the Special One

Donnie was good at making Kira laugh. Even though she knew for years that he wouldn't live to be a ripe old age, his death still was unexpected. Kira didn't really understand diabetes—and still doesn't that much—but she knows it can take you quickly if you don't take care of yourself and take the insulin that you need. Donnie couldn't afford to buy it when he was out of work and it was so hard for him to find a job. Kira knows he loved them, and her mom knows that you're with her during this hard time. Kira can only imagine what her mom is going through, just because she knows what it would feel like if she lost a child of her own. Of which Kira didn't lose one of her kids...thankfully to you.

Lord, thank you for helping all of us to cope with his loss. Even when Kira knows that there wasn't anything, they could have done to prevent it, a person still has a hard time with losing someone they love. They always, thinks I should have done this, or I should have done that, but no one could have stopped it. It was his time to be with you, or you wouldn't have let him go.

Don't take this wrong, but Kira does grieve his passing. However, she just knows he is with you in Heaven and in a much better place. "And she thought he pestered all of them before!" (Chuckle)

Donnie was ready to be with you, Lord, At the end, it sounds like he was giving up on the earthly life. So many thoughts ran through Kira's head like a whirlwind.

Patty Scott

Lord, thank you for this glorious day!!

It's funny how you chose when to allow something to happen. You're trying to show Kira more and more that the industry she works in is not the only thing in the world and in her life. Lord! You'll show her and help them get more work done in less time! Now that she is back from the funeral, and she must face what is piled in her office. You do know it's tax season! Whew!! What a time ...... they are going to have!! It seems like everything she gets to touch is not issue free!!

Lord, you're amazing. Kira can't wait to see what all she gets to learn from <u>this</u>!! This lesson in love! Faith, trust, hope ......

Even in our everyday living and our work, Lord, you have promised us your never-ending love, you say you bring us to it; you'll get us through it.

Lord, Kira can see what you have been telling her. Yes, hard times are there, but she trusts you, Jesus, to get her and the others through it!! As you have and always did in the past, why would she start doubting you now?

Kira loves you and she thanks you for your guidance and your love. You were there with her in the office, looking over her shoulder to see and to

Having Coffee with the Special One

show her an easier or better way to get it done. Lord, you did it for her.

Lord be with Kira's daughter-in-law too as she is having a rough time too. There are blessings even in sadness.

At least, Kira can feel.

Lord, you do have a sense of humor, don't <u>you</u>!

Lord, you're right: we do have choices. Kira can either be miserable and stressed out, or she can hang on to your peace and love.

Kira trusts you, Jesus! Love and family are what matters, and you can't replace a family member, as she is fully aware of.

Lord, you know what their family is facing now just like other families are too. It's so hard when marriages and plans in your life don't go as you had planned. You sort of forget that and you start just taking things for granted. You forget that your life can change at any moment, and nothing in life is promised to be there forever.

In fact, it you don't know when it can change or will change. That's why Lord, you teach us to take one day at a time and take what happens in that day as it happens, you need to be in the present moment.

It makes sense now. Kira will miss her brother Donnie and miss the people that may leave her life other ways, but you have given her great memories that she can think about and find the silver lining in the gray clouds.

Kira can be thankful to you that they had a great relationship and they didn't have a disagreement more than a couple of times. Her family all wish they could have spent more time with Donnie, given him a call or something, but for some reason that didn't happen. At times Kira thinks they did something wrong, but as she has seen on posts on social media, they just don't have that much power. They can't stop life from happening as it's supposed to. We all have a "life" time clock, and we can't stop it if we wanted to.

It says in the Bible that you can't add one second to your life to prolong it nor can you do anything to speed it up, it's all in God's hands. Yet there are times we all must be reminded you're the one in control, you're the one with the power. It was his time to be with you, Lord. Donnie is in Heaven with you. He is looking over Kira's shoulder now with you, Lord, so she better keep on track, right?! Donnie must know how much they all loved him; he was kind of spoiled by us all.

Kira remembers the picture of Donnie feeding flour to his horse, the green plastic one on wheels. Sitting in the corner of her mom's kitchen, Kira doesn't think he was even two yet. He was their baby. There just aren't many bad memories with

Having Coffee with the Special One

him. Kira even remembers waking up in the middle of the night and when she walked out into the living room, she found

her dad was rocking holding Donnie. That was a rare occasion, but so touching.

Kira's dad must have enjoyed him. Lord, Donnie was good about staying in touch with us all. Yes, Kira will admit that he drove her nuts at times of course, but that's what she'll miss the most. Getting him those t-shirts from a bar in Dallas—how would he have known about a bar in Dallas—he hadn't even been to Texas!

Lord, tell him we are sorry on one hand, but we are glad he is with you. He is at peace, and what better place is there to be.

Lord, you reveal to us what you want us to learn or to know. It's not up to us to play these guessing games.

In all circumstances in her life, Kira needs to take each moment one at a time. Why does she try to handle something that hasn't even come to pass? Sometimes it's hard enough at the moment that Kira must face at the time she is dealing with it. You keep telling her she needs to get to the basics in life. You'll counsel Kira, guide her, and give her the wisdom that you want her to have. Kira can say or hear this a hundred times, but it still comes to the fact that if it comes from the heart it comes from you. One day it'll stick with her, or Kira will just automatically realize it, so she knows she is making the right choice or decision.

We aren't supposed to look back at history, or forward into the future. Sometimes looking back shows us, Lord, Kira didn't think she could survive this life if you weren't with her.

She can see every area of her life where you're and where you have been. Some of it isn't pretty: it's full of sin and not such a pleasant person. The areas in her life that are good, is you being with Kira. Kira is so thankful you forgave her for the stupid things she has done and what she still does. You love her even when she does stupid stuff.

Thank you, Lord, for when you're with her.

"Trust in the Lord, with all your heart, lean not on our own understanding."

Yes, Lord, Kira is going to need to hold on tight to you and hang on to your love and forgiveness. Thank you for cheering her on and letting her know not to give up. You'll lead the way, perseverance. Kira loves you and she trusts you, <u>Jesus</u>!

Having Coffee with the Special One

No human being can give to us as you have given. No human can love us as you do either!! The peace of the Lord is with us always.

Lord, there are so many people praying for Kira's family. They can't let you down. You'll shine through this and your peace will hold them tight. Stay focused on you and keep you close to her heart and soul. You're Kira's soul mate. The gospel groups that she listens to, Lord, they have a gift from you, and you can feel the love and trust they have in you. Your spirit flows through them. They are blessed by you. Kira hangs on to what they say because it comes from you.

Our whole purpose in life is to glorify you, but we don't do a very good job at times. In fact, Kira is sure that she has let you down at times. She is glad that you forgive her sins that are known and unknown.

Thank you, Lord.

Kira also realizes that she doesn't have the power to ruin what you have planned; she needs to lighten up sometimes. People post similar messages on social media a lot. Kira she really needs to remember that. She cannot ruin what you have planned for her or in her life.

Lord, when Kira was evaluating herself, she thought at times she was trying to see where she went wrong, or where she could improve. Oh, and

Patty Scott

yes, she did make the mistake of thinking that her way was the only way.

Forgive her now that she can see that there are other ways, but the right way, is your way. It's up to you to determine how successful or blessed she is, not her. Kira is not the ultimate decision maker even though she may have thought that she was at times.

Dear Lord, thank you for being with her family and one of Donnie's friends. With your presence, they could all feel your peace and love for them. We know Donnie is in a better place, where he belongs.

Lord, Kira has learned that forgiveness is a powerful part in life. She needed to learn not only to forgive others but also herself for not doing what she should have done, or what she did do. Each step and phase of Kira's journey has taught her that when she leans on you—and she does that a lot now—you'll carry her when she can't do it on her own, (of which she isn't supposed to either.)

Now Kira understands why you keep telling her to keep her focus on you. One reason is so she doesn't go off the deep end or fall into the pit of anger and pain, when someone hurts her, or something goes wrong. There will be sad times in our lives and there will be times when we lose someone that we

Having Coffee with the Special One

love. We just must hang on to what time we had with them, think of the laughter and joy we shared with them, and hang on to the memories.

Just because we believe, and we have faith in you it doesn't mean that we won't have trials and tribulations. Kira had to really learn that, and you have showed her. You have been with her all the way, and there is more yet to come. Kira has also learned that maybe it was someone else that needed to learn something, and you used her for them to learn. Kira doesn't know if it did teach them or not, and she doesn't know who it is. Again, that's why you really need to do the best you can because you don't know when someone is watching you, and maybe they can learn from what you're going through.

Dear Lord, Kira knows you're there, and, she does allow doubts to stop her at times from what she thinks you're telling her.

Dear God!! She cannot back down, she can't give up now. You have brought Kira too far in her journey, and she knows you're leading her and working with her; you haven't let her go.

Kira can't allow the negative to wear her down. There are days when just feels like giving up and walking away, then something will show up in what she reads, a song on the radio, or even a billboard on the way to church.... expect Miracles!

Patty Scott

Well you know Kira needs a miracle because no one wants to help or get involved with some of the stuff she is going through. It would be so easy to just walk away. But that's not like her, and really that wouldn't be the best either because if she thinks it haunts her now, just imagine how it would haunt her if she didn't do all that she could do. Kira understands she could do what she could do, and you'll do the rest.

Well God it's your turn, so do your stuff. When we write about it your glory will shine, and people can see that you're there. This must end, and there comes a time with a situation that a resolution needs to be met. Your way God, not Kira's way. She sees that now.

Lord, you have already shown others how Kira has grown and it's hard for others in her life to believe she is where she is; it was all you. You know that throaty laugh Kira always had, well it's coming out more and more. Look where you have led her and what you have done in her life!! You have given her several blessings and gifts.

Kira needs to be more thankful and accepting of your gifts, it's up to you not her, so she can accept the blessing just as they are pure and simple. They are blessings from you and Kira doesn't need to feel guilty or not like that she is worth it. It's all up to

Having Coffee with the Special One

you how you bless her and when you do it. Kira needs to enjoy all that you have given her.

You gave Kira her kids, her grandkids, and her friends that she has.

Lord, you have given her hope, peace, and love.

You're right, no human can give Kira what she needs or love her as she wants and needs to be loved. Only you can. You're the one and only – one true <u>God</u>!! You're the Alpha and the Omega. They can touch the surface, and love her, but nothing like the love that you have for us.

All Kira can do is pray that others may be touched by what you have given her. And it isn't always the material things, it's so much more than that.

No Lord, they can't always understand what you have chosen to do with her. And yes, Lord, Kira doesn't always understand your ways with others. In fact, sometimes it's a mystery to her.

Kira just hopes she'll just learn to accept that this is the way it is. You know Lord, it's fun, yes!!

She'll admit sometimes that she gets scared. Kira just needs to remember you're leading the way and you're with her. So, who can be against her when you're leading the way?

She also needs to remember; it's all done in your timing, not hers.

You have surprised Kira. Her family is proud of her for what you're doing within her. They have seen the change in her, and they are getting on board with some of what you're doing with and for Kira.

You know not all of it, but hopefully somewhere along the way, they will realize "what harm is it doing"?

It's a fun ride, and Kira is living on the edge with you. Kira is so glad you know what you're doing, because she doesn't. She's believing with blind trust that you won't harm her, and you'll keep her from harm. You know, Lord, this has been a big step for her, and it's even getting bigger at times.

Wow, the mountains you have helped Kira climb and the boulders you have moved out of her way: something good is around the corner and has already been happening.

God is on the move......

Lord, it has been five years since the car wreck.

You have carried Kira through this, and you have healed her. With each passing year there has been something new that she could see you have healed. Lord, thank you for healing Kira.

Having Coffee with the Special One

As much as this is coming out in this story, Kira needs to complete this portion of her journey so that she can tell about the true saving grace you have brought upon her life.

As Kira is aware, you haven't left her side since the day of the accident.

Lord, Kira knows since she was born, you haven't left her side. You have taught her that there's nothing in this world that's her security: it's you, Lord, who is her security. This is what you have taught Kira and what she has learned through the journey you have carried her through so far.

You don't lie to her, and you don't tell her what you think she wants to hear. Lord, you tell the truth no matter how hard it may be to face.

You don't lie and you don't <u>cheat</u>!

Lord, others do. Kira may even do it without knowing it, but it isn't on purpose if it should happen.

Lord, you're the truth, the way, and the light.

Thank you, Jesus, for the love, the care, and the peace you have given Kira. Kira depends on you and she trusts you Jesus. She knows that you'll make a way for her to get back to or move forward with what you have planned for her. Help her open her heart and mind unto you, Jesus Christ, and see what you want her to see, listen to and follow you.

Lord, Kira really is excited to know you have a great plan for her, and that the two of you're going to have fun. Yes, Lord, she feels as though you're sitting right here with her. You have blessed Kira with the privilege of seeing things that you want her to see. The clouds in the sky that are angels with trumpets.

Jesus, she knows that that all comes from you. You give Kira the guidance and answers she needs to do what is right. Now she sees this. Wow! Did Kira ever misunderstand what it meant to have your yoke upon her? Here Kira was asking you to remove them and she should have asked for you to put them upon her.

Lord, Kira is sorry when she doesn't fully comprehend what you're trying to show her or tell her. Kira does realize now that you may put your yoke upon her to keep her safe, and she realized sometimes it was there to protect her.

Yes, Lord, you filled her with your very <u>life</u>! You gave her another chance here on earth sort of like her mom. You're giving her several chances to get things right. Look at what Kira learned just watching what you did for Olivia in her life. But it just didn't soak in like it does now. Now Kira can really see how Olivia's faith kept her safe all those years. It doesn't mean there weren't rough times, but you kept Olivia safe so she could be around for her family. For all the things given unto me, are from you, Lord, help me be right with them and do your will.

Having Coffee with the Special One

Jesus, hear our prayer. Kira loves you and thanks you for forgiving her for all her sins.

Dear Lord, you protected Kira from harm by placing your shield of amour around her. Kira says I love thee, Lord, Jesus. You're there no matter what. Praise be to God.

Dear Father in Heaven above, now Kira has learned why she should thank you even for the rough times. Kira needs to share so that others know of your steadfast love for us. No matter what, we just must invite you, repent our sins, and ask you to guide us.

Lord, you're Kira's savior, the giver of life. Kira knows her life is full of problems, but you'll guide her so she can get through them one at a time and remove the boulders that block her path along the way. Lord, you're the rock that she stands on.

Kira thinks about Sheila: it didn't particularly go the way that Kira planned, but as usual it worked out the best for both Sheila and Kira, and also it worked out good for another person. Sheila has a gift of helping others through hard times so now, with your help and guidance, Lord, she can work where there isn't much pressure, and it's a calmer atmosphere. That's what Sheila wanted and needed in her life at this time.

Jesus, help them all stay close to you and let Sheila do what you intended for her to do. Sheila is a spreader of the word and your love and will help others that cross her path. At first Kira wasn't excited to hear where she went, but all in all it's the best for them all.

No matter what is done in life, God is in control. If we choose to defy him, the problems at hand are like a stumbling block, and we have a difficult time getting through it. Kira chooses to trust the Lord, and then she can thank him for the problems and the opportunity to make it right.

Several opportunities have been presented where Kira has gotten to be involved with Sheila and where she went to work, and now a lot is opened. That's the way Kira looks at it. It's true, Jesus, if we look through the eyes of the Lord, we see what is good.

One of the mistakes that Kira sees that she did was not talking more to Sheila about what was going on with her, rather than trying to push her into something that she didn't want. One thing about Kira is she must learn from her mistakes, so she doesn't continue to make the same ones over and over.

Hopefully now, Kira is in a position to where she will watch for and pay more attention to the signs, and do something sooner rather than let it get to the point where she loses someone that she put so much time and heart into.

Having Coffee with the Special One

When Kira thinks back, she realized that it was about two years ago when Kira saw that Sheila didn't want what Kira was trying to offer her. Sheila didn't want to be a business owner or be in charge of some of the things that Kira put on her. Sheila just wanted to go into the office, do her work and then go home at the end of the day to her family. Kira can't fault her for that: she and Sheila just handled things differently and different needs or desires.

Kira found that you can't make someone want something just because Kira may want it for them. You're helping Kira stop some of the mistakes that she made in the past and she is learning how to not do some of them again. But, Lord, she must admit there are some that she can't quite master yet. Is it a flaw or weakness in her?

Kira hopes she is understanding what you're saying. For example, if someone acts like or does something that Kira doesn't like, she will calmly talk about it rather than scream at them. Is that what you're talking about?

Each day Kira can see, Lord, where she is hanging on to more of your peace and not allowing others to push her buttons. Or, if they do say something, then Kira says something right then, so she doesn't build up anger or resentment. This is all thanks to you, Lord, and how you're working through her, as she sees it in her eyes.

Patty Scott

Lord, you're correct that if we look for you in all our life, we will see you and how you're working through us, in our life. Kira can clearly see that now because she is looking for it, before she wasn't looking for it, and of course couldn't see how you were working through her.

You know, Jesus, a lot has been brought to my attention. May I ask you about where in the Bible it talks about so many killings. Babies, women, and children were hurt. How horrible when someone so young is just starting out.

Reading about this in the Bible hits Kira hard. Why didn't you stop some or all of it, Lord?

I wonder that, Lord, because we don't want to think of you as a horrible, mean person that's selfish and just out for yourself. I too myself at times, wonder how this kind of stuff could go on. But in my mind, I have come to understand that our Free Will has a lot to do with this.

You're not a controlling God: you want people to come to you freely and not be forced. You want us to have you in our hearts and minds so that we can fully understand the kind of relationship you want to have with us. You do honestly forgive us for <u>all</u> our sins—past and present—not just some of them.

It doesn't mean that what was happening, wasn't cruel, or mean, back in the Bible days, but it does show that something good came out of it. God could have protected us in other ways too, but

Having Coffee with the Special One

that's what we all don't understand. Harod could have been stopped, yet he wasn't.

Kira knows there is so much more she must learn here, but it's part of what has been presented to her, from others. Jesus, it's hard for someone to understand when they are trying to find someone great to believe in.

Kira knows that everyone has their own journeys to go on with you and in life, and she can't speak for others, but it's something that's asked quite often. At Christmas is when most of this comes out, because it's around the time period when you were born and brought into this world.

Through these questions, help Kira talk to others and tell them so that they don't think you're a cruel God that doesn't care. Lord, you're love and you're kindness. You're firm and strong as Kira knows too.

Please, Lord, let the love shine through me as you have taught me to see.

Lord, Kira pictured you reaching for her hand. She sees the high walls of the mountains. She sees your smile and the sparkle in your eyes. You have cleared the path for her and will help guide her through all her trials and tribulations through life.

Patty Scott

Dear God, I would like to thank you for getting us through it all and some of it ahead of time.

Kira knows, Lord, that you'll provide her answers as she is guided through her tribulations and hold on to her helping her get through where you want her to be. You, Lord, have cleared the path for Kira, and are leading the way.

Kira can feel your presence and she knows it's your guidance that's giving her the answers. Thank you, Jesus.

Kira knows she cannot let go of your hand, and she doesn't want to let go. She knows that "we", Lord, have come a long way, and Kira can't turn back now. She loves you Lord, and she doesn't want it the way it was in the past. You pushed it back like it was just a curtain, but you opened the curtain—and path—for Kira.

Lord, it sure is a good thing that you're timeless and working on what Kira needs help with because she would be so overwhelmed with situations if she didn't have you. Kira knows her peace and acceptance comes from you too because there is such a relief within her. The tension and the stress just go away and diminishes within her. The peace that surpasses all understanding that's what you're talking about isn't it? That's what you mean, when we involve you and ask you in. You lead the way, and we can feel your help!

Having Coffee with the Special One

Jesus, Kira can't wait to see the outcome. She knows that the outcome is up to you—not her or anyone else—it's all up to you. Kira can't wait to be able to tell others finally how you helped her. She's really getting excited because she knows the ending is near.

Thank you, Lord, for caring about Kira and helping her. She knows you're there. "<u>**She knows it**</u>."

There were three creditors Kira wanted to thank you for watching over and taking care of. Jesus, this brings tears to Kira's eyes when she thinks of how you have helped them stay afloat and maintain what you have given them. Now Kira really knows what you meant when you told her to keep her eyes and stay focused on you because you would get her through ... and you did Jesus, you did!!

Kira's business is growing again. Her customers are coming in and thanking Kira for the way she and her staff took care of them in the past, and why they stay with her company. It's all thanks to you, Lord, for directing them Kira's way. You're giving Kira and her staff what you want them to have.

Lord, in your mercy hear my prayer.

"Thank you."

Patty Scott

This is the season for us to give thanks as it's Christmas! You know that it's one of Kira's favorite times of the year! It's about spending time with family and friends, celebrating your birth and reflecting on all the things you have done for us.

Jesus, this is the time when Kira can look at what all you have done for Kira, her family, and the people around her throughout the past year. Each year it gets better and each year you show Kira where you're answering her prayers she has prayed for during the year. Sometimes, it's small baby steps but at least it's steps in the right direction.

You have made her marriage better. It's getting back to where it was but with a more mature and better understanding about what it really means to love someone unconditionally. Even though we have problems in our lives, it doesn't mean that you, Lord, aren't there for us, it just means that you'll help us through them. Or they will just go away and work themselves out.

In the past there were times when Kira forgot about you, or just wouldn't invite you in to help. Now Kira can see where she was wrong in that. You sure make the path more enjoyable and she gets to skip along the way with you, Lord. Holding you close is much more fun. Kira loves the sparkle in your eyes and your smile, or the smile of the angel that you keep putting in my sight. Thank you for the angels Lord, and the helping hands.

Having Coffee with the Special One

<u>Lord, Jesus</u>, do what I can.... you'll do the rest.

That has been put in my sight several times. I am listening Lord, I am listening.

Kira knows that you'll get her through this.

Trust in the Lord, with all your heart, lean not on your own understanding.

Acknowledge the Lord in all your ways. He will lead you straight. Until now you haven't asked in my name. "Ask," you shall receive, and your joy will be complete.

Dear God, thank you for being here with me. Thank you for sending your son, to save us all, even the ones that don't truly understand it yet, thank you for saving them too.

Isn't it kind of hard for us to skip in your yoke? Kira knows Lord, that you're amazing with all you do. Lord, you're the Almighty father, the spirit and the son. "<u>Wow</u>."

Kira has learned something particularly important and valuable remembering that family is the most important thing in the world, next to the Lord.

When you have your priorities right and you're right with God, it all falls into place. It doesn't mean you don't have issues or problems; it just means they aren't the center of being.

Patty Scott

Thank you, Lord, for putting your foot down and getting my attention. You have opened Kira's eyes and heart unto you, Jesus Christ. Everything is different. Kira is different. She responds with love and compassion, something she didn't really know before. Sometimes Kira still responds wrong, but then she sits, thinks about it, apologizes, and tries to see things the way others may see it.

Kira doesn't know if a hundred percent of her strong will and stubbornness will go away, but she knows however it ends up, the Lord is with her. No matter what, the Lord will love her and help her thorough whatever circumstance Kira is faced with.

Jesus, I thank you and I am ever so grateful for the time that you have taken and spent with me during these past five years.

It's funny we have worked on this for over five years, and so many others have had a hand in it. So many have given me inspiration, and chances to become a better person. I will try so hard, to step back and remember that my world, is so much bigger than myself. There is much more to it.

Kira just needed to get out and see what all you, Lord, are doing in the lives of others, and in her life.

Fear, love, and trust in God above all things.

Yes, Lord, Kira would like you to stay with her and help her today. We can make some Christmas pies,

Having Coffee with the Special One

and get the food ready to nourish everyone while we enjoy the season, and your love for us.

There will still be a lot of challenges ahead that need to be dealt with and Kira will tackle one at a time, with your help.

Dear God, Kira knows that she can depend on you. She knows she can't and doesn't want to do it alone. Kira knows you'll lead the way, and you have her back.

Jesus, Kira is so glad that you can laugh with her. That shows the joy you have put in Kira's heart and that's the joy in your heart.

Lord, you're showing Kira in such a gentle way where she could have made better choices, better decisions. At first, it was hard for Kira to see where it was her—and not others— that was doing wrong as she had been thinking.

Look at the friends that Kira has, and the love they show her and her family. Look at her sisters and their husbands. God, Kira is so fortunate. Not everyone has that, and they all are so blessed by you and your love. Love wins, doesn't it? Every time............

Patty Scott

You know what Lord, Kira doesn't even mind realizing that you're in control and it's not her.

You're so gentle with her, not forceful or ordering her around.

You're handling her with kindness and care.

You have the power and you could do it differently, but you don't.

You know how it was with Kira about the "man thing" and the "control thing".

You know how hard it was for her to give in and to become submissive.

Jesus, you have showed Kira that you weren't just trying to control her you were trying to give her something better than what she had.

She was wearing herself out. Running in circles and not going anywhere. What a cycle.

Kira feels so loved by you, Lord, Jesus.

Thank you for having coffee with her and joining her.

Having Coffee with the Special One

Thank you again for forgiving her. Can she ever say it enough?

Showing her the way, the truth, and the light.

You make her heart sing!!!

Glory to God in the highest.

Your glorious face shines upon Kira and gives her peace. Each one of the problems she faces, oh Lord, are a gift from you.

Kira doesn't know why she lost sight of you, because you have shown her so many times how each bad thing in her life turned into something good. You have given Kira so much more than what was ever taken from her.

Look at how her immediate family has grown, and the love and the joy that has been given to them. Each one of them has so much to offer and share. They are a blessing in Kira and Tims' life. Every single one of them.

One of the main things Kira has learned is that she often wants results immediately, and that just isn't the way that you work. We must always wait upon you. You know it just dawned on Kira that it isn't always true: there have been times when she prayed with groups of people in Bible study and they got instant results in what they were praying for. For example, when Kira's Bible study group prayed for the safety of one of Kira's nieces, you, Lord, saved her from harm within a 24-hour period.

So, Lord, you don't always make us wait forever, as it seems. The times your work is done quickly just don't seem to stand out like the ones that take forever to be resolved. HA HA.... you do know how to make us view how quickly you answer our prayers, don't you?

That's just another example how we need to be careful how we think about things. We need to be able to separate "us" from "you", Lord. And that you, Lord, will not hurt us, but you do teach us lessons and discipline us...but with oh, so ever-loving kindness.

"Do not be afraid for I am with you" says the Lord. Be slow to anger.

You give Kira the strength to face the day.

Kira loves you Lord, Jesus, with all her heart, mind, and body. You, Lord, are deep into her soul.

Lord, Kira has turned it all over to you.

She keeps messing up! Kira knows it's way above her pay grade because it's you, Lord, who knows what is in others' hearts and minds. Only you, Lord, know what the result will be before it even

Having Coffee with the Special One

gets to that point. Lord, you can alter how everyone looks at it, and you can change their minds. You do that for all of us, Lord, Jesus.

You don't always have a lot to say. And we all get busy and aren't listening. But then when we listen—and hear you Lord, —then we know what we will hear is especially important.

Jesus, in all this time you have spent with Kira she has learned that she can rely on you. You honestly do listen to people's prayers and you have listened to hers. Even if the problem didn't go away you taught her how to get through it...you showed her the way.

Thank you, Jesus. Thank you for showing the way.

Dear Lord, Kira keeps catching herself looking for you and your face, or the face of the angels in the clouds, in the formations.

She is finding you're surrounding her with people who have had a stroke, some serious illness or misfortune in their lives, and giving them the opportunity to share your love for them.

Looks like Kira got behind on what she was supposed to do, oh Lord. Help her seek you in all that she does, so she doesn't get behind. Always help Kira hang on to the joy and the peace that you instill in her, so that she remembers you in all that she does, and she does it with great joy in her heart.

Kira does look for you everywhere Lord. She hopes and prays that she listens to you and she knows it's from you Lord. Kira wants to get it right. So often when she doesn't wait for you to answer, she does it wrong. You know what Kira is talking about. Kira wants to work with the right people in all that she is doing, and she wants the ones that you pick for her.

Yes! It just came to her again, she doesn't have the power to mess up what you intend for her, or what you want for her life. Kira just doesn't have that power.

Dear God, there are times when Kira doesn't know how to say it or what to say, so she needs you to teach her the right way. You know the problem she has, no filters.

There were times, when Kira felt as though she was at a turning point or at the crossroads of life. But, which way should she go?

Lord, she feels like you're leading her to writing so she can share her stories and your messages. Lord, it's so much fun to sit and talk to you and when she

Having Coffee with the Special One

writes what you want her to say, Kira just feels so close to you.

Lord, sometimes after talking with you the lightbulb goes off in her head, and there is the answer she was looking for! You show her the way, through this way.

Lord, in your mercy and love direct her to where you want her to be. If Kira is not mistakenly thinking, she has realized that you want her to stay right where she is for now as that's by your reason, Lord.

The Lord is giving Kira what she needs to put in the stories. If she didn't take time to talk to the Lord, every morning, then she wouldn't have experienced the opportunities to learn from and use to help others and pray with them.

Lord, you're showing Kira your way. Help Kira to listen to you and know it's you. Give her the wisdom and the knowledge that she needs. Lord, you're working through Kira and others, and bringing them together for your purpose. Thank you, Jesus.

Lord, in your mercy hear our prayers. And thank you for this journey we are on.

Kira looks forward to seeing you every day and talking to you each morning, sharing the good and the bad with you. She has even stopped to think about your conversations and be thankful for what you have done and are doing in her life, and in the lives of the people around Kira. She loves the end results: like the person's cancer that has gone into remission.... the couple who has reconciled...or the ones who separate, gain acceptance, and learn to move forward in a positive manner.

"Do not be afraid for I am with you says the Lord."

Good morning Jesus.

Kira has been sleeping well lately. Thank you very much for that.

Thank you for waking Kira up so you can have coffee together and talk.

You know what today will be like, so Kira doesn't want to forget to ask you to come with her and to help guide her through the daily challenges she faces. You keep telling her you won't give her more than she can endure; you sure are blessing their company with opportunities. You have brought them a lot of new business and other challenges.

Kira can laugh now about how they were in the middle of tax season and all sorts of issues kept popping up. You do know at times Kira will get stressed out and "lose it" but when she remembers to step back, think about it, and looks up to you, it makes a difference. It's in what you would think

Having Coffee with the Special One

versus how Kira thinks, that allows her to handle it.

Jesus, tax season is a stressful time. It seems the computers issues just drive Kira insane. She swore up and down in the very beginning that she would always do work by hand, so if something happened, she could always revert to that if she needed to. But in today's computer-driven world, that's not the way to work. Even the workload requires her and her team to use computers to stop addition errors, and sloppiness.

But really, why all the additional problems?

HA Yes, I know why! I just thought I would vent a little. Lord, you would know my frustration. You know if everything is working, everything is fine.

If you want me to sit and talk to you can't you pick another way to do so? Or is this really the only way you'll get my attention? Kira thought, guess, I need to work on this more too.

As Kira is thinking, she has got to put a timer or bell somewhere close to her, to go off when it's time to sit back and thank you for the day, or to say Hi, how are you doing?

You know she hasn't forgotten you, and she is grasping on to your peace again. Somehow, she has got to do this.......

Patty Scott

Kira says, oh, by the way, thank you for letting me have a nap yesterday. Yes, that's what I am thinking about right now. I loved the fact that I could relax enough and rest, to take a nap. Thank you for your peace so I could rest.

Kira has found that she is sleeping so much better since she has let you in and you gave her a new spirit. Lord, she thanks you for that.

Even though at times Kira's world around her is spinning and chaotic, she knows your peace surpasses all understanding, and that's what gives her the opportunity to rest. Kira has said many times in the past that she wished she could slow down and take time to enjoy life.

Lord, well you're affording Kira the chance to do so now. She is grateful for that. Just one more thing showing that you have helped Kira even in some of the small things in her life. While it may seem small, it's important. Taking time to relax and rest was something she couldn't do much in life—because Kira thought she had to always be doing something and could never to sit idle. Through you, Lord, Kira has learned that, well sometimes, you need to just rest.

Funny thing is you told Kira that she was the only one that could slow it down, and, Lord, you helped her do that very thing.

Having Coffee with the Special One

Life on earth is too short for our worldly lives, but I guess when you're ready to take us for our eternal life with you, we will live forever.

Kira thinks that maybe she shouldn't say she guesses, because she does believe you, Lord. She just wasn't sure what to say there. When it's her time, you'll take her. Kira believes that everyone has a time clock, and no one can lengthen their life or shorten it because it's all in your time. For now, she gets to live her life to the fullest; you have given her the peace and the joy.

The center of calm in Kira's life is you, Jesus, with the Holy Spirit, you have given her and the Lord, our Savior.

Since you came back in Kira's life, or should she say since she opened to you and let you back in, now, Lord, Jesus. Kira realizes it's you, because you're the only one that can fulfill her inner most wants and desires.

You, Lord, provide the emotional connection she needed. No one could fill that empty hole in her; only you could because you, Lord, knew what was missing in her. You're the only one that knows how Kira needs to be loved and who wants to love her that way. It doesn't mean that others don't love her, there is just something about your love that's above all else. Your love, Lord, suffices her needs.

Kira doesn't know how to properly explain it, but your love, Lord, is a love that no-one else can give.

You, Lord, were the missing piece in her, and it was you she pushed out of her life when she needed you most (like when Kira turned 40, leaving her kids, and all the other crap in her life.)

Kira couldn't believe all of the things that others could do. She couldn't understand why she had to move away from two of her kids. It was so devastating, and so hard for Kira. It was the one thing that could hurt her the most, and it happened. She always knew that she had to get ready for her kids to grow up and move away...but she wasn't prepared to move away from them. Kira wondered if you really are ever prepared for your kids to leave you either, but that's the way you're raised so you know it will happen.

Kira was so busy going to school and trying to build something for the future that she forgot to live in the present and cherish what she had at that time. Now when it was all said and done, most think it would be to late to change things, but Kira realized that she could still have her kids in her life while they lived their lives which would be different. Kira still doesn't like it that she doesn't get to see all of them as often as she would like, but she knows they are all just a phone call, text or quick flight away.

Kira guesses that maybe that's what makes it easy is that they aren't that far away. Kira hasn't quite figured out yet why she doesn't spend more time with them, but she knows that everyone is so busy with their lives and raising children is a 24/7

Having Coffee with the Special One

adventure. She knows the grandkids go to school and have homework and everyday things that must be done. So, it's hard still to go spend time with them.

Each year Kira says she will try harder, and each year she does. Yet, it still isn't what she thinks or imagines it should be like. In some ways Kira really doesn't know how to be any different. After she and Tim moved away from their families, and traveled a lot, they stopped trying to be close to others or form friendships. That's kind of dumb especially with your own family.

Kira doesn't want to be in their faces every second of their life, but she wants to hold them close to her in her heart and mind. Kira knows the wants and needs she has with her own siblings and mom. She misses her family and the fun they had when they were growing up. Now Kira can remember the good times and when a memory pops in her mind, she will chuckle. Like the time her sisters were messing around in the bedroom...jumping between the beds...falling off...and giggling.

When they were growing up there were times when all four of the girls would be in one bedroom where they shared two sets of bunkbeds. You know there was a time in Kira's life where she strongly disliked the way she had to grow up, and there are still some things that she wishes never happened. But now Kira knows that the love that she and her sisters share today (and shared then) and the good times they experienced while growing up are memories that they will have together, forever.

This is showing Kira that you, Lord, want us to establish good relationships, and love one another. Love is one of the strongest—and most important—attributes a person can have. There is nothing like a hug from someone you hold dear in your heart.

Kira and her siblings are better now at keeping in contact with each other. A lot of it has to do with age and now that they have raised their kids, they have a little more time to think of each other and give each other a call. It's amazing how Kira and Dawn can pick up the phone and have a two-hour conversation. It's like they have never been apart. Lord, you know how important it is to have someone like that in your life.

Jag, one of Kira's other sisters, can talk on forever. Kira enjoys talking with her because Jag really has some fun stuff to talk about (she always finds interesting stories on the Internet to discuss!.) Kira is the oldest of all four girls but sometimes she feels like she is the youngest because Kira and her sisters all have strong personalities and are basically bossy. Dawn and Kira seem to take things in stride a little more, while Jag and Gay are more shakers and movers, and they like to run the show. Kira says this as she chuckles, because it really is funny to see all four of them together at times.

Having Coffee with the Special One

When you're an outsider looking in, sometimes you might get overwhelmed, because Kira knows sometimes, she does.

During the years, Kira has learned more about her sisters and grown to love them even more. She will take what she can when she gets to see them because Kira knows what it's like to be away from them, and not in their lives. Kira would rather be with them, than not. When they lost one of their brothers it makes you realize how quickly time flies by and when you start to lose the ones you love, you start holding them closer to your heart, and really try to make more time for them.

Kira's mother and God really did a good job with holding her family together with all they went through when Kira was growing up. When she looks back at those hard times, Kira can see that it could have been so much worse. It's funny when Kira's dad wasn't around it was mostly fun for her family: there was a lot of laughter in the home, and when they didn't have to clean the house, there was a lot of play. Now that the walls, are down Kira gets to see and remember the good times.

Thank you, Jesus, for helping her remember the love and the strength that each one has. Kira has learned you don't want to forget where you came from, and how it all started. It's good for you to see the roads you have traveled, and how far you have come in life. You get to see the transitions, and lessons you have learned, and how you, God, change the way she can look at them. You teach

Patty Scott

Kira how to look at things through your eyes. She can see that you were there all along, and there were many times when the laughter outweighed the tears.

Remember that one-time Kira was teaching or trying to teach Jag how to drive? They were at the grocery store a few blocks away from their house in Kira's Volkswagen. They drove over the bushes and onto someone's yard. (HA HA) That was so funny, the bouncing and the bumping. And then they took off. The news had already reached home before they even got home. Jag and Kira didn't realize they had gone over the bushes that belonged to someone they went to church with them.

Of course, as Kira and her siblings found out, in a small town like where they grew up there weren't too many places one of the couldn't go, that someone didn't know them. They had one of the biggest families, and well, let's say, one of the kids were always getting into something, so people knew who we were.

One of Kira's younger brothers was ornery and well, let's say, he kept Kira's older brother busy with getting him out of messes. Kira's older brother was very protective of his siblings, and man you didn't want to mess with Kira or one of her sisters because no matter where he was, or what he was doing, if he found out someone was messing with or picking on them, he wouldn't tolerate it and would protect them.

Having Coffee with the Special One

When Kira was growing up, she didn't take too kindly to that, but now she looks back at it and realizes that having a big brother who protected her was kind of nice to have around. Kira knows that God was always close, but so was her brother. Kira didn't miss having an older sister because she and her other brother, Chip, got along so well. It was almost like having another sister except he didn't want to talk girl talk, that's for sure.

Kira has found that growing up in a big family is awesome. In addition to her immediate family, her mom had thirteen siblings. Of course, everyone got married and had families, so the family continued to grow.

The sad thing is though, when they start dying, you get to go to a lot of funerals, too. Which is hard to take at times. Once you get over the mourning, then you see and accept it for what it is. Since Kira's family is so close to God it just seemed to make it a little easier to handle the losses. Kira had noticed that the funerals where God is involved with the people, it's more peaceful and acceptance by the family and others who loved the departed.

In Kira's mind, that makes a lot of the difference in the world.

When there are trying times, and sad times in our lives, it's easier to get through them with the help of the Lord.

You see everyone must go through the tough times, why not let him in and let him help? What would it hurt?

Kira got to attend the Christmas candlelight service at her church last night. While singing the Christmas songs she felt so privileged to be able to share that with her daughter's mother-in-law. Kira thought about the songs' words, and what she was reading in the order of the sermon.

You don't have to go to church to feel close to God, but it doesn't hurt to either. For Kira she gets so much out of going: she gets more than it ever has taken from her.

She is filled with Hope, Mercy, Love and Forgiveness.

It's so hard for her to understand, why a person wouldn't want what she has. Yet it's so easy to have it.

It's like saying the common table prayer: Come, Lord, Jesus, be my guest and let these gifts to us be blessed. We are asking the Lord, to come share the food that we have prepared, and he has given us, and be in our homes. Those words carry a powerful punch..............................

Having Coffee with the Special One

When Kira was younger, she didn't really think of them that way.

What Child is this who lays on Mary's lap sleeping....

Can you imagine getting to raise that child and kissing his beautiful face, that you're holding the Lord, in your arms? Wow!!!

That has made a wonderful impact on Kira's life, maybe it can yours too.

God Bless you all.

Remember that we celebrate the Lord's beginning on Christmas but don't forget him the other days of the year. Know that you're not alone.

God is there to help you no matter what.

In Jesus Name I pray for you all. Amen

www.ingramcontent.com/pod-product-compliance
Lightning Source LLC
Chambersburg PA
CBHW021757220426
43662CB00006B/90